Cheating Welfare

Cheating Welfare

Public Assistance and the
Criminalization of Poverty

Kaaryn S. Gustafson

NEW YORK UNIVERSITY PRESS
New York and London

NEW YORK UNIVERSITY PRESS
New York and London
www.nyupress.org

Some portions of text that appear in this book have appeared in the
author's article "The Criminalization of Poverty," first published by
the *Journal of Criminal Law and Criminology*, Volume 99, Issue 3.

References to Internet websites (URLs) were accurate at the time of writing.
Neither the author nor New York University Press is responsible for URLs
that may have expired or changed since the manuscript was prepared.

Library of Congress Cataloging-in-Publication Data
Gustafson, Kaaryn S.
Cheating welfare : public assistance and the criminalization of poverty /
Kaaryn S. Gustafson.
p. cm.
Includes bibliographical references and index.
ISBN 978-0-8147-3231-1 (cl : alk. paper) — ISBN 978-0-8147-3291-5 (e-book)
1. Welfare fraud—United States. 2. Public welfare—California—Case studies. I. Title.
KF3720.G87   2011
362.5'5610973—dc22   2011005522

Manufactured in the United States of America
c   10 9 8 7 6 5 4 3 2 1
p   10 9 8 7 6 5 4 3 2 1

To Anneke, Solveig, and Mark Gustafson

Contents

Acknowledgments

This project was nurtured through the supervision and support of Kristin Luker, Lauren Edelman, and Jane Mauldon. Kristin's encouragement, not to mention her monthly meetings over coffee and cookies early on in this project, allowed me to pursue this study even when I was unsure where it would lead. Her comments on drafts were invaluable. In the early stages of this research, a number of insightful, scholarly friends helped me make my way through the research and writing: Catherine Albiston, Beth Bernstein, Simon Halliday, Mark Harris, Anna Korteweg, Idit Kostiner, Laura Beth Nielsen, Jackie Orr, Amy Schalet, and Diana Selig. Others who offered helpful advice early in the course of this project include Ed Barnes, John Gilliom, Susan Silbey, and Frank Munger. For Pam Strayer's assistance transcribing some of the interview tapes I will be ever grateful.

I must thank Debbie Gershenowitz, my editor at NYU Press, for encouraging me to publish this study as a book. Sincere thanks to those who read manuscript drafts and offered comments: Mario Barnes, Jill Davies, Mark Gustafson, Alexandra Lahav, Frank Munger, and Lucie White. I also owe a debt of thanks to several research assistants: Sri Chalasani, Elizabeth Martinez, Anton Petrov, Tovah Ross, and Leslie Shanley. And I owe many thanks to the institutional support I received from the University of California at Berkeley and from the University of Connecticut School of Law. A Vice Chancellor for Research Grant provided recording and transcribing equipment. A Chancellor's Dissertation Year Fellowship and Graduate Opportunity Program Dissertation Year Fellowship gave me time to invest in the research and writing. Research funding from the University of Connecticut Law School Foundation provided me time to think and write.

Most of all, thanks to my daughter, Anneke, and to my parents, Solveig and Mark, who spent a lot of time as a threesome while I worked at the library or the dining room table. I'm grateful for your patience and support.

List of Abbreviations

ADC	Aid to Dependent Children
AFDC	Aid to Families with Dependent Children
CalWORKs	California Work Opportunity and Responsibility to Kids Program, California's program of cash assistance to low-income families
FAP	Family Assistance Program
MediCal	California's Medicaid program, a health insurance program for low-income individuals who are not eligible for Medicare
MFY	Mobilization for Youth
NWRO	National Welfare Rights Organization
PRWORA	Personal Responsibility and Work Opportunity Reconciliation Act, the federal legislation reforming the welfare system in 1996
Section 8	A federal housing subsidy program, first established under Section 8 of the Housing Act of 1937
SIP	Self-Initiated Program
SSA	Social Security Act of 1935
SSI	Supplemental Security Income
TANF	Temporary Assistance to Needy Families
WIC	Special Supplemental Nutrition Program for Women, Infants and Children

Introduction

Mention the word *welfare* in a room full of people in the United States and you can expect to see brows furrow and mouths tighten in disgust. *Welfare,* the colloquial term for some public benefits in the United States, no longer holds its original meaning: well-being. Instead, it has become a pejorative term used to label "welfare mothers" or "welfare queens." And while welfare use has always carried the stigma of poverty, it now also bears the stigma of criminality.

Welfare rules assume the criminality of the poor. Indeed, the logics of crime control now reign supreme over efforts to reduce poverty or to ameliorate its effects. As government policies targeting the poor have changed with time, so have the experiences of poor families who use welfare. Many of today's welfare policies are far removed from basic goals of ensuring the well-being of families. Rather, policies are, first and foremost, intended to deter welfare use, to guard against misuse, and to punish welfare cheating. Policing the poor and protecting taxpayer dollars from fraud and abuse have taken priority over providing security to economically vulnerable parents and children. Today's welfare system treats those who use public benefits, or who even apply for benefits, as latent criminals. Nationwide, welfare recipients are treated as presumptive liars, cheaters, and thieves. Their lives are heavily surveilled and regulated, not only by the welfare system, but also by the criminal justice system. Changes in public attitudes and government practices have led to what can be described as the criminalization of poverty.

The term *criminalization* is used in this book to describe a web of state practices and policies related to welfare. There are several different strands of criminalization. First, there are a number of practices involving the stigmatization, surveillance, and regulation of the poor. These practices are historically embedded in aid programs to the poor but seem to be expanding.

Second, many welfare policies and practices assume a latent criminality among the poor. Reforms over the last two decades have been aimed at excluding from welfare those individuals who have engaged in illicit behavior in the past and have also aimed at imposing harsh penalties on those who engage in illicit activities while receiving public benefits. These policies adopt the get-tough-on-crime approach once relegated to the criminal justice system.

Third, criminalization involves the growing overlap between the welfare system and the criminal justice system. This intersection includes not only overlapping goals and attitudes toward the poor but also collaborative practices and shared information systems between welfare offices and various branches of the criminal justice system. Very concrete examples of this criminalization exist—most notably, aggressive investigations of and prosecutions for welfare fraud.

Despite this criminalization of the welfare system, poor families continue breaking the rules of welfare receipt and continue hiding information from welfare officials. Many of those who receive public benefits actually do cheat. But they do not all cheat for the same reasons. Some cheat because of the need to provide food and shelter for themselves and their families, some cheat because they have figured out how to avoid getting caught, some cheat because they perceive no risks of cheating, and some cheat because they cannot comprehend the complicated rules of the system. Some cheat for several of these reasons.

The title of this book, *Cheating Welfare*, is intended to rouse readers to think about not only the ways welfare recipients cheat the welfare system but also the ways the existing system is at odds with the welfare of families and the welfare of society. This study looks at the welfare system from two vantage points: from the policy level and from the perspective of those who use public benefits. It provides insight into the history, social construction, and lived experience of welfare and shows why cheating is all but inevitable—not because poor people are more immoral than anyone else but because ordinary individuals navigating complex systems of rules are likely to become entangled despite their best efforts. It also challenges readers to question their assumptions about welfare policies, welfare recipients, and crime control policies in the United States. The book examines the creation of welfare rules by the lawmakers; the reconstruction of those welfare rules by administrators; the acceptance of or resistance to those rules in the abstract by the poor; the day-to-day negotiation of the rules by welfare recipients; and, finally, the punitive responses of the state to rule violations. It examines the construction of the crime we know as welfare fraud and, relying on in-depth interviews with welfare recipients in Northern California, examines the hold that welfare rules have—and do not have—over low-income and no-income parents in the wake of federal welfare reform.

With an eye to the rules and penalties instituted under the United States' federal welfare reforms of 1996, the book's empirical research is driven by four main questions: First, what knowledge do welfare recipients possess of welfare rules and the consequences of rule breaking? Second, to what extent do welfare recipients comply with the welfare rules—both the formal rules and the rules as they understand them? Third, do individuals immersed in a system of complex rules with which compliance is difficult question the legitimacy of and resist either the welfare system or the broader legal system? Finally, do welfare recipients display the potential to transform the system?

The findings reveal that while all too often treated as a monolithic group, welfare recipients display significant variation in their rule knowledge, rule compliance, and views about the rules' legitimacy. The personal stories the interviewees share are startling, angering, and heartbreaking. Most respondents in this study found it difficult to comply with the rules and therefore cheated routinely. Some of the rule breaking was done knowingly, some done unknowingly. Surprisingly, the state's zealous pursuit of welfare fraud in the county where the interviewees lived was actually capturing those who were trying best to comply with the rules and who were most likely to believe the rules were fair.

The data undermine the rational actor model so commonly applied to welfare recipients, a model based on the assumption that the welfare rules are known and understood, are guiding behavior, and are the reason welfare rolls dropped dramatically after the federal welfare reforms of 1996. In addition, the types of resistance the interviewees displayed were not those that would challenge the welfare system and create change that would improve their lot but instead resistance that merely reinforced legal understandings, cultural symbols, and punitive policies deployed against them. Most of the interviewees, despite receiving welfare themselves, embraced negative stereotypes of welfare recipients and supported punitive welfare policies. Rather than challenging widely held views of welfare recipients as morally deviant, they simply described themselves as different from, and better than, other welfare recipients. In the end, welfare recipients reified rather than resisted law's power over the poor.

This book engages with—and addresses gaps in—three bodies of literature: empirical research on welfare policies and their effects; criminology; and law-and-society literature on legal consciousness and resistance. The following sections outline some of the questions drawn from those bodies of scholarship.

Examining the Root Issues of Welfare Policy

Over the last three decades, welfare policies have been informed by popular beliefs that welfare fraud is rampant. As a result, welfare policies have become more punitive, and the boundaries between the welfare system and the criminal justice system have blurred—so much so that in some locales, at certain points in time, prosecution caseloads for welfare fraud have exceeded welfare caseloads. And though the welfare and criminal justice systems have been converging in many ways, scholars who study poverty, public policy, and crime seem not to have taken notice.

Welfare policies are informed by rational choice models of behavioral social science. Much of the policy literature examines changes in policy and subsequent changes in behavioral outcomes, such as rates of welfare use or employment rates. Much of the quantitative research about welfare receipt and welfare cheating has emerged in policy studies of the efficacy of welfare fraud prevention strategies and relies upon administrative data, thus examining welfare recipients in the aggregate (Lange 1979; Chi 1984; Gardiner 1984; Gardiner and Lyman 1984; Hutton 1985; Wolf and Greenberg 1986). These studies examine, for example, discrepancies between calculations of need and the benefits actually provided. Or they triangulate income and resource data from governmental databases to search for income sources that welfare recipients have failed to report. These studies can uncover only a limited amount of rule breaking, for they measure only noncompliance that can be observed in administrative records. In addition, these studies examining welfare recipients in the aggregate cannot discern intentional from unintentional rule breaking, though intent is central to notions of culpability in American criminal law.

Other studies of welfare rule violation examine the sanction rates for welfare recipients who fail to meet their work requirements or other requirements (Cherlin et al. 2002; Kalil, Seefeldt, and Wang 2002). While these studies may give an indication of how many individuals failed to comply with the formal rules, they can offer no indication of how many decided to break the rules, how many simply could not comply, or how many broke the rules unknowingly. And, of course, these studies do not discuss the cases where individuals broke the rules without getting caught. Much of the welfare research of the last two fifteen years has examined the effects of welfare rules on welfare recipients' wage earning (Bloom et al. 2000) or the effects of policy changes on welfare recipients' departures from the welfare system (commonly known as "leaver studies") (e.g., Anderson, Halter, and Gryzlak

2004; California Department of Social Services 2000; Lower-Basch 2000; Verma and Hendra 2003). All of these studies problematically assume that welfare recipients know the rules well enough to factor them into their decision making and that complying with the rules and regulations is a choice they can fully exercise. As a result, these studies assume causation between rule changes, individual choice, and policy outcomes when, in fact, there may be less informed choice and direct causation involved than these studies conclude.

Most researchers, in fact, have failed to ask some of the most interesting, relevant, and basic research questions about welfare policy. For example, there has been little research on what would seem to be crucial questions for both welfare policy analysts and criminologists, namely, whether individuals who are subject to rules—particularly punitive rules—possess accurate knowledge of the rules and the consequences of rule breaking. This question, it would seem, is antecedent and necessary to any convincing discussion of the effects of policy changes and rule enforcement.

Herbert Simon writes that perfect rationality "requires a complete knowledge and anticipation of the consequences that will follow on each choice" (1997, 93). Therefore having knowledge of, or even access to gaining knowledge of, the rules and the consequences of complying or not complying with them is important in the exercise of rationality, whether in the context of welfare or elsewhere. Most studies of welfare policies employ simplistic behavioral models and take for granted that welfare recipients fully comprehend both the vast set of rules that govern their behavior and the consequences for violating these rules. For the most part, however, policy analysts have not tested assumptions that welfare recipients possess complete knowledge of rules and regulations.

Rather than assuming perfect information and unconstrained choice, Herbert Simon has urged scholars to acknowledge "bounded rationality" (1997, 89), the notion that individuals and organizations must sometimes act despite limited information and constraints on available choices and actions. Simon writes that the neoclassical economic models of human action—the very models predominant in public policy studies of welfare recipients— fail to "ask how the actors acquire the information required for these decisions, how they make the necessary calculations, or even, and this is the crux of the matter—whether they are capable of making the kinds of decisions postulated in utility-maximizing or profit-maximizing theory" (20). Many welfare policy studies based on economic models fail to consider bounded rationality.

This book examines a bounded rationality and contextualized negotiation of welfare rules. It looks at how individuals obtain information about rules, rights, and the consequences of rule breaking. The study makes clear not only that rule knowledge is rarely complete among individuals who are subject to the welfare rules but also that the level of rule knowledge is not uniform among individuals subject to the rules. Moreover, this study goes beyond analyses of rule compliance based on simple economic models—models that assume rule knowledge—and offers a more nuanced analysis of legal knowledge, where both action and inaction are viewed not only in relationship to formal rules and rights but also in relationship to individual competence, in response to the hegemonic power of legal symbols, and in resistance to or in flow with law's power.

Studying the Intersection of Welfare Law and Criminal Law

Generally, the welfare system and the criminal justice system have been treated as distinct realms of law. That is not the case. The logics of criminology have come to reign over means-tested public aid programs. And though the welfare and criminal justice systems have converged in many ways, only a few scholars seem to have taken notice (see Garland 2001; Wacquant 2001, 2008, 2009a, 2009b). Many poverty law scholars and criminal law scholars seem to have overlooked the trends, even as the federal government and many states have been implementing policies that punish welfare cheating increasingly harshly and that punish through criminal prosecution rather than civil penalties. Much of this book explores and questions the convergence of the welfare system, traditionally the benevolent arm of the state, and the criminal justice system, the punitive arm of the state. It also examines the effects of this convergence on the individuals in the midst of this shifting state power.

The body of qualitative research on the lives of welfare recipients is growing (e.g., Berrick 1995; Edin and Lein 1997; Gilliom 1997, 2001; Kingfisher 1996; Rank 1994; Sarat 1990; Schein 1995; Seccombe 1999; Soss 2000; Stack 1975). Recent literature on the economic coping strategies of the poor has revealed rule breaking as common practice among welfare recipients (Berrick 1995; Edin and Lein 1997; Edin and Jencks 1993; Gilliom 1997, 2001; Kingfisher 1996; Seccombe 1999). These findings about rule breaking, however, have been only tangentially related to the central questions of these studies. These works include individual stories that hint at the motivations behind noncompliant actions with welfare rules, some of which might lead to prosecution for welfare fraud. These writings also reveal practices that are not captured in statistical analyses or discovered by welfare fraud investigators. They point to the negative effects of welfare fraud investigations for families on aid. They also lead to a couple conclusions: first, that some welfare recipients have to break the rules to make ends meet; second, that welfare recipients who break the rules may not necessarily do so intentionally.

Criminologists have neglected the possibilities of research on noncompliance with welfare rules and criminal welfare fraud in particular. This is a significant oversight for many reasons. First and foremost, fraud is a common criminal charge, with felony fraud making up between 20 and 30 percent of the prosecutions in California at the time of the data collection in this study. Violent crimes, however, tend to capture the attention of researchers more easily—to be "sexier"—than property crimes.

A second reason why welfare fraud is a surprising omission in scholarly work on crime is that it would appear to fit well within Marxist analyses of crime and social inequality. In an overview of Marxist analyses of the causes of crime, David Greenberg discusses numerous studies examining the links between crime rates and levels of inequality or unemployment, many of them studies of property crimes (1993, 69). It is easy to envision studies of welfare fraud contributing to this literature. While this study does not pursue that analysis, the data may be of some interest to Marxist scholars, particularly those who might wish to see data on property crimes that have occurred later than the nineteenth century.

Finally, crimes of fraud—or at least the ones prosecuted—tend to be perpetrated by women rather than men, making those crimes unusual. While women made up only 17 percent of U.S. felony convictions in 2002, they made up 42 percent of felony fraud convictions that year (Durose and Langan 2004, 6, table 5 (defining fraud charges to include forgery and embezzlement)). Data assembled by the U.S. Department of Justice on arrests and convictions in forty large U.S. urban counties revealed that in 2002 women made up 41 percent of defendants charged with felony fraud (Kyckelhahn and Cohen 2008, 2), down from 52 percent in 1998 (Reaves 2001, 4, table 3). In no other categories of felony convictions do women come even close to making up such large percentages of convictions (Durose and Langan 2004, 6, table 5). Moreover, in contrast to other felonies, the majority of those charged with fraud (55 percent) have had no prior convictions (Cohen and Kyckelhahn 2010, 5, table 4).

The gender disparity in felony fraud convictions is also interesting because men have a higher rate of arrest for fraud. In 1994, there were 158 men arrested for fraud per 100,000 men in the population, and 98 women arrested for fraud per 100,000 women in the population (Daly and Tonry 1997, 210, table 1A). There appears to be a dramatic and unexplained gender difference that occurs somewhere between arrest and prosecution and that results in such a large number of felony fraud prosecutions brought against women despite the higher arrest rate for men. Also, between 1975 and 1994 the number of fraud arrests increased more quickly among women than among men, with a 140 percent rate of increase for women and a 108 percent increase for men (Daly and Tonry 1997, 212, table 1D). One would expect the distinctiveness of fraud statistics to spark social scientists and legal scholars to delve deeply into the nature of fraud. Until now, however, such has not been the case.

Even scholars in the area of feminist criminology have sidestepped analyses of welfare fraud. The gendered aspects of fraud prosecutions should make welfare fraud particularly interesting to feminist criminologists. Perhaps one explanation for the oversight is that much of the scholarship within feminist criminology examines women as the victims of crime (especially rape and domestic violence) rather than the perpetrators of crime. Dana Britton has rightly complained that better understandings of women's interactions with the law "require a new, more nuanced conception of women offenders that disrupts the dichotomy in which they have been seen only either as innocent victims or as hardened offenders" (2000, 72).

Feminist legal scholars have sometimes argued that gender-neutral theories of rationality are problematic for women (Okin 1989, 71). Most women are mothers and therefore factor both the interests and the outcomes of others (their families) into their decisions and their actions. As Martha Fineman explains, women are more likely than men to experience "derivative dependency" as a result of the "inevitable dependency" of their children or of others relying upon their caregiving (1995, 8). This dependency—distinct from the commonly disparaged "welfare dependency"—leaves women more economically vulnerable than men. However, issues of dependency, economic opportunity, and need have been underexamined in the scholarship on women's criminal behavior generally and welfare fraud specifically. This study is not intended to, nor could it possibly, address all of the gaps in criminological research. It may, however, provide some perspectives on welfare rule breaking that motivate more extensive research on women and crime.

Treating Welfare Law as Law

For most people, even for many legal academics, it is unusual to think about welfare policies, welfare rules, and welfare regulations as "the law." These, however, are just as much part of the law as any criminal prohibition on the books or as any Supreme Court decision. Law regulates behavior. It expresses collective visions of the social good, of future goals, of moral values. It punishes and marginalizes those who deviate from social norms. Government assistance to the poor in the United States is "law" in each of these senses.

Law and legal rules are nothing abstract for poor families who use government aid programs. Austin Sarat, in his study of legal consciousness among the poor, writes that individuals who use welfare experience law as something "repeatedly encountered in the most ordinary transactions and events in their lives" (1990, 344). Sarat continues: "Law is immediate and powerful because being on welfare means having a significant part of one's life organized by a regime of legal rules invoked by officials to claim jurisdiction over choices and decisions which those not on welfare would regard as personal and private" (344). Thus research on welfare recipients is inherently research about the law, about rules that are intricately woven, if not carved, into the daily lives of legal subjects. This book specifically addresses how welfare recipients understand the law and how they negotiate moral and rational conflicts that arise while living under the law's rules and regulations.

One of the goals of this book is to complicate notions of rules and rule compliance, to step beyond positive law notions of law as written law and beyond notions of legal formalism which hold that the only significant effects of law are those that can be measured. Rules that guide behavior and individuals' understandings of their status as rights bearers are not informed only by written rules and regulations. Individuals' understandings of law, and of their relationships to the law, are also informed by legal and political symbols. This book treats law as a vague and fuzzy set of commands and symbols, some of which are embodied in rules and some of which are merely individuals' interpretations of legal norms. It also looks at the legitimacy individuals invest in the law and their resistance to law's power, both in attitude and in action.

Compliance and Legality

A traditional notion of why individuals obey the law is that they comply when they fear sanctions. Under deterrence theory, the threat of sanctions for rule breaking prompts individuals to comply with the law. Sociolegal scholars, however, have complicated the notion of rule compliance, looking at how people understand rules, when they play by the rules, and when they do not (e.g., Tyler 1990). One of the questions this study pursues is whether people obey legal rules that are difficult to follow, whether they attempt to comply, and if so, why. Another question is how individuals respond when they have incomplete knowledge of the rules.

The legitimacy that people subject to a legal system place in that system and their adherence to the rules of that system is sometimes called *legality*. Legality involves different levels of analysis. First, a discussion of legality requires an examination of whether individuals subject to the rules invest their support in them. Do people believe in the rules, find them fair, and consider them binding guides of conduct, both for others and for themselves? If people find that rules are legitimate, then they may be more likely to obey them (Tyler 1994, 5).

Second, legality involves consideration of the goals society has established and an examination of whether the laws and policies, as enacted, conform to those goals. In short, is there means-ends rationality to the policies that have been enacted? If rules and policies serve multiple and contradictory goals, then the system as a whole may lack coherence. If laws are designed to reflect collective beliefs, to communicate in clear fashion shared understandings of the social good of right and wrong, and to unite people, then incoherent rules may unsettle the expressive functions of law rather than foster social cohesion.

Third, an analysis of legality requires an examination of whether laws are consistent with organizing principles that inform legal policies—principles such as economic efficiency. We generally recognize limits to the social and economic costs we will invest in enforcing laws and punishing offenders. Enforcement that becomes too vigorous or costly may undermine the legitimacy individuals invest in the underlying laws. These three aspects of legality are considered in the analysis of welfare recipients' descriptions of welfare rules and their enforcement and their perceptions of whether the rules are fair and just.

Scholars have offered only cursory examinations of legality and welfare law. According to Kathryn Edin and Christopher Jencks, the welfare system may seem arbitrary or nonsensical from the perspective of the recipients. On the basis of their study involving welfare recipients in Chicago, Edin and Jencks concluded: "We have . . . created a welfare system whose rules have no moral legitimacy in recipients' eyes. This feeling is not confined to second-generation welfare recipients in poor neighborhoods—the so-called underclass. It is shared by mainstream women who have finished high school, held jobs, married, had children, and ended up on welfare only when their husbands left them. It is a feeling bred by a system whose rules are incompatible with everyday American morality, not by the peculiar characteristics of welfare recipients" (1993, 212).

The data Edin and Jencks relied upon, however, could not truly substantiate their conclusion about welfare recipients' sense of the lack of moral legitimacy of the welfare rules. The study simply showed that families faced big gaps between their welfare checks and their basic expenses and that full compliance with the welfare income-reporting rules was therefore almost nonexistent. Because the researchers focused not on welfare recipients' attitudes toward the rules, but only on their sources of income, they could not truly measure welfare recipients' moral evaluation of the rules—how they categorized their rule transgressions or how they evaluated the fairness of the rules themselves or the welfare system overall. In addition, while Edin and Jencks found that welfare recipients were unlikely to be caught for failing to report income, they did not explore welfare recipients' perceptions of their risks of getting caught. If the likelihood of getting caught was low, then it could be that welfare recipients went without reporting their income sources because it was a simple and low-risk way of bringing in income. If, on the other hand, welfare recipients feared the risks of getting caught and violated the rules anyway, then it might be that their economic needs overrode either a fear of getting caught or beliefs that the rules were legitimate and needed to be followed. Karen Seccombe, a researcher who did ask welfare recipients their opinions about the welfare system, found that their opinions varied about the need for and legitimacy of punitive welfare policies (1999, 170-77). The final two chapters of this book analyze the legitimacy of the welfare system in the United States.

Legal Consciousness and Resistance

The interviews that come later in this book examine not only individuals' knowledge of welfare rules but also their understandings of self and others as objects of law's power and as agents of social and political change. Over the last decade, there has been a growing body of scholarship on what is known as *legal consciousness*. Scholars who study legal consciousness have explored how people construct their understandings of law through their experiences with the legal system. Legal consciousness scholars suggest that "we abandon an understanding of the law as a single, coherent entity" (Ewick and Silbey 1998, 17). Legal consciousness studies begins with the view that law consists of something more than rules or rights, that rules and rights can have multiple meanings for or effects upon their subjects, and that notions of law can be complicated and even contradictory. According to Susan Silbey, "The study of legal consciousness traces the ways in which law is experienced and interpreted by specific individuals as they engage, avoid, or resist the law and legal meanings" (2001, 8626). Legal consciousness scholars view law as ever-pervasive in the lives of individuals (Sarat 1990). Thus, even when individuals are avoiding or resisting the law, legal rules, legal interpretations, and legal meanings, they are nonetheless in some kind of relationship with the law.

Many legal consciousness scholars take a "constitutive" view of law, within which law's meaning and law's power are constituted by the understandings and day-to-day practices of the individuals who are subject to those laws. The constitutive approach "emphasizes the roles of consciousness and cultural practice as communicating factors between individual agency and social structure rather than expressions of one or the other" (Silbey 2001, 8627). It also assumes "the mutuality and inseparability of law, culture, identity, and experience" (Engel and Munger 1996, 14). Rules and rights are given meaning not only by lawmakers but also by everyday people who are subject to the rules or who hold the potential to exercise rights.

In studying law, then, legal consciousness scholars focus on how individuals interact with the law. Many of these scholars also trace the broad reach of law, examining how law might matter outside the context of legal institutions. As part of the bottom-up approach, legal consciousness scholars focus not on elites but rather on everyday citizens and on people who may be socially, politically, or economically disadvantaged. Because welfare policies are intended and constructed to regulate the minutiae of everyday life and because welfare recipients tend to be disadvantaged along a number of axes of status and identity, this study has an allegiance to this bottom-up approach.

Studies that explore the constitutive nature of law and legal consciousness commonly examine the interplay between law and identity, focusing on how negotiations between law and identity affect individuals' abilities and desires to mobilize law or legal rules. For example, a number of studies have found that while individuals' identities and the injustices they experience as a result of those identities establish bases for legal claims, their identities also work in complicated ways to dampen their desires to call upon the law for their own benefit. For example, Kristin Bumiller's interviews with racial minorities who had experienced discrimination revealed that they avoided making discrimination claims because they wanted to avoid being seen, or seeing themselves, as disempowered victims (Bumiller 1988). Similarly, David Engel and Frank Munger found that individuals who had experienced discrimination based on their disabilities were reluctant to take legal action to address it, sometimes because they considered rights-claiming disempowering or stigmatizing (1996, 24-25). And a study of hate speech by Laura Beth Nielsen found that the people of color she interviewed, despite being silenced by racial slurs, were those least supportive of legal regulations of racist hate speech because they were cynical about law's capacity to change behavior (2004, 124-47).

These studies of legal consciousness examine when people mobilize the law and when they do not. They also look at how the use and nonuse of rights and legal institutions constantly redefine what law is and how it works in society. They find that individual identity—that is, how one views oneself in relationship to the larger society—shapes one's view of both law and of society and affects one's ability or willingness to mobilize the law. The studies additionally suggest that identities and stereotypes may prompt individuals to distance themselves from legal rights and from law's power, especially law's power to assign stigma.

Three recurring themes in the legal consciousness scholarship are relevant to this study because they emerge as themes in the data: (1) polyvocality and contradiction in individuals' descriptions of law; (2) resistance, counterhegemony, and empowerment; and (3) the increasing criminalization of everyday life. The first theme, of polyvocality and contradiction, addresses the many ways that individuals think about law. Legal consciousness scholars have revealed that individuals interact with the law in complex, contradictory, and even self-defeating ways. Patricia Ewick and Susan Silbey (1998), in their study of the law in the lives of everyday citizens, identified three schemas to describe the way individuals interact with the law. According to one of the schemas, individuals envision themselves *before the law*, where law is an orderly system of authoritative rules, "a separate sphere from ordinary social life" (1998, 47). When individuals possess a consciousness of being *with the law*, they engage with legal rules in their everyday lives, using law to pursue their self-interest (48). At other times, individuals may find themselves *against the law*, caught in law's power (49). They may even experience multiple consciousnesses at once. Recognizing the multiple ways that individuals may experience law proves useful in the context of welfare, where recipients are subject to a complex array of rules and regulations and to complicated relationships with the state.

The second theme—which includes the related issues of resistance, coun-terhegemony, and empowerment—has been a prominent theme in the legal consciousness literature (Ewick and Silbey 1992; McCann and March 1996; Merry 1995; Gilliom 1997, 2001; White and Gilliom 1998). Several of these studies attempt to document accounts of resistance to law's power, legal rules, and legal meanings. Resistance, counterhegemony, and empowerment are important to this study because, despite rampant noncompliance with welfare rules and regulations, there has been little examination of what that noncompliance means—both to individual welfare recipients and to law's power.

Most of the obvious resistance to welfare rules is through individual noncompliance, not through legal or political challenge. This lack of formal resistance and its implications have been little explored in the context of wel-fare. Joel Handler, meditating on Steven Lukes's theory of power, has pon-dered the question of how quiescence might be interpreted. He notes that "power and empowerment is a relational process, a dynamic process. It has both psychological and material or substantive aspects. Relationships are not stable. Resources and perceptions change; power changes as well" (1998, 149; also 2002, 278). Handler's body of work (e.g., 1998, 2002) demonstrates his particular interests in when and how individuals who are dependent upon government bureaucracies become empowered to make bureaucracies work for them.

But the welfare system is a site of both empowerment and disempow-erment. John Gilliom, in his study of welfare recipients, places the issue of disempowerment in context, finding that women receiving welfare do not define their financial troubles or administrative complaints in terms of gov-ernment or political power. Gilliom writes, "It seems clear that their legal consciousness is one of entrapment, fear, and some mystification, rather than the sort of empowering ascension to rights we might see elsewhere" (2001, 92). Gilliom finds that rather than drawing individual or collective power from the legal claims that might be available, welfare recipients engage in constant acts of individual resistance. However, acts of resistance that may be perceived as individually empowering may ultimately be disempowering to the larger group.

As with Gilliom's study, resistance is a theme in this book. One of the questions addressed in this study of welfare recipients who violate welfare rules and regulations is whether they are doing so out of conscious attempts to resist the welfare system or as a result of misunderstanding the rules. Another question is whether welfare recipients, or at least some welfare recipients, have developed understandings of law or of their own identities that contest the dominant paradigms. Yet other questions revolve around whether resistance that welfare recipients exhibit bears the potential to transform law. Finally, a goal of this book is to articulate a better definition—or definitions—of resistance.

The Power of Condensation Symbols

The political scientist Stuart Scheingold (1974) writes that studying the effects of law must include analysis of the organizing legal symbols, especially the myth of rights. With the welfare system in the United States, however, there are no substantive constitutional rights to government support and no longer any unconditional statutory entitlements. Thus there is no widely shared myth of rights to basic public support. There is, however, the myth of the welfare queen, a powerful stereotype described in chapter 2. While this may not be a typical legal symbol, the welfare queen has been an organizing political symbol over the last several decades (Hancock 2004; Lubiano 1992). Some political scientists describe symbols such as the welfare queen as *condensation symbols* (Edelman 1964, 36; see also Gusfield 1986; McConahay 1988; Scheingold 1974). Condensation symbols capture and distill collective anxieties about morality, politics, and the economy. They serve as rallying points for broader ideological issues.

Analyzing individual and collective attitudes about and actions around welfare without reference to the symbol of the welfare queen would be inapt. The welfare queen serves as a vehicle—for those across the political spectrum—to discuss the proper role of government and to discuss individual behavior and personal responsibility. The symbol reflects anxieties about race, gender, class, sexuality, motherhood, and criminality. It also influences federal and state policies and informs individual decisions and individual identities.

This Book: A Reader's Guide

This research project has been inspired by the research—and the gaps in research—in various disciplines. While the broad, interdisciplinary approach of this book poses the threat of offering too little to each discipline, the aim of the project is to unearth some new findings and begin some new analytical inquiries that will make some progress in both filling the gaps within the various disciplines and in building bridges across them.

Though a typical social scientific study includes little or no historical backdrop, a discussion of welfare policies in the United States would be decontextualized to the point of absurdity without one. Thus chapter 2 offers a history of U.S. welfare policies and welfare politics, with particular focus on the genealogy of the complex, sometimes contradictory, and increasingly punitive welfare rules and regulations. Chapter 3, "The Criminalization of Poverty," describes the growing overlap between the welfare system and the criminal justice system and the ease with which welfare recipients find themselves entangled in law's expansive punitive power.

Chapter 4 describes some of the salient background characteristics and histories of the individuals who participated in the interviews for this book. Chapters 5 and 6 describe the findings of interviews with welfare recipients. Specifically, chapter 5, "Living within and without the Rules," describes welfare recipients' compliance and noncompliance with the welfare rules and regulations. Chapter 6 then portrays the variation in rule engagement by welfare recipients by describing three types of welfare recipients: the Informed, the Misinformed, and the Preoccupied/Disengaged. The descriptions of the welfare recipients and their engagement with the rules highlight how problematic some of the assumptions about rule compliance and rule breaking have been. They also make clear that rule compliance and beliefs in rule legitimacy are not necessarily as consistent as some scholars have suggested.

Chapter 7, "Contextualizing Criminality, Noncompliance, and Resistance," critiques existing analyses of resistance in the growing literature of legal consciousness. It focuses on the ways resistance can maintain and reinforce systems of domination and highlights the limited capacity of welfare recipients, given law and legal symbols as they now exist, to mobilize for political change. Chapter 8, concluding the book, returns to an analysis of the legitimacy of welfare law by offering frameworks other than the governing frame of criminal regulation to guide welfare policies. Finally, the Appendices outline the critical methodology underlying this study.

2

Reconstructing Social Ills

From the Perils of Poverty to Welfare Dependency

Assistance to the poor has never been provided without strings attached. Aid to the poor, particularly government-sponsored aid to the poor, has been designed to regulate—markets and the economy, families, morality, even motherhood.

That is not to say that providing for the poor has been divorced from a public desire to do good for the poor. From the beginning, the provision of welfare in the United States has rested upon some core moral values, particularly the belief that poor and vulnerable members of society require society's assistance. At the same time, this belief has been accompanied by the idea that only some of the poor deserve assistance—usually the very young, the very old, and the disabled.

The welfare system in the United States, a lightly regulated free-market economy, has also been guided by beliefs about how individuals will or should behave as members of the labor force. One of these ideas is that individuals will participate in the paid labor market only if working will put them in significantly better economic circumstances than not working. Another guiding belief is that individuals living in a free-market society implicitly covenant to engage in economic risk, whether the risk leads to benefit or peril. Further, to maintain a free-market economy where individuals are motivated to take economic risks, society must refrain from protecting individuals too much from the hardships of economic failure.

The underpinnings of the American welfare system, however, have created contradictions and stresses within the design and the functioning of the system itself. Both law and social science have heavily influenced the ideals behind social welfare programs, the discourses framing social problems, and the structure of the social welfare system itself. Past welfare policies, programs, and motivations echo in today's welfare politics. That history is outlined below.

From Charitable Aid to Government-Sponsored Relief

In the United States, early efforts to aid poor families grew from efforts to create morally upright mothers who would then raise morally upright children. In the early twentieth century the discipline of social work dominated the framing of the social issues and social problems, including poverty. As is the case today, women and children found themselves particularly vulnerable to poverty. Perhaps in contrast to today's political context, however, women constituted the strongest political force shaping aid programs for the poor.

During the first two decades of the twentieth century, female reformers sought wide-ranging political and economic transformation. Many of the female reformers represented the elite—white, economically privileged women drawn from the first great wave of women college graduates. They brought about transformations in the areas of health, education, and welfare, including the adoption and implementation of aid programs known as Mothers' Pensions. Mothers' Pensions, programs established first through private charities and later implemented as state-level relief programs, provided aid to poor children (Leff 1973; Skocpol et al. 1993). The goals of Mothers' Pensions were twofold: first, to provide aid to poor, white widows who, with the loss of their husbands, had few legitimate means of financial support; second, to inculcate poor immigrant families with the moral ground rules of the dominant, middle-class American society (Gordon 1994, 44-47). These dual purposes of providing for the sympathetic deserving poor and policing and surveilling families at the margins have held steady through American aid programs, both private and public.

Social reformers of the Reform Era believed that creating good mothers was good for the greater welfare of society. America's privileged classes wanted younger generations to be raised in an atmosphere of traditional middle-class values. Providing aid and social services gave social workers a way to regulate what went on in poor homes. Social workers overseeing state aid programs considered routine surveillance of poor families essential to determining their "deservingness" of aid (Katz 1989; Gordon 1994). Whether a family was deserving depended not only on a family's economic need but also on a host of other criteria related to hygiene and morals used to gauge whether a family maintained a "suitable home" (Katz 1989; Bell 1965). Immigrants and working women, whose cultures and practices were commonly most at odds with the motherhood ideals held and fostered by the privileged social workers, were those least likely to receive state-sponsored aid (Ladd-

Taylor 1994, 149-50). African American women were generally excluded from both the early private charitable aid programs and, later, the state Mothers' Pensions. Molly Ladd-Taylor writes that African American women, while the poorest demographic group in the nation in the Depression era, were virtually absent from the welfare rolls nationwide (1994, 149). When African American women did receive aid, it usually came from middle-class charitable aid societies organized by other African American women (Gordon 1994, 114-17).

Early aid programs provided poor single mothers with little money. These mothers usually had to generate additional income to survive. However, to maintain the appearance of a suitable home, poor mothers often, according to historian Molly Ladd-Taylor, had to hide "jobs, income and lovers from their caseworkers" (1994, 151). Ladd-Taylor notes that "because recipients were not given enough money to live on, but might lose their pensions if they were resourceful and got some money from another source, cheating became part of the system" (151). Thus the early welfare system created a culture of hide-and-seek between poor families and aid administrators.

The Social Security Act and Its Early Years

Provisions of the federal Social Security Act of 1935 (SSA) creating aid to poor children paralleled the private and state relief programs from which they took root. An attempt to address the instabilities suffered during the Great Depression, the SSA established a minimal safety net for Americans who were most vulnerable to the risks of the free market. At the same time, the act created a dual-track welfare system that distinguished between the deserving poor and the undeserving poor, between wage earners and those who did not work for wages, between whites and nonwhites, and between men and women (see Abramovitz 1988; Jensen 1990; Ladd-Taylor 1994; Nelson 1990; Sapiro 1990; Boris 1993; Gordon 1994; Mink 1990; Quadagno 1994). As a general matter, the most generous benefits flowed to the old and disabled, especially elderly and disabled workers. Entire categories of workers— including agricultural workers and domestics—were excluded from receiving benefits under the Social Security Act. These categories of work were those dominated by African Americans and by working women of all racial and ethnic groups (Quadagno 1984, 643).

Aid to Dependent Children (ADC), the program specifically designed for needy children, was intended to support the dependents of deceased working men (Nelson 1990). The state took the place of the wage-earning father.

While the program did provide some cash assistance to families, the assistance was inadequate to sustain a family. ADC adopted the "suitable home" requirements that had been an element of the state Mothers' Pensions. Again, it was generally assumed that good mothers would not spend their time engaged in wage labor. Welfare stipends, however, paid too little to support children and their mothers (Gordon 1994, 298). Poor mothers caught working could be, and were, deemed unfit mothers and their children deemed undeserving of aid. According to historian Linda Gordon, "Luck and skill at dissemblance, not rules, determined who got caught" (1994, 298). In the end, poor mothers were damned if they did work for pay and doomed if they didn't.

It was not until the 1950s that the federal government began to provide states funds to support a caretaker relative for a child receiving ADC. Until the early 1960s, government aid available to the poor was provided in cash; few people received food assistance, and there was no broad-based system of medical insurance for the poor. All of the government relief programs—from federal programs such as aid to the blind and aged, joint state-federal programs such as ADC, and county aid programs known as Home Relief—were distributed by local welfare agencies. These local agencies wielded great power and broad discretion in determining who was eligible for aid, how much aid would be distributed to anyone deemed eligible, and who would or would not receive aid if funds were insufficient to meet everyone's needs (Quadagno 1994, 119). The vast discretion in the system tended to reinforce rather than remedy existing economic disparities among social groups.

The level of benefits varied dramatically from locale to locale, and racial and ethnic discrimination against mothers influenced the distribution of aid within locales. Southern states typically used a number of tactics to exclude African Americans from the welfare rolls altogether. Some southern counties established priority lists for small pools of cash aid. White families were given priority over African Americans, leaving many people of color without relief in times of dire need. Kenneth Neubeck and Noel Cazenave note that in southern states only a small fraction of eligible African American children received government aid (2001, 52). Some states, including Arizona and New Mexico, excluded Native Americans outright from their welfare rolls (55-56). Many localities also used "suitable home" requirements to exclude women who bore children out of wedlock and women who social workers determined had a man living, or even staying, in the home for any length of time (59-61).

The Growth of Aid to Dependent Children

After World War II, the ADC rolls grew—from 701,000 people in 1945 to three million in 1960 (Patterson 1994, 85-86). The proportion of families headed by divorced or unmarried mothers also grew, while the proportion of families headed by widows declined (Patterson 1994, 106). In addition, the number of African American and Puerto Rican families receiving welfare rose, especially in the industrial hubs of the North (Handler and Hasenfeld 2007, 162-64). Along with these changes in welfare recipient populations came perceptions among middle-class whites that aid was no longer going to those who had originally been given primacy as the deserving poor, namely, white families who had lost their male breadwinners.

Welfare offices in many states and locales adopted "suitable home" and "substitute parent" rules, essentially morality standards that were arbitrarily and discriminatorily applied and that commonly excluded women of color from the welfare rolls, especially in the South (Bell 1965, 76). Notwithstanding a 1961 rule issued by the secretary of Health, Education and Welfare barring the arbitrary application of "suitable home" requirements, many welfare offices continued to engage in midnight raids on the homes of ADC recipients in order to police "man in the house" rules (Reich 1965, 1248; Handler and Hasenfeld 2007, 164). The stated reason for surprise visits was to catch men sleeping in the homes of women receiving welfare. Unmarried women with men in their beds were deemed morally unfit and their households therefore unsuitable for assistance (Bell 1965, 41-46). In addition, the men discovered in the homes were considered household breadwinners who had hidden their income support from the aid office (Bell 1965, 77-78). The unstated but underlying goals of the rules were to police and punish the sexuality of single mothers, to close off the indirect access to government support of able-bodied men, to winnow the welfare rolls, and to reinforce the idea that families receiving aid were entitled to no more than near-desperate living standards.

Midnight raids on welfare recipients continued for most of the 1960s. During that time, a number of publicized cases of welfare fraud charges resulted from the raids (Neubeck and Cazenave 2001, 96-97). In many of those cases, though, the men, not the women, were charged with fraud. Men found residing with women receiving welfare aid were treated as the welfare cheats. The prosecutions of men, rather than women, suggest that the welfare and law enforcement officials considered women to be easily manipulated by the men but ultimately blameless in the cheating (Neubeck and Cazenave 2001, 102). This view of the innocence of women, however, would change over time.

Controlling welfare benefits also became a way of controlling the political and economic power of the poor. In the South, welfare policies became a target for state legislature engaged in civil rights retrenchment following the Supreme Court's antisegregation decision in *Brown v. Board of Education of Topeka* (1954). For example, in 1960 Louisiana legislators, in response to a school desegregation order by a federal court, passed twenty-nine bills known as the legislature's "segregation package." Included in the segregation package were stiffened suitable home welfare requirements (Neubeck and Cazenave 2001, 70-71). Mothers considered unsuitable were those who had given birth outside marriage, those who had given birth while on welfare, or those who were involved in common-law relationships (71). The "suitable home" rules were applied retroactively, and welfare recipients were given no right to appeal (72). The effects of the these requirements were dramatic: "The legislation removed over a quarter of Louisiana's ADC recipients from the state's welfare rolls by eliminating the eligibility of 6,000 families with 22,500 children—95 percent of whom were African American" (71).

Welfare became a hot political issue outside the South too. Nationwide, the needs of the poor outstripped the welfare aid available. Many poor families were denied assistance. Only a small proportion of the eligible poor actually received the welfare benefits they were entitled to receive under the Social Security statute. And as the 1960s rolled around, many of the welfare regulations were mere pretexts for winnowing the welfare rolls. In June, July, and August of 1963, for example, New York City rejected 45 percent of the welfare applications that were submitted (Pope 1989, 15).

Social workers in welfare offices played a central role in the provision of welfare, and they possessed vast discretion in the welfare process. Aid payments under ADC were based on a number of factors that a caseworker might include in calculating a family's need. In addition to the basic level of need that the federal government expected states to meet (though the basic level varied dramatically from state to state), states had their own "special needs grants," which took into account the particular needs of each family (West 1981, 23). These grants were numerous and extensive. Special needs could include things from home furnishings to basic articles of clothing to the purchase of a washing machine, an appliance some welfare departments considered essential for a parent with an infant (Pope 1989, 13). New York City even had a special allowance for families whose homes were infested with rats: these families received a small monthly payment to be paid to the utility company for the cost of keeping a light on in the kitchen all night (Piven and Cloward [1971] 1993, 292). Thus a poor mother's good standing with a caseworker was important to the family's receipt of discretionary grants.

In the 1960s, the welfare system was opaque to most welfare recipients. Welfare rules and regulations were not published or made available to welfare recipients. Because the specifics of special needs grants were largely unknown to recipients, and because caseworkers were supposed to establish eligibility for these benefits on the basis of routine visits to the homes of recipients, grant levels varied from one family to another. With a lot of room for discretion, though, there was also a lot of room for arbitrary treatment, as well as racial and ethnic discrimination, in determining the amount of aid poor families received—and in determining whether families received aid at all.

The War on Poverty

The War on Poverty, heralded in American policy debates by John F. Kennedy and mobilized by the administration of Lyndon B. Johnson, brought a pivotal change to public perceptions of poverty and its causes. The discourse of the War on Poverty promoted the idea that poverty was a widespread problem and that Americans had a moral duty to see that postwar affluence, or at least stability, extended to those who had not received a share of the wealth. The War on Poverty also placed the responsibility for alleviating poverty on the government, the federal government specifically.

While this moment held the potential for transforming perceptions of poor families and securing the limited safety net available to them, that potential went unrealized. The spotlight on poverty shone on only some pockets of poverty. For example, President John F. Kennedy publicized the plight of poor, working whites in Appalachia. He also brought attention to the horrible poverty suffered by the elderly who were unable to work. The federal policy changes that resulted from the War on Poverty had the greatest impact on these populations.

The 1960s brought changes to a number of public assistance programs. Even before the broad-scale War on Poverty began, the U.S. Congress under President Kennedy enacted changes in the Social Security Act, expanding ADC to allow states to provide aid to two-parent families where the breadwinner (assumed to be the father) faced a long spell of unemployment (Piven and Cloward [1971] 1993, 126-27). This program, which was a state option, was called Aid to Families with Dependent Children–Unemployed Parent (AFDC-UP). Until this time, two-parent families had been excluded from ADC programs altogether. Support for AFDC-UP was fostered by the view that the exclusion of two-parent families was forcing men to desert their wives and children and contributing to the disintegration of families. In 1961 Congress funded a food stamp program, providing nutrition to the hungry. ADC became Aid to Families with Dependent Children (AFDC) in 1962. In addition, amendments to the Social Security Act in 1965 created Medicaid, a medical program for low-income families and disabled individuals that was, and is, jointly funded by the federal government and the states.

While new policies did bring some improvements for poor families, the antipoverty policies of the early 1960s in other ways contributed to existing social inequalities. They did this by reinforcing and reinscribing the idea that the guidelines for administering aid to the poor were properly delineated by age, gender, race, and attachment to the paid labor force. As a result, the policies helped widen the gaps between the "haves" and "have-nots," even among the poor. And moral devaluation of the "have-nots"—the less deserving or undeserving—easily followed. AFDC remained at the bottom tier of federal antipoverty programs in its generosity, and its recipients—and even more, those eligible poor who were denied AFDC benefits—sat on the bottom tier of the social and economic hierarchy.

The Welfare Rights Movement

In the early 1960s, the welfare system was awash with problems. Social workers had more clients than they could handle. The welfare system was individualized, discretionary, arbitrary, and discriminatory. Midnight raids conducted by welfare caseworkers on the homes of poor mothers, notwithstanding the Flemming Rule, were being used to police the "man-in-the-house" rules and throw women and their children off the welfare rolls (Reich 1963). Welfare offices were not required to give welfare recipients advance warning before decreasing their payments or cutting them off aid entirely and often doled out aid capriciously (Piven and Cloward [1977] 1979, 297). Moreover, welfare recipients, unaware that appealing administrative decisions was an option, rarely sought appeals when their payments were reduced or their cases closed. Administrative hearings to dispute aid reductions or terminations were, in fact, almost nonexistent before the late 1960s. As late as 1964, New York City, with a welfare caseload of half a million people, heard only fifteen appeals on welfare cases (Piven and Cloward [1971] 1993, 173).

But changes were afoot. The welfare rights movement arose amid the swirling tide of civil rights reforms for minorities and increased demand for women's rights. The movement was instigated by a triumvirate of social agents—the federal government, grassroots reformers, and legal reformers. For the federal government, antipoverty efforts were part of a broader effort to shift the balance of power within the system of federalism from the individual states to the federal government. With judicial substantiation of federal powers through *Brown v. Board of Education*, and presidential efforts to find solutions to the seemingly intractable problems of racial discrimination and poverty, the shift was well in progress in mid-1960s despite southern resistance to civil rights.

The federal government, perhaps surprisingly, contributed greatly to the welfare rights movement. Although the privately funded Legal Aid Society had existed since the turn of the century, the federal government—for fear that money provided to lawyers would blur the boundaries between the legal profession and the government—did not fund lawyers until the 1960s. Against the resistance of the American Bar Association, which sought to maintain regulatory independence from the federal government, the Johnson administration began funneling money into legal services for the poor (Auerbach 1976, 269-97). Energetic lawyers, funded by the federal government, provided a wide array of legal services to the poor, handling both minor individual cases and broader actions challenging government policies (Auerbach 1976, 296). Welfare issues provided ample legal work for these eager lawyers.

In the mid-1960s, government policy makers and the legal profession collaborated to improve the social welfare system. An Advisory Council on Public Welfare, appointed by the secretary of Health, Education, and Welfare under a directive of the 1962 Public Welfare Amendments, issued a report to the secretary in June 1966. The report recommended that the federal government establish nationwide standards for welfare provision, that financial need be the sole measure of welfare eligibility, that social services become widely available to the poor, and that legally enforceable rights become attached to welfare payments (Advisory Council on Public Welfare 1966, xii-xiv). It attacked state eligibility requirements, especially rules that required that a welfare applicant reside in the state for a specified length of time, as harmful to families and the nation (30-32). It claimed that aid to the poor in the form of cash was essential to the dignity of the poor (72). The council's recommendations—particularly the destigmatization of poverty through the emphasis on need, and the legal protections for welfare recipients—were consonant with the views of those lawyers and recipients trying to reform the system. The report stated: "Public assistance is a remedy for the risk of economic deprivation. . . . But a protection which is not available to all who incur the risk under a rule of enforceable law is a gratuity subject to elements of chance or the caprice or prejudices of those who determine its policies or control its administration. . . . The federally aided programs of public assistance under the Social Security Act are the one area of social protection against the risk of actual poverty which carries built-in provision for legally enforceable entitlement" (xix). The focus, then, was not on the pathologies of poor individuals or families but on the risks of both economic instability and government intrusion, risks over which individuals and families had no control.

The grassroots movements for welfare rights arose among low-income mothers, mostly women of color, in urban areas (Kornbluh 2007). Local welfare rights groups arose almost simultaneously in a number of cities spanning the United States, including Los Angeles, San Francisco, Oakland, Chicago, Detroit, Cleveland, Manhattan, Brooklyn, and Roxbury (Bailis 1974, 11; Cloward and Piven 1966, 513; Jackson and Johnson 1973, 22, 103; Pope 1989, 40-51; West 1981, 22). The early groups had no shared plan for action, few political or material resources, differing grievances, and little to no knowledge of each other's efforts. In demanding changes in welfare provision, their demands were largely self-interested and practical. They wanted sufficient government-provided aid to help them raise healthy children in a secure setting. As the various groups coalesced and the movement became more focused, the welfare rights activists began to seek a broader goal that was more menacing to the status quo: they wanted mothering, specifically the mothering of poor children of color, recognized as legitimate labor and as a social good. They believed they had the political power to bring about political change.

Lawyers became involved in the welfare rights movement, at which point the movement developed strategies for structural legal change. Columbia University professors Richard Cloward and Lloyd Ohlin established the Mobilization for Youth (MFY) project in Harlem. MFY was designed to address the needs of the community as those various needs arose. In 1963, its first year, the MFY Legal Unit filed numerous requests for fair hearings and filed suits against the New York City Welfare Department on behalf of welfare recipients who had been denied benefits (M. Davis 1993, 26-27). Harlem's MFY, especially its legal unit, had a meaningful role in the early mobilization of the poor and in the first attempts to jostle the welfare system through strategic litigation. The head of MFY's Legal Unit, Edward Sparer, would come to play an important role in the welfare rights litigation over the next decade. In 1965 Sparer convinced Columbia University to house the new Center on Social Welfare Policy and Law and then left MFY to run it (M. Davis 1993, 35).

The strategies chosen by MFY and the Center on Social Welfare Policy and Law were informed by provocative new ideas put forth by legal scholars of the time. Charles Reich's 1964 *Yale Law Journal* article "The New Property" proved particularly influential. Reich's central idea was that individuality, in terms of liberty and self-expression, is tied up with possession and control of property. The article began: "The institution called property guards the troubled boundary between individual man and the state. It is not the only guardian; many other institutions, laws, and practices serve as well. But in a society that chiefly values material well-being, the power to control a particular portion of that well-being is the very foundation of individuality" (733). In the article, Reich suggested that individuals' increasing reliance on government benefits was creating risks of government control over individuals and should prompt Americans to develop new notions of property and property rights. He argued that individuals' dependence on government-controlled benefits created greater opportunities for the government to control lives, coerce behavior, and curtail liberties. Under Reich's analysis, government benefits such as welfare should be given the status of property and the legal weight of traditional forms of property. If they were, Reich argued, their deprivation would trigger due process protections. A changing society, according to Reich, where individuals' lives were increasingly regulated by and reliant on government rules and government largesse called for new language, new understandings, and new interpretations of the U.S. Constitution.

Legal scholars followed Reich's lead and sought economic protections in constitutional law. Edward Sparer in 1965 wrote an article that called for equal protection guarantees for what he saw as discriminatory application of federal welfare programs and a constitutionally recognized "right to live" that would ensure basic subsistence to all Americans (35). Robert Cover, who in 1966 was a first-year student at Columbia Law School (later a law professor at Yale), drafted what became an influential and widely circulated legal memo on possible welfare rights strategies (M. Davis 1993, 59). Cover noted the lack of uniformity among states in the administration of federally mandated social welfare programs. He suggested pursuing litigation in the federal rather than state courts in order to bring national uniformity to welfare administration. This is precisely what lawyers for the poor began doing—arguing for a federal legal right to welfare, a right anchored in the U.S. Constitution.

Two of the most prominent leaders of the welfare rights movement were neither welfare recipients nor lawyers. Richard Cloward and Frances Fox Piven, two professors at the Columbia University School of Social Work, published an article titled "A Strategy to End Poverty" in the *Nation* in 1966. The article put forth a "crisis theory" to end poverty. Cloward and Piven noted that the political will at the time was to drive the poor from the welfare rolls, not to address the poverty that made AFDC a heavily used program. They also noted that only about half of the families eligible actually received AFDC. Cloward and Piven argued that if every individual who qualified for AFDC applied for the benefits, demanded every dollar available under the rules, and protested anything they were denied, then the federal, state, and local governments would be overwhelmed. "If this strategy were implemented," they argued, "a political crisis would result that could lead to legislation for a guaranteed annual income and thus an end to poverty" (510). A mass redistribution of wealth in the United States would be the only way to close the wide economic and racial gaps in the country. Central to this strategy was urging the poor to make claims to statutory benefits and to seek administrative redress if those claims were not fully satisfied. This strategy set in motion a decade-long shift, moving welfare from the domain of social work to the domain of law.

Grassroots welfare rights groups and activist lawyers gathered any information they could from welfare offices and pinpointed underutilized special grants that were available to recipients. The first large-scale welfare rights actions began in New York City with the 1965-66 campaign for winter clothing (Piven and Cloward [1971] 1993, 293-95). Although New York had a written policy allowing the poor a small amount of money in the fall to buy winter coats and boots for family members, very few welfare recipients knew of this policy and even fewer received the money. Led by an organizer from MFY, welfare recipients in Harlem filled out applications for winter clothing and went to their welfare offices en masse to demand winter clothing allowances. The welfare administrators, taken by surprise and overwhelmed by the action, provided the funds. Actions of this sort spread across the country. For example, a similar winter clothing action occurred in Ohio (West 1981, 23). The poor, newly aware of benefits potentially available to them, demanded the money to which they were entitled. Often, to avoid confrontations, the welfare offices simply provided the money. When welfare offices were not so acquiescent, situations grew more volatile.

More and more of the poor realized they were eligible for assistance and applied for welfare; and more and more welfare recipients demanded special needs grants. The sheer volume of applications was overwhelming the already overburdened social workers in welfare offices. Social workers in large cities were supposed to conduct home visits, but the number of cases each one had to handle prevented the workers from making visits *and* handling all of the paperwork. Welfare system insiders resisted welfare rights activism by reformulating policies. The first things to go were special needs grants. In September 1968, the New York State Board of Social Welfare ended its special needs grants in favor of a flat grant based on family size with a quarterly supplementation of twenty-five dollars to cover clothing and school-related expenses (Piven and Cloward [1977] 1979, 305). Other states followed suit.

The welfare rights movement moved from welfare offices to the courts. The welfare rights lawyers followed the NAACP's pattern of filing strategic test cases in federal courts. They saw *King v. Smith* (1968), first filed in federal court in 1966, as an ideal opportunity to establish precedent for federally recognized welfare rights. The plaintiff, Sylvester Smith, was an African American widow and mother of four whose welfare case had been closed when the welfare department found that a man (with a wife and nine children of his own) sometimes spent the night in her house. The case challenged the "substitute father rule," which stipulated that any man cohabiting with a mother should be responsible for supporting the entire household. The brief submitted by the plaintiff in the Supreme Court case identified a host of problematic issues associated with man-in-the-house rules: various constitutional claims; statutory claims; and, most notably, a claim that state practices were depriving the poor of a "right to live" (M. Davis 1993, 62-67). In 1968, the Supreme Court, avoiding the constitutional issues, handed down a decision halting the substitute father rule, declaring that it was inconsistent with the Social Security Act's intent to provide for needy children (*King v. Smith* (1968), 329). As a result, welfare offices devoted markedly less attention to the men involved in the lives of women receiving welfare. While the ruling lifted the stigma of welfare cheating from fathers and boyfriends, it also redirected attention to mothers.

As the 1960s progressed, low-income women of color were increasingly blamed for all sorts of social problems. An oft-cited 1965 report by Daniel Patrick Moynihan promoted the idea that the problems of inner cities—poverty, joblessness, and crime—could be traced to a "tangle of pathology" perpetuated by unmarried black mothers (30). The Moynihan Report identified family disorganization and disintegration among poor African Americans as a source of social, moral, and economic instability in the United States (5-6, 14). It stated that "as a direct result of this high rate of divorce, separation, and desertion, a very large percent of Negro families are headed by females. While the percentage of such families among whites has been dropping since 1940, it has been rising among Negroes" (9). Even worse, according to the report, many of the children in female-headed households received AFDC, a program originally designed for widows and orphans (12). In Moynihan's popular portrayal, low-income African American mothers were a social threat because they gave birth to and raised sons who became the criminal, urban underclass. This portrayal made it increasingly hard for grassroots welfare rights activists to have their voices heard.

The specter of the "black matriarch" described in the Moynihan Report became a powerful figure haunting efforts to expand economic security programs for the poor (Fineman 1991). Rather than focusing on the low educational attainment and high unemployment rates among African American men in urban areas, politicians and public opinion focused on the threats that independent black mothers posed to the future of the American family and American society. According to the portrait painted by the Moynihan Report and the many analyses that followed, low-income African American women were responsible for producing a dangerous threat: young, black—and likely criminal—men.

During the late 1960s and early 1970s, welfare rights lawyers argued a number of Supreme Court cases that brought about changes for poor families receiving welfare. Many of those changes imposed legal rationality on the system. For example, recipients became entitled to notice before their benefits were reduced or ended and rights to fair hearings to challenge negative actions (*Goldberg v. Kelly,* (1970)). The arbitrary exclusion of new state residents from the welfare rolls was curbed (*Shapiro v. Thompson* (1969)).

Not all of the Supreme Court decisions, however, favored welfare recipients. While the procedural rationality of AFDC was stepped up, the substantive foundations of the welfare program remained in question. The Supreme Court repeatedly ignored arguments for a guaranteed minimum income, for a governmentally secured "right to live." In fact, the Supreme Court ruled that states possessed the authority to cut welfare benefits and to set maximum aid payment levels even when those levels would leave families with unmet needs (*Rosado v. Wyman* (1970); *Dandridge v. Williams* (1970)). Moreover, the Supreme Court rejected arguments that programmatic distinctions between categories of the poor—specifically those that provided higher benefits to the white and elderly and lower benefits to the black and young—amounted to invidious discrimination (*Jefferson v. Hackney* (1972)).

The legal arm of the welfare rights movement and the grassroots arm, while working together in many ways, were also making fundamentally different claims about government assistance to poor families. The grassroots activists focused on the particular plight of poor mothers of color in inner cities. They demanded recognition of their particular needs and of the importance of taking good care of children as they grew up. Theirs was a call for government to recognize and remedy the economic effects of race, class, gender, and parental status disparities. The legal reformers, however, downplayed the racialized, classed, and gendered lives and experiences of poor mothers, highlighting instead the universality of rights.

Both the failures and the successes of the legal efforts led to the undoing of the grassroots welfare rights movement. The legal efforts triggered the demise of special needs grants and other discretionary welfare benefits. With those grants gone and with individuals able to pursue problems with benefits through the fair hearings process, incentives for individual participation in a broad movement of the poor withered (Handler and Hasenfeld 1991, 120). By 1970, in fact, the National Welfare Rights Organization (NWRO), an umbrella group to local welfare rights organizations around the country, had virtually ended its earlier collaborative relationship with the lawyers who were litigating the welfare rights cases and was devoting more and more of its time to lobbying (M. Davis 1993, 52; West 1981, 287).

Many legislative reforms occurred during the early 1970s. The Nixon administration expanded the food stamp program and established Supplemental Security Income for low-income elderly and disabled persons (Katz 1989, 102; Leiby 1978, 327). In 1972 President Richard Nixon proposed the Family Assistance Program (FAP), a guaranteed income program offered as an alternative to the existing AFDC program. The proposed guaranteed annual income for a two-parent family of four was $1,600, a meager figure but actually higher than the annual benefits some southern states provided at the time to families under AFDC (Patterson 1994, 192-93). Nonetheless, those welfare rights activists who were still doing battle opposed the plan's low benefits and its work requirements (Patterson 1994, 195). Members of the NWRO attacked FAP as "institutional racism" (Moynihan 1973, 226). With no enthusiastic support from either liberals or conservatives, the FAP bill failed in Congress (Patterson 1994, 194).

The movement for welfare rights was effectively dead in 1973. Grassroots organizations were gone. Attempts by lawyers to secure rights to welfare had pushed the issue as far as the courts appeared willing to allow. In addition, instead of committing its resources to fighting poverty, the federal government began curbing earlier efforts to ameliorate poverty. The Legal Services Program, established by the federal Office of Economic Opportunity in 1965, was transformed in 1974 into the Legal Services Corporation, a quasi-independent, nonprofit source of legal aid money established by Congress (West 1981, 332). This change was prompted by a desire among members of Congress to dampen the efforts of Legal Services attorneys who, despite receiving government money, had devoted significant time and resources litigating claims against the government. Under the new rules, the corporation could not have poor clients as members of the board of directors, and the corporation's lawyers were prohibited from some political activities (West 1981, 332). With both grassroots activists and legal activists quieting their efforts, there was little counterpressure to the punitive changes to welfare policies that were to come.

The 1970s: Growing Concerns about Government Waste and Fraud

The welfare rights movement and all of its players did produce some dramatic effects on the welfare system. The number of people receiving AFDC tripled between 1960 and 1974 (Patterson 1994, 171). The efforts of welfare rights activists contributed, both directly and indirectly, to this surge. It also became harder to live on welfare. As the U.S. economy slowed down in the 1970s, welfare benefits were devalued as a result of rapid inflation (Piven and Cloward [1971] 1993, 371-72). This would begin several decades of decline in the real value of welfare benefits (Gustafson 2009, 651).

As a result of the welfare reforms passed during the Nixon administration, the AFDC system became less discretionary and more bureaucratic. Specifically, welfare offices increased the amount of paperwork welfare recipients had to submit and began mailing welfare checks rather than having welfare recipients pick them up at the offices. These changes were made for two reasons: first, to make welfare receipt more cumbersome and reduce the welfare rolls; second to prevent welfare recipients from gathering at welfare offices, sharing information with each other, and starting riots (Piven and Cloward [1971] 1993, 374-79). Welfare offices replaced trained social workers with office caseworkers who processed paperwork. Caseworker visits to the homes of welfare recipients virtually ended (Casey and Mannix 1989, 1386).

Quality control measures implemented in 1973 imposed increased reporting requirements for welfare recipients (Brodkin 1986, 30; W. Simon 1983).

Through a practice known as "churning," the federal government increased the amount of information and paperwork required to determine welfare eligibility and disqualified welfare recipients who failed to submit paperwork in a timely manner (Casey and Mannix 1989, 1385). Welfare officials knew that increasing the paperwork requirements would discourage some recipients from applying for aid and would disqualify others—even eligible poor families—who failed to fulfill their obligations. It was an effective strategy, eliminating a growing number of poor children from the welfare rolls (Piven and Cloward [1971] 1993, 379; Lipsky 1984, 13).

Concerns about welfare cheats, in particular, began to rise. Following amendments to the Social Security Act in 1974, AFDC recipients were required to report their Social Security numbers, and soon computers began being used routinely to monitor for fraud (Greenberg and Wolf 1986, 19). The welfare system involved more paperwork and fewer and fewer caseworkers, thus depersonalizing welfare receipt (Patterson 1994, 200).

President Jimmy Carter offered Congress welfare reform proposals that included punitive provisions that would cut off benefits to adult members of families receiving AFDC if those adults refused to work (Patterson 1994, 206-7). The War on Poverty rhetoric about individuals being at the mercy of economic forces was long gone: Carter's rhetoric implied a direct relationship between individuals' unwillingness to work and their poverty. Efforts to condition government assistance on participation in state-supervised work programs ran contrary to the "new property" theories of the 1960s, which had promoted economic support contingent only upon need.

The federal government began tracking state error rates in welfare and food stamp payments. The federal rules penalized states for overpayments in benefits but not for underpayments to or exclusion of the eligible poor, thus creating incentives for states to err on the side of caution in determining eligibility (Casey and Mannix 1989; Lipsky 1984). As a result of the Food Stamp Act of 1977, those who applied for food stamps were required to provide their Social Security numbers to welfare officials. This marked the first widespread use of data exchange among government agencies and the beginning of computer data tracking of the poor.

To keep government waste in check, President Carter signed into law the Inspector General Act of 1978, which authorized him to appoint inspector generals to oversee twelve administrative agencies. Data collection and fiscal oversight increased. A 1979 inspector general report on the Department of Health, Education and Welfare revealed costly fraud and abuse—by students defaulting on their government loans and by medical care providers overcharging the Medicaid and Medicare programs (Office of Inspector General 1979, 58-68, 122). Overpayments to AFDC recipients and fraud by government officials in both the cash aid and food stamp programs were cited in the report but were described as problems less significant than the student aid and medical aid abuses.

Crowning the Welfare Queen

Concerns about welfare cheating have been a recurrent theme in poverty politics. Senator Robert Byrd made a highly publicized investigation of welfare fraud in Washington, D.C., in 1962 (Gilens 1999, 115). In 1972, when President Richard Nixon was considering an overhaul of the welfare system, Senator Russell Long of Louisiana declared that "the welfare system, as we know it today, is being manipulated and abused by malingerers, cheats and outright frauds" (Long 1972, 1). While a distrust of poor adults has always existed in the United States, that distrust appeared to grow during the 1970s.

That is not to say that no individuals defrauded the welfare system. In fact, there have been a few notable cheats. In the late 1970s and early 1980s, there were some well-publicized cases of welfare fraud in large U.S. cities. The first nationally publicized case made news in 1974 when police investigated a forty-seven-year-old Chicago mother, Linda Taylor, for welfare fraud. Taylor herself triggered the investigation by reporting to police that fourteen thousand dollars in cash, jewelry, and furs had been stolen from her home. Early newspaper accounts of the investigation reported that Taylor was being investigated for using as many as fourteen different aliases over twenty-eight years to collect perhaps hundreds of thousands of dollars in welfare and social security payments (New York Times, December 15, 1974). The early estimates of her fraud were apparently overstated. In March 1977, Taylor—whom investigators and the press called the "welfare queen"—was found guilty of welfare fraud and perjury for using two aliases to collect eight thousand dollars in wrongful payments over the course of twenty-three months (*New York Times,* March 19, 1977).

Then, in 1978, a thirty-three-year-old African American mother from Compton, California, Barbara Jean Williams, was convicted of ten counts of welfare fraud and twelve counts of perjury. According to a newspaper account of the investigation, an anonymous tip prompted officials to check her alleged aliases in the computer, which revealed several welfare cases opened under identical or similar names (Washington Post, December 2, 1978). At the time she applied for aid, the welfare system had not yet been computerized, making it easy for a willful criminal to open multiple cases under different names. Williams, described by the *New York Times* as the "Queen of Welfare," was sentenced to eight years in jail (*New York Times,* December 29, 1978). In coverage of her court case, the *New York Times* and *Washington Post* repeatedly noted that Williams drove a Cadillac.

It was not by happenstance that welfare fraud cases involving double-dipping were discovered in the late 1970s, as it was then that the AFDC system was computerized, making it easier for welfare officials to identify and document cases of fraud. What may have appeared to the public and to legislators as a spike in welfare fraud cases was actually a sudden improvement in the abilities of officials to root out fraud. While this transformation—the computerization of the welfare system—might have been celebrated as a means of providing aid more efficiently and effectively, it instead sparked a period of zealous attacks on welfare recipients and welfare programs.

The 1980s: The Rise of the Welfare Queen

The election of Ronald Reagan to U.S. president in 1980 marked a shift in government priorities along with a shift in public rhetoric about the poor and about welfare. From the first moment of his bid for presidential election in 1980, Ronald Reagan used anecdotes about welfare queens to exemplify everything he believed wrong with government programs—excessive spending on domestic programs and misuse of government money. Reagan apparently merged the identities of Taylor, the Chicago "welfare queen," and Williams, the Cadillac-driving "Queen of Welfare" from Compton, into one persona that starred in an often-used anecdote. And he regularly exaggerated the number of aliases so that his welfare queen had a hundred of them (Broder 1981). The symbol of the welfare queen played a prominent role in Reagan's presidential campaign.

In December 1980, after Reagan's successful presidential election, another large welfare fraud case surfaced in California. Dorothy Woods, a thirty-eight-year-old African American mother of six living in Pasadena, was charged with welfare fraud for creating twelve aliases for herself and using the names of fictitious children to receive large payments from the AFDC program (New York Times, December 21, 1980, and March 17, 1983a). Woods was jailed in November of 1981; in March of 1983 she pleaded guilty to forty-one criminal counts, including forgery, perjury, and welfare fraud. According to prosecutors, Woods fraudulently collected $377,458 in welfare fraud between 1974 and 1980 (New York Times, March 17, 1983a). The media dubbed Woods—who possessed a Rolls Royce, a Mercedes Benz, and a Cadillac and who lived in a large house with a pool—the "Welfare Queen" (New York Times, December 21, 1980).

Rather than treating the three welfare fraud cases of Linda Taylor, Barbara Jean Williams, and Dorothy Woods as the exceptional instances of criminal activity they were, politicians—and the media and public as well—adopted these cases as typifying poor, African American women on welfare. These "welfare queens" were treated not merely as stereotypes of poor black mothers on aid but as archetypes—perfect examples of what welfare recipients become over the course of years on the dole. Ronald Reagan's reelection campaign was spearheaded by an attack on "waste, fraud and abuse" in welfare programs. Just as in his first bid for the White House, the welfare queen became a powerful symbol in the 1984 presidential campaign.

The figure of the welfare queen offered contradictory stereotypes about the rationality of poor women. On the one hand, the welfare queen stereotype embodied someone hyperrational who was working the system, milking government money from taxpayers. The welfare queen was someone who had decided to maximize her income by having more and more children and increasing her government benefits rather than working. She also represented a mother who refused to marry—because entering into marriage would jeopardize her government benefits.

At the same time, the welfare queen stereotype portrayed welfare recipients as uneducated, lazy, and irrational. A welfare queen was someone who did not, or perhaps would not, pursue the long-term well-being of her family. She was someone unmotivated to seek an education to improve her station, someone who refused to take the economic risk of becoming independent of the welfare system. Worst of all, she had children without regard for her inability to raise them in middle-class comfort. She neither participated in the paid labor market nor took on the caretaking responsibilities for a working husband. She simply drew upon taxpayer dollars, displaying neither gratitude nor remorse.

Where the welfare queen stereotype was accurate was in its characterization of poverty and welfare as women's issues. Indeed in 1984, two-thirds of the adults living below the poverty line were women. And with rising divorce rates and an increasing number of nonmarital births in the United States, the disproportionate representation of women and their children would become a growing trend.

Poverty reduction was not a government priority under the Reagan administration. Whereas Nixon, during his State of the Union Address in 1973, proudly stated that federal spending on food assistance programs had tripled during his presidency, Reagan regarded those very programs as government waste (Pear 1982). Under Reagan's direction, the federal government cut funding for food stamps (Roberts 1981). It also tightened the eligibility requirements for the federal school lunch program, eliminating 2.6 million children from eligibility (Pear 1982).

Congress passed policies that contributed to hardships among low-income families rather than reducing poverty in the United States. For example, the Omnibus Budget Reconciliation Act of 1981 reduced income disregards that had previously been available to poor working families. By reducing a family's aid by one dollar for every dollar earned through employment, it effectively rendered welfare benefits unavailable to poor parents who worked. Between 1978 and 1985, the number of poor Americans increased by ten million, and those who were poor found themselves even farther below the poverty line (Lelyveld 1985).

The attacks on the disempowered were not limited to attacks on welfare recipients; President Reagan also took aim at legal aid attorneys. Many of the welfare policies and welfare reforms Reagan instituted as governor of California had been challenged, often successfully, by class-action lawsuits filed by legal aid lawyers on behalf of poor clients. In his first two annual budgets, Reagan sought an end to congressional funding of the Legal Services Corporation altogether; when he faced resistance, he turned to funding cutbacks. These reductions left many legal aid offices, which were for many poor people their only access to administrative appeals and to the courts, without the resources they needed to serve clients. The reforms also prohibited Legal Services employees from engaging in lobbying and restricted Legal Services attorneys from filing class-action lawsuits against state and federal governments (New York Times, November 29, 1983b). These class-action suits had, of course, been the engine in the welfare rights movement in the 1960s and 1970s.

Finally, both Reagan and members of the Senate Finance Committee began to attack just those welfare reforms that had been secured through welfare litigation during the welfare rights movement, specifically the federalization of oversight of welfare programs. Policy makers began pushing for a "New Federalism," a movement that included shifting the responsibilities for welfare benefits from the federal government to the states.

Reframing Poverty: The Underclass and Government-Bred Dependency

During the 1980s social science took hold as the dominant professional discourse guiding welfare policies. No longer were lawyers guiding welfare policies or welfare rhetoric. The Supreme Court, Congress, and the state legislatures had settled the boundaries of welfare reform on the legal front. No longer were social workers influential in welfare design. Instead, statisticians examined administrative data in an attempt both to gauge quality control figures and to detect welfare fraud (e.g., Chi 1984; Gardiner 1984; Gardiner and Lyman 1984; Greenberg and Wolf 1986; Hutton 1985; Lange 1979; Little 1983; Wolf and Greenberg 1986). And economists measured the costs of government outlays for welfare and proposed policies for reducing those costs. At the same time, sociologists proved very influential in guiding debates about welfare. Drawing upon the work of the anthropologist Oscar Lewis in the 1950s (Lewis 1959, 1968) and Daniel Patrick Moynihan in the 1960s (Moynihan 1965), sociologists examined why welfare rates remained high among certain subpopulations and wrote about the "culture of poverty" in poor communities where families were dependent upon government aid for their subsistence, particularly African Americans living in large cities. The culture-of-poverty hypothesis was transformed into research on "welfare dependency" and "the underclass" in the 1980s.

Academics and policy makers began labeling welfare itself, rather than poverty, as the social problem to be conquered, the social ill that deserved public attention. The analyses put forward during the 1980s fostered public beliefs that effective remedies for poverty lay outside the ken of the government and that poverty had simply become ingrained in the culture of inner-city, African American neighborhoods.

Charles Murray, a prominent author and welfare pundit, used the term *welfare dependency* in his popular book *Losing Ground* to describe the long-term use of welfare by poor families (1984, 38). He employed an economic model of welfare use, describing the receipt of welfare as an individual choice that stood in opposition to work. Murray used the image of the "carrot and stick" to describe state-created incentives and disincentives for work that the state created or could create (176). He also used the language of desert, arguing that the welfare policies of the sixties had transferred resources from "the most capable poor to the least capable, from the most law-abiding to the least law-abiding, and from the most responsible to the least responsible" (201). His implication that welfare recipients were less law-abiding and responsible than other Americans was common in the 1980s.

Murray admitted that working failed to lift many families much beyond poverty and that many poor adults had little incentive to work. Still, he argued, these people should work, and society should create penalties that would make existence uncomfortable for anyone who failed to work (1984, 177). He argued that means-tested government assistance programs had eroded both the work ethic and the pride that Americans had once taken from work, even low-paid work (178-91). He also popularized the argument—or perhaps gave voice to a popular belief—that the welfare system, encompassing the government generally and the welfare system particularly, was to blame for the social and economic problems in the United States. Murray's rhetoric became influential in the popular and elite debates, soon leading to policy changes. The debates included other conservatives, including Lawrence Mead (1986) and George Gilder (1981), who relied on rational actor models of welfare use.

Examining the effects of social policies of the 1960s and 1970s, the University of Chicago sociologist William Julius Wilson wrote about the growth of "the underclass." He defined the underclass as "the most disadvantaged segment of the black urban community, that heterogeneous grouping of families and individuals who are outside the mainstream of the American occupational system. Included in this group are individuals who lack training and skills and either experience long-term unemployment or are not members of the labor force, individuals who are engaged in street crime and other forms of aberrant behavior, and families that experience long-term spells of poverty and/or welfare dependency" (1987, 8). Wilson's work on the underclass was influential in shaping the focus and nature of debates on poverty over the next decade for two main reasons. First, he examined only poverty in northern, urban centers populated by African Americans. By limiting his examination to what seemed to be the site least affected by the War on Poverty and its reforms, his focus had the effect of shifting policy debates from poverty generally to the urban segment of the poor. And while whites made up a larger proportion of welfare recipients and rural poverty remained a persistent problem, African Americans living in inner cities absorbed more of the attention of research and public debate. Second, Wilson examined long-term welfare use—what he described as "welfare dependency"—as a pathology on a par with criminal behavior. Public benefits became the problem, not the cure, when it came to poverty. *Welfare dependency* became a catch-phrase in the decade that followed.

Social scientists' interest in studying welfare and welfare fraud contributed to a rise in the policing of welfare. On the street level, fraud control measures brought about increased surveillance of poor families. Computers were increasingly used to organize and store information about families receiving welfare. These computer files could also be—and were—used to search for inconsistent information and errors in benefit calculations. The files could also be cross-checked with other administrative data files, including those kept by state tax boards, state employment agencies, health care providers, and the Internal Revenue Service.

States and counties revved up the number of fraud investigators who were in welfare offices. Their actions echoed welfare policies of old. While the midnight raids conducted by welfare officials in the 1950s and 1960s to police the man-in-the-house rules largely ended as a result of the Flemming Rule, similar unannounced visits and searches continued under the guise of welfare fraud investigations. In addition, during the 1980s and 1990s many states and localities opened up welfare fraud hotlines that anyone could use anonymously to report suspected fraud.

The increased attention of social scientists, as well as their growing role in designing welfare policies, changed the way Americans thought of poverty and poor families. In macro-level studies of welfare recipients, "the poor" became an undifferentiated group in social consciousness and public discourse, a group perceived as urban, African American, and female. Moreover, this group frequently described as the underclass was increasingly treated as a group that lay outside the American mainstream—not only with regard to income levels, but also with regard to work habits, family structure, and morals.

These scholars influenced the policies implemented under President George Bush. The Family Support Act, signed by President Reagan one month before the 1988 presidential election, demonstrated the effects of the court decisions of the 1960s and 1970s on the drafting of legislation. Congress no longer left the intent behind the legislation unclear or stated that welfare provisions were designed to meet economic need. The act explicitly stated that the reforms were intended to prompt individuals' transitions from welfare to work. These transitions were hoped to occur through two routes—mandatory job training for welfare recipients with children over the age of three and workfare programs for principal wage earners in two-parent families receiving welfare (Handler 1987-88; Trattner 1994, 376).

The Family Support Act of 1988, designed by Daniel Patrick Moynihan, who had by then become a senator, offered—at least in theory—some supports for the working poor. Those supports included money for child care and transportation expenses for families, as well as continued Medicaid coverage for families who left welfare but continued to have low incomes (Trattner 1994, 377). But the policies did little to help the poor. The historian William Trattner notes that the statute failed to establish minimum AFDC benefits or to encourage states to increase benefits, thereby ensuring that "real" dollar values of welfare would continue their decline (1994, 377). In short, the statute allowed the poor to get poorer. In addition, the training and work programs developed under the Family Support Act never received the funding they needed for job training, child care, and supportive services (Katz 1998, 75; Trattner 1994, 381). Many of the family supports for working families simply never materialized.

This welfare reform effort marked a dramatic shift away from the rights rhetoric of the welfare rights movement. No longer were the individual rights of welfare recipients a pressing legal concern. Instead, the rights of states and the rights of employed taxpayers—now the "public" to whom the government owed its full commitment—dominated the discourse. But the commitment to the public did not include a commitment to cut government expenditures on welfare programs: the Family Support Act of 1988 actually increased social welfare costs by $3.5 billion over five years (Melnick 1990, 226).

In addition, under President George H. Bush, devolution—the extraction of the federal government from government works and the shift of responsibility from federal to state and local governments—began in earnest in the context of aid to the poor. Changes in government assistance to the poor were a significant part of the devolutionary process. State welfare waiver programs began the development of state-controlled welfare policies. Waiver programs were nothing new in the 1980s; they had been available long before their surge in use during the Bush era. As part of the 1962 amendment to the Social Security Act, Congress granted the Department of Health, Education and Welfare (later to become the Department of Health and Human Services) the ability to waive federal public assistance requirements where states proposed experimental or demonstration projects "likely to assist in promoting the objectives of [the statute]" (Section 1115 of the Social Security Act, 42 U.S.C. § 1315a). These experiments began with small site projects where welfare offices tried alternative administrative rules to see whether the changes streamlined the delivery of benefits to the poor (Williams 1994, 11-12, 14-15).

The Bush administration took advantage of this waiver rule, actively encouraging states to submit waiver proposals to the secretary of Health and

Human Services. Many states accepted the invitation, and the projects were generally approved without delay. (A challenge to this rubber-stamping was taken up in *Beno v. Shalala* (1994).) Many of these experimental waiver projects simply provided a pretext for the states to reduce welfare expenditures, and many states instituted the very rules that had come under attack during the welfare rights movement. California's 1992 waiver, for example, sought to reduce the level of AFDC cash payments below that mandated by federal legislation. The Ninth Circuit Court opinion, addressing a challenge to California's waiver, stated, "California's waiver application alleged that the instant benefits cut would promote the objectives of the Act by creating a 'work-incentive' experiment, which would 'encourage able-bodied adults to find work'" (*Beno v. Shalala* (1994), 1062).

Many of the state waiver proposals imposed new punitive conditions upon parents receiving welfare. For example, Wisconsin had a waiver program called "Learnfare" that cut the cash AFDC families received if the teen-aged children in those families missed too many days of school (Trattner 1994, 380). Other states, including New Jersey, established policies whereby newborn children would not be recognized as members of the welfare recipients' household in the calculations of cash aid (though they would be considered in food stamp calculations). These "family cap" or "child exclusion" provisions were primarily designed to discourage welfare recipients from getting pregnant and bearing children while receiving welfare by eliminating the small increase in cash aid that would have otherwise been triggered by an increase in family size. The waivers were designed to regulate not only economic behavior but also sexuality, morality, and family planning.

While scientific rhetoric infused these policies, and while welfare waivers were touted as "experiments" giving states a chance to evaluate the effectiveness of policy changes, some social scientists questioned the scientific value of these experiments. Some of the waiver policies, for example, were instituted statewide, meaning there was no control group against which to compare the effects of the policy changes. Moreover, these so-called experiments commonly violated ethical guidelines that social scientists generally follow in conducting research with human subjects, namely, guidelines prohibiting experiments that might bring physical, psychological, or emotional harm to human subjects and guidelines requiring that experiments be performed only upon persons who have given their informed consent to participate and who are not vulnerable to coercion. Indeed the welfare waivers of the Bush era turned poor parents and their children into the unconsenting subjects—or some might say objects—of social experiments designed to modify behavior through economic deprivation and its attendant psychological and physical harms. Studies of the family cap policies in New Jersey, where abortions were more easily available than in other states, found that the family cap was associated with lower birthrates and higher abortion rates, though only among black welfare recipients in certain neighborhoods (Jagannathan and Camasso 2003; Camasso 2007).

By the end of the Bush era, the welfare rights movement's notion that welfare recipients were rights-bearing members of the general citizenry had faded into distant memory.

The 1990s: Welfare Reform and the Convergence of the Welfare and Criminal Justice Systems

Vilifying the low-income mothers receiving welfare became a bipartisan project in the 1990s. Survey research revealed that Americans associated welfare with African Americans and viewed the welfare system as a program that rewarded laziness among African Americans (Gilens 1999, 3). *Welfare dependency* became a key term associated not only with economic risk and social disorder but also with crime (Hancock 2004, 93-94). In an interview during his presidential campaign of 1992, Bill Clinton said, "What I am in favor of doing is breaking the chain of dependency through putting more people to work" (Scheer 1992). The issue of welfare dependency was in active play during the 1992 presidential campaign. Once in office, President Bill Clinton carried forward his predecessor's efforts to decentralize public assistance programs, impose conditions upon welfare receipt, and preclude the efforts of lawyers in challenging welfare provisions.

The welfare reforms crafted during the first Clinton administration were the result of rare bipartisan effort. Social scientists, including liberal Paul Ellwood and conservative Charles Murray, played prominent roles in proposing policies that would require welfare recipients to work (Bane and Ellwood 1994; Ellwood 1988). Ellwood argued that the AFDC system served as a disincentive to work. He and Mary Jo Bane wrote, "For the welfare system to be morally legitimate in the eyes of its clients and the taxpayers, it needs to embody not only the values of self-sufficiency and responsibility but also the values of fairness and rationality" (Bane and Ellwood 1994, 133).

Work was central to the policies crafted by both liberals and conservatives, though they differed on the role of the federal government. Bane and Ellwood promoted the idea that government should "make work pay" by expanding redistributive tax policies, such as the Earned Income Tax Credit, and by making medical insurance available to all workers. Murray, on the other hand, disapproved of most government supports, arguing that they made Americans dependent on government. His proposal involved "scrapping the entire federal welfare and income-support structure for working-aged persons, including AFDC, Medicaid, Food Stamps, Unemployment Insurance, Worker's [sic] Compensation, subsidized housing, disability insurance, and the rest" (1984, 227-28).

Making clear to the courts that welfare reform was not simply or essentially about serving the needs of the poor, members of Congress titled the 1996 welfare reform measure the Personal Responsibility and Work Opportunity Reconciliation Act of 1996 (PRWORA). The legislation eliminated the broad, federally governed AFDC program. In its place came block grants, distributed by the federal government to the states, and a cash assistance program known as Temporary Assistance for Needy Families (TANF).

The "congressional findings" that appear at the beginning of the PRWORA statute, which authorizes TANF, are telling of the concerns and priorities members of Congress brought to the development of legislation. The first two findings address the importance of marriage to society; the second addresses the need for "promotion of responsible fatherhood and motherhood." The remaining seven findings—and their subsections—describe the social and economic harms suffered by—and it is suggested, caused by—female-headed households and nonmarital childbearing. The given purposes of the statute were to give the states flexibility to "provide assistance to needy families" and to "end the dependence of needy parents on government benefits," two goals that are in many ways contradictory.

President Clinton promised that the welfare reforms would, above all, "make work pay." (This statement disregarded the caretaking work that poor parents were doing in their homes, for that work has never paid.) The clear implication was that if poor adults played by the rules they would get ahead. At the same time, the new welfare system threatened that those who failed to play by the rules would be harshly punished with new penalties. Those who failed to meet their obligations under the new welfare system would be excluded from the benefits of social participation by having the safety net pulled out from under them, in some cases permanently.

PRWORA, the federal legislation authorizing the transformation of the welfare system, was signed in August of 1996. It did away with a statutory entitlement to aid based solely on need. It allowed states themselves to determine the rules for receipt and restrict benefits to individuals who would otherwise be income-eligible for cash assistance under the federal guidelines.

The federal law also allowed states to determine the maximum grants available to the poor. States generally maintained the aid levels they had in place under the AFDC program. Just as they had under the AFDC program, the monthly benefits varied dramatically from state to state.

The federal law instituted a host of new rules and regulations. For example, it mandated a sixty-month lifetime limit on receipt of TANF cash aid. Whether a welfare recipient received welfare over a full five-year stretch or was on and off aid for years, once she reached her sixty-month limit, she could receive no more TANF aid. The federal sixty-month time limit was set as an outer limit; PRWORA allowed states to institute even shorter time limits. Twenty-one states implemented time limits shorter than five years (Schram 2002, 92). In California, once a welfare recipient reached her time limit, the recipient's children could continue to receive cash assistance, and the recipient, if working, might continue to receive work supports such as transportation assistance and child care. Because the TANF block grant program was not implemented in California until January 1, 1998, the first welfare recipients did not reach their sixty-month time limits until December 31, 2002.

PRWORA required states to implement welfare-to-work programs and required welfare recipients to participate in work activities within twenty-four months of receiving their first aid checks under TANF. Again, states could choose to require welfare recipients to work sooner than twenty-four months into their aid receipt, and twenty-six states did (Schram 2002, 92). California legislators used the money from the federal block grant to implement the California Work Opportunity and Responsibility to Kids program, better known as CalWORKs. The legislation required all families who had received AFDC and who would continue to receive aid to participate in work activities after eighteen months; all new applicants had twenty-four months to either engage in work activities or face sanctions. The CalWORKs program began with an orientation program. Orientation either included or was followed by a series of assessment tests to determine a welfare recipient's level of literacy and skill. After the orientation, individuals were required to meet with an employment specialist—the new titles given to the welfare caseworkers who had until then been known as eligibility workers—and to sign a "welfare-to-work" plan.

The federal rules passed in 1996 required welfare recipients to engage in "work activities" but initially left it to the states to define what counted as a work activity. California was one of many states known as "work-first" states. In work-first states, welfare recipients were pushed to take jobs—any jobs—rather than engage in training or education. Under AFDC, welfare recipients had been allowed to pursue educational programs, even college, if they were motivated to do so. Some who argued for the work-first approach complained that allowing welfare recipients to go to school undermined a general work ethic, allowed individuals to linger in the welfare system longer than necessary, and prompted a sense of unfairness among the many students who put themselves through college without direct cash assistance from the federal government. The CalWORKs program instituted after the federal reforms allowed a welfare recipient to participate in education programs only with the approval of her employment specialist. These programs, known as "Self-Initiated Programs" or "SIPs," were rarely pursued, in part, the interviews suggest, because often neither welfare recipients nor welfare workers knew about them. Welfare recipients who initiated and pursued education plans were allowed only a few months of education and even then were pushed toward low-paid vocational courses, such as cosmetology, that could directly lead to employment.

Once they signed their welfare-to-work plans, welfare recipients in California were required to work, or be engaged in a work-related activity such as a work-skills training program, for thirty-two hours a week. The requirement for two-parent families was thirty-five hours a week, which could be performed in full by one parent or divided between the two. For single parents with children under age six, the work participation requirement was reduced to twenty hours a week.

Welfare recipients engaged in work had available to them some work supports through the CalWORKs program. These supports included subsidized child care, though finding providers who would accept the low state payments and who did not have long waiting lists was often difficult for welfare recipients. Transportation supports—for example, payments for auto mileage or bus passes—were also available to working welfare recipients.

PRWORA allowed the states to exempt some welfare recipients from the work requirements, although it initially limited those exempt to 20 percent of the welfare caseload. The states were given the discretion to determine what the exemption categories would be. California identified twelve exemption categories under which welfare recipients could avoid the work requirements without being sanctioned.

Congress and the states also implemented punitive policies that affected parents and children who had not violated the eligibility rules. PRWORA allowed states to adopt the "family cap" policies that prevented children born to welfare recipients from receiving cash aid. California adopted the policy, calling it the maximum family grant. It was one of twenty-three states to adopt family cap policies (Schram 2002).

Welfare reform brought additional requirements and regulations for parents receiving aid. First, to receive money under the TANF block grant and under CalWORKs, parents had to show that their children's immunizations were up-to-date. Second, mothers had to cooperate in measures to determine the paternity of their children and to collect child support. Failure to cooperate could lead to benefit sanctions or to a denial of aid altogether. Third, teen parents were required to live with their own parents and to attend school to receive cash aid.

The federal welfare reform legislation, which politicians commonly described as the "carrot and stick" approach to welfare during the movement for the 1996 reforms, included a number of sticks. The biggest stick: sanctions. Sanctions applied to individuals who failed to comply with state welfare requirements. When it came to sanctions, California was not one of the most punitive states. While thirty-six states instituted full-family sanctions, which cut off a family's entire cash grant if the adult or adults failed to meet state-mandated work requirements, California employed an adult-only sanction (Pavetti et al. 2004). In other words, if a welfare recipient in California failed to satisfy her work requirement hours (or attend her CalWORKs orientation or meeting with her employment specialist), then only her portion of aid was withheld from the cash grant. A parent who failed to meet her work requirements also faced the loss of any ancillary benefits she used as work supports, such as transportation subsidies and child care services.

The Early Effects of Welfare Reform and the California Context

Because each state adopted its own unique welfare program, an overall analysis of welfare reform or specific welfare reform programs proves difficult. There can be no doubt, however, that the welfare caseloads nationwide dropped dramatically between 1996 and 2002. Between January 1994, when the AFDC caseload peaked in the United States, and January 2002, the welfare rolls nationwide dropped more than 60 percent, from more than 14.3 million recipients to 5.3 million recipients (U.S. Department of Health and Human Services 2010). It is not clear how much of the decrease can be directly attributed to welfare reform. In the two years before welfare reforms of 1996, the caseloads had already begun to decline. In addition, the U.S. economy was robust and growing from the mid-1990s to well into 2000.

Work participation rates among welfare recipients rose after welfare reform was instituted. The jobs that welfare recipients took, however, generally provided low pay—too low to raise them out of poverty. The average wage for parents who left the welfare system for employment was between seven and eight dollars an hour (Lower-Basch and Greenberg 2009, 175). The jobs that welfare leavers took tended to lack stable hours, health care coverage, sick leave, or vacation time (Lower-Basch and Greenberg 2009, 175-76). Because the state welfare caseloads dropped precipitously, however, welfare reform was widely described as a success. Sanford F. Schram and Joe Soss note that "when advocates established dependency as a synecdoche for underclass pathology and as the central target for reform, they simultaneously highlighted caseload decline and employment among leavers as preeminent standards for judging the success of reform" (2001, 56).

Still other indicators of economic hardship persisted among the low-income families using, and leaving, the welfare system. During the first five years of welfare reform, the child poverty rate declined only slightly and then rose again, where it has since hovered around 18 percent (Chau and Douglas-Hall 2008, 6 table1). Rates of extreme poverty—meaning an income at less than half the poverty line—rose; so, too, did measures of food insecurity and hunger (Burnham 2002, 46-48).

Despite the lingering problems of hunger and poverty, food stamp participation declined dramatically between 1996 and 1999, from a monthly average of 25.5 million families to 18.5 million (U.S. General Accounting Office 1999). Most of the families leaving welfare should have remained eligible for food stamps on the basis of their low incomes. However, the state TANF programs and their application procedures appeared to be one of the factors affecting underutilization of food stamps (U.S. General Accounting Office 1999; Zedlewski and Brauner 1999a, 1999b). In most locales, food stamps were administered through the same offices as TANF cash assistance. Some welfare offices instituted programs that dissuaded poor families from even applying for assistance. The Department of Agriculture cited seventeen states for these practices, which tended to deter hungry families from applying for food stamps (U.S. General Accounting Office 1999).

Dramatic shifts in welfare discourses, welfare benefits, and welfare administration occurred during the twentieth century. Throughout the century and across all of the changes, the idea that welfare should be used to regulate morality was inherent in the discourses and policies. But the ideas about what the moral threats were changed over time. At the beginning, private charities and, later, state aid programs assumed that mothers were the moral guides within families, and aid programs were intended to replace missing fathers by offering the financial stability that would provide mothers with the ability to provide moral instruction for their families. By the end of the century, though, dominant public rhetoric and welfare policies cast poor mothers as threats to morality, both within individual families and within society more generally. Popular descriptions of poor mothers as dependent—or even parasitic—members of the national economy and as uncaring mothers fueled the reforms that eventually took place. The reformers at the end of the twentieth century considered it best for families and for society to coax, or push, poor mothers out of the household and into the workforce.

There were also shifts in the legal rationality of welfare administration and in the view of poor mothers as rational economic actors. When private charities began administering aid to the poor, the benefits they provided were individualized and discretionary. Aid was inconsistent, unstable, and usually insufficient to support families. The early social worker model was designed to mold poor women into a standard model of motherhood. By contrast, the welfare system at the end of the century was designed to mold poor women into wage earners in the model of the gender-neutral economic man. The welfare system became legally rational: it was bureaucratic, with numerous rules, routine requirements, standardized forms, and interchangeable unskilled workers. As procedurally regulated and routine as the system became, however, the ultimate goals of the system were muddled, multiple, and conflicting.

By the turn of the twenty-first century, social science had become the dominant discourse shaping the welfare system. It was not, however, a vein of social science aimed at improving the conditions of society for the poor; instead, it was aimed at restricting the flow of tax dollars from the rich to the poor—or, in the rhetoric of reform advocates, from workers to nonworkers. The social scientific discourse informing welfare reform focused not on minimizing the risks of poverty or hunger but instead on minimizing the risks of "welfare dependency" and crime.

The current U.S. welfare system has arisen from a hodgepodge of legislative efforts over the last century. Throughout that century, multiple professions with different discourses and different goals have, at certain points, been dominant in setting the course for the welfare system. As a result, the welfare system now serves multiple and often contradictory goals. As a simple example, the welfare system was designed in part to lessen the brutality of poverty and provide support—if only meager support—to families lacking other financial resources. At the same time, the welfare system now has the stated goal of "ending dependency" by eliminating poor families from the welfare rolls. Welfare offices' successes are measured today not by how many families they serve but by how quickly they reduce their caseloads of welfare recipients—whether or not the families need assistance.

3

The Criminalization of Poverty

The 1996 welfare reforms were designed, so then-president Bill Clinton said, to "make work pay." Work, however, was only one of the many areas of life regulated by the welfare reform measure. As a result of the reforms, the federal government and the states instituted a host of policies and practices that equated welfare receipt with criminality; policed the everyday lives of poor families; and wove the criminal justice system into the welfare system, often entangling poor families in the process. David Garland notes that the "themes that dominate crime policy—rational choice and the structures of control, deterrents, and disincentives, the normality of crime, the responsibilization of individuals, the threatening underclass, the failing, overly lenient system—have come to organize the politics of poverty as well" (2001, 196). Current welfare policies were designed to punish the poor; to stigmatize poverty, particularly poverty that leads to welfare receipt; and to create a system of deterrence to keep low-wage workers attached to the labor force.

Other scholars have begun tracing the ways that crime control strategies have seeped into various realms of social life. John Gilliom, for example, traced the emergence of drug testing in the workplace and how it involved a process of "reclassifying largely criminal policies as administrative and colonizing the workplace as a site of surveillance and control" (1996, 119). As another example, Jonathan Simon offers evidence to show how Americans are now "governing through crime": in other words, using the fear of crime as the "occasion and rationale for governance" (2002, 1418). Both Gilliom and Simon highlight the many ways that crime control mechanisms are becoming part of the normal landscape of daily life. Not only are individuals subject to more intrusive forms of crime control, they are also adopting and perpetuating the measures themselves.

Certainly a vast regulatory and punitive system developed under welfare reform. The welfare policies the states put in place under the block grant system included a broad range of punitive approaches to the poor designed to punish not only poor adults who failed to transition to work but also entire families where the head of the household failed to live up to governing standards of morality. The reforms ended aid to families as a federal entitlement and allowed states to develop their own eligibility rules.

The influence of criminology on welfare policy is evident not only in the specific policies of welfare reform but also in the rhetoric used in policy development. For example, in the early 1990s the routine experience of a family's leaving the welfare system for work and then returning to the system later was commonly described as "cycling" by welfare researchers. By the early 2000s, however, this experience had been relabeled "recidivism" by the Department of Health and Human Services and was being adopted by social scientists (e.g., Gurmu and Smith 2006). The term *recidivism,* of course, is pejorative and borrowed from criminology, where it is used to describe repeated engagement in crime.

This chapter examines the increasing criminalization of the welfare system and welfare recipients. Because the empirical study was conducted in California, this chapter gives special attention to the welfare policies there.

The Welfare System as a Tool of Law Enforcement

The policing that occurs through the welfare system spans various fields of social life. Current policies are geared to regulating the sexual morality of the low-income mothers, regulating the formations of family and the details of family life, and regulating the labor market. Jacques Donzelot, in his book *The Policing of Families* (1997), borrows Michel Foucault's use of the term *policing,* not "in the limiting, repressive sense we give the term today, but according to a much broader meaning that encompasse[s] all of the methods for developing the quality of the population and strength of the nation" (6). It is this expansive definition of policing that is usually used in this book in discussion of welfare policies. In this section, though, the term *policing* is used more specifically to describe policies that reflect a merging of the welfare system and the criminal justice system. Indeed, numerous sections of the federal welfare reform legislation of 1996 and many of the laws and policies implemented by the states as a result embrace both the goals and the methods of the criminal justice system.

For example, the fugitive felon prohibitions, Operation Talon, and the drug felony lifetime ban have little to do with aid to the poor. These rules and programs are essentially new ways for the criminal justice system to make use of welfare administrative data to capture poor individuals who are also wanted by the criminal justice system. Through changes in statutes and practices, then, the welfare system has become an extension of the criminal justice system.

Fugitive Felon Prohibitions

The federal welfare legislation of 1996 included a provision that prohibited any individual who is wanted by law enforcement officials for a felony warrant or for violating the terms of parole or probation from receiving government benefits, including not only TANF benefits but also food stamps, SSI, and housing assistance. According to a report by the U.S. General Accounting Office, "About 110,000 beneficiaries [were] identified as fugitive felons and dropped from the SSI, Food Stamp, and TANF rolls" (2002, 3). While government officials claim that fugitive felon rules remove dangerous criminals from the streets, it is not clear that dangerous criminals are those who are ensnared. According to the GAO report, more than one-quarter of the SSI recipients excluded from aid under the rule were dropped because of parole or probation violations; in more than 37.4 percent of the cases, the offense on the warrant was not indicated in the data (39). Not all parole or probation violations, however, are direct threats to public safety. An individual may have a warrant issued for arrest for parole or probation offenses that, while they may be violations of parole, are not criminal acts. For example, an individual may have a warrant issued for missing a meeting with a parole or probation officer, missing a substance abuse meeting, or being determined to be psychologically unstable.

Thus it is not clear whether this rule is reining in threatening criminals and keeping public housing safe or merely reducing the government costs of providing aid to individuals with outstanding warrants. Excluding felons—even those who have served their sentences—from the full benefits available to citizens without felony convictions certainly draws upon precedents under some state laws. A number of states exclude convicted felons, including those who have completed their sentences, from voting (Manza and Uggen 2006, 74). However, the drug felony exclusion and the fugitive felon rules extend beyond political disfranchisement to encompass deprivations of economic citizenship. While withdrawing the right to vote may have little impact on an individual's daily life, economic disfranchisement can substantially and detrimentally affect not only daily life but also physical well-being.

The fugitive felon provisions raise several concerns: first, the denial of benefits to needy adults and their children; second, the suspension of procedural rights within the welfare system for individuals who have been involved in the criminal justice system; and third, the denial of economic citizenship.

Operation Talon

The federal legislation also loosened the confidentiality that once pro-tected poor families' personal and financial information. Before 1996, law enforcement officers could access welfare records only through legal pro-cess. Now, however, welfare records are available to law enforcement officers simply upon request—without probable cause, suspicion, or judicial process of any kind. Under the federal regulations, both welfare offices and public housing agencies are required to "furnish any Federal, State, or local law enforcement officer, upon the request of the officer, with the current address, Social Security number, and photograph of any recipient of assistance." This exchange of information is available to law enforcement officials not only when the welfare recipient herself has violated the law but also when an offi-cer believes the aid recipient, or anyone in her household, "has information that is necessary for the officer to conduct an official duty" (7 U.S.C. 2020(e) (8); 42 U.S.C. 1437z).

The information exchange between public assistance files and law enforcement, however, has expanded beyond mere investigatory use. Under a program titled Operation Talon, food stamp offices are used as the sites of sting operations for arresting individuals with outstanding warrants. Under the program, individuals with warrants who receive food stamps typically receive a call telling them to report to a welfare office at a designated time to resolve a problem with their benefits or to receive some kind of bonus. When they show up, an officer from the sheriff's department is waiting to serve the arrest warrant. Thousands of low-income citizens have been rounded up under the program. Between early 1997 and September 2006, Operation Talon led to the arrest of 10,980 individuals across the country (Office of Inspector General 2006).

Operation Talon has made the welfare system an extension of the crimi-nal justice system, transforming welfare offices into traps for hungry law-breakers. Bayview, the research site for this study, was, in fact, one of the one hundred sites in the country where these sting operations began. While the Inspector General's Year 2000 Update on Operation Talon indicates that some individuals arrested under the program faced charges on violent or serious crimes, many others did not. For example: 31 percent were for offenses known as "Group B offenses," which are considered less serious (e.g., writing bad checks). And many of the Group A offenses were nonviolent offenses: 11 percent for fraud charges and 10 percent for larceny/theft offenses, categories that may include welfare fraud; 23 percent for drug-related offenses (Viadero

2001, Exhibit A; Office of Inspector General 2000, 6). More than three-fourths of the California warrants were on fraud charges (which include but are not limited to welfare fraud charges) (Office of Inspector General 2000, 6). Thus it is not clear whether this program is protecting public safety by capturing violent criminals or simply providing law enforcement officers a new tool in making easy arrests.

The Drug Felony Lifetime Ban

The federal welfare legislation encourages states to adopt rules excluding adults with drug felony convictions from receiving aid. By December 2001, forty-two states had adopted the drug felony ban either in part or in full, though the number dropped to thirty-two by 2005 (Gustafson 2009, 672). State lawmakers choose the criteria used to determine whether an individual is ineligible for government aid on the basis of a past drug conviction. These criteria vary dramatically.

In fifteen states, including California, all drug-related charges—from possession of small quantities to major trafficking—will disqualify an individual from welfare receipt for life (U.S. Government Accountability Office 2005, 33-34, table 5). Low-income adults with drug records may receive neither cash aid nor food stamps. The other states that exclude convicted drug felons have modified their exclusions in various ways. For example, some of the states disqualify individuals convicted of manufacturing or distributing drugs but allow those who have been convicted of using drugs to remain on aid. Some states allow parents who are participating in or who have completed drug treatment programs to requalify for aid. And in some states adults are ineligible for aid for the first twelve months after incarceration but are eligible thereafter.

As well as anyone has been able to count, approximately ninety-two thousand adults had been removed from the welfare rolls because of felony drug convictions between 1997 and 2002 (Allard 2002, 4). According to data analysis by Patricia Allard at the Sentencing Project, California disqualified 37,825 adults from welfare receipt under the felony drug exclusion between 1996 and 1999 (Allard 2002, 5, table 2), meaning Californians accounted for more than one-third of the adults excluded under the felony drug exclusion nationwide.

While California's TANF program is supposed to make substance abuse treatment available to individuals who need it to become work-ready, it is unlikely that parents with substance abuse problems who know about the felony drug exclusion will reveal their problems to caseworkers, given the penalties for being arrested with drugs. Rather than deterring welfare recipients from drug use, these rules—assuming they are known and understood by welfare recipients—may have the countereffect of discouraging individuals with drug problems from inquiring about or seeking out help with their problems.

Given the limited knowledge of the elements of welfare reform, it is unlikely most recipients are aware of the felony drug exclusion. This lack of knowledge and the diversity of rules nationwide make it difficult for the felony drug exclusion to serve as a clear deterrent to drug use. In some states the drug exclusion rules are so complex that it is unlikely that any welfare recipients know or fully understand them unless or until they find themselves subject to those rules.

It could be argued persuasively that the drug felony ban is unfair—that it punishes not only parents but also their children. It is a harsh punishment for first-time petty drug offenders. In addition, it is arbitrary to target drug offenders when individuals convicted of other crimes, such as homicide and rape, can receive benefits after serving time. The drug felony lifetime ban, again, makes the welfare system an instrument of the criminal justice system. And here, again, the policies push those who are already economically marginalized to the periphery of society.

Conflating Poverty and Crime
Biometric Imaging and Data Sharing between the Welfare and Criminal Justice Systems

In the late 1990s some federal studies began to examine welfare cheating and welfare overpayments. Some studies found that some individuals might be receiving food stamp benefits in more than one state or collecting cash aid in multiple states (U.S. General Accounting Office 1998; Office of State Systems 1997). Reports also began to surface that government benefits were flowing to men and women who were incarcerated (U.S. General Accounting Office 1997).

The 1996 federal welfare reform legislation required states to institute fraud prevention programs. The legislation did not, however, specify what the fraud prevention programs should look like. The three most populous U.S. states—California, New York, and Texas—as well as some other states—Arizona, Connecticut, Illinois, Massachusetts, and Pennsylvania—instituted biometric imaging, in most cases fingerprint-imaging programs, as part of their welfare fraud control measures. These biometric data collection requirements have been applied, depending on the state, to recipients of food stamps, TANF grants, and General Assistance grants (available to indigent adults without children). Individuals who apply for cash aid or food stamps in these states are required to submit fingerprints—and sometimes photographs—through an electronic imaging system. New fingerprints are cross-checked with those on record to identify cases where a person might have tried to apply for aid in two different welfare offices. The stated goals of these programs are to deter and catch individuals who might attempt to "double-dip" by using aliases to open multiple welfare cases.

While there were several well-publicized California and Illinois cases of double-dipping welfare fraud between 1975 and 1983 (discussed in chapter 2), in all of those cases the welfare recipients had signed up for aid before applicants were required to submit Social Security numbers and before extensive computer verification systems existed. With computerized records and substantial documentation requirements now in place, individuals would have great difficulty opening multiple cases: even if they used fake Social Security numbers, computer checks on the numbers would be likely to reveal earnings or assets associated with those numbers. The fingerprint-imaging systems, then, are largely superfluous to existing efforts to reduce fraud. But fingerprint imaging serves another purpose: the collection of biometric data scrutinizes and stigmatizes low-income adults in a way that equates poverty with criminality.

In states with biometric imaging, applying for welfare mirrors the experience of being booked for a crime: after being interrogated about family and finances, individuals are photographed and fingerprinted. The fingerprint images are entered into statewide computer systems and then used to check for duplicate applications. Few duplicates—indicating one person submitting more than one welfare application—are found. In California, for example, the state identifies only three matches per month and typically refers only one of these cases per month for more extensive fraud investigation or prosecution (Rivera 1994). A report by the California state auditor in 2005 berated the legislature for the fingerprint-imaging system, stating it was impossible "to determine whether SFIS [State Fingerprint Imaging System] generates enough savings to cover the estimated $31 million the State has paid for SFIS or the estimated $11.4 million the State will pay each year to operate it" (California State Auditor 2005, 1).

Policy makers claim that the real motive behind fingerprint imaging is deterring, not catching, acts of fraud. There is, however, evidence that procedures deter not only fraudulent applications but also legitimate applications by needy families, particularly eligible immigrant families (Services, Immigrant Rights and Education Network 2000). The Asian Pacific American Legal Center (APALC) conducted a survey of community-based organizations to determine why, despite such high poverty rates about Asian and Pacific Islander communities, food stamps were being underutilized by eligible members of those communities. The report listed fear of the state fingerprint-imaging system as one of the top four barriers to food stamp use among the eligible poor (Asian Pacific American Legal Center 2000). The fingerprint-imaging requirements create another hurdle poor people must clear in what is an otherwise demanding application process. In some counties in California, fingerprint imaging is done only on certain days, sometimes requiring aid applicants to make an additional trip to the welfare department and delaying the time between initial application and first day of aid receipt. (In fact, while recruiting interviewees outside a California welfare office for this study, I routinely ran into welfare applicants who were showing up for their second or third fingerprint-imaging appointments because the machine had been broken on previous visits to the welfare office.)

Studies in the states that fingerprint welfare recipients have blasted the practice as costly and ineffective. According to the testimony of Celia Hagert, a senior policy analyst at the Center for Public Policy Priorities, Texas began fingerprint imaging on a pilot basis in 1996 and implemented it statewide in August 1999 (Hagert 2001). According to the report evaluating the program in Texas, fingerprint imaging did not reduce caseloads and, instead of saving taxpayer dollars, cost the state $1.7 million during the first seven months of operation (Schexnayder et al. 1997). By the end of 2000, fingerprint imaging had cost the state $15.9 million. The fingerprinting program did not reveal widespread fraud. According to Hagert, between 1996 and the end of 2000, fingerprint imaging had "resulted in only nine charges filed by the DA, 10 administrative penalty cases, and 12 determinations of no fraud" (Hagert 2001). The high costs and low yield of criminal wrongdoing, though, did not prompt repeal. While in 2002 the Texas Board of Human Services voted to allow certain seniors and the disabled to request exemption from the fingerprint-imaging requirement of the food stamp application process where the imaging would pose an undue burden, the fingerprint-imaging system was otherwise left intact and remains in use today. Evidence of the cost-effectiveness of California's fingerprint-imaging system was similarly elusive (California State Auditor 2009).

While lawmakers and the public seem unwilling to devote tax dollars to providing cash benefits to the poor, there seems to be great willingness to spend money to police the poor—even when doing so appears to be economically inefficient or ineffective. By instituting these programs, states signal that crime control—specifically preventing the receipt of excess government benefits—takes priority over relieving poverty, relieving food insecurity, and containing state administrative costs.

Drug Testing

The welfare system is moving beyond efforts to punish people for drug convictions; there have been efforts to use the welfare system to root out drug use. There have been numerous proposals to identify drug use among the welfare poor by making drug tests a condition of welfare receipt. Michigan, for example, instituted a pilot drug-testing program in three counties, and policy makers hoped to institute the program statewide. Under the program, all adults who applied for welfare were to be tested as part of the application process. In addition, every six months 20 percent of the recipients would be randomly tested. Welfare applicants and recipients who refused urine testing or refused to comply with a treatment plan after a positive test were to be refused benefits.

Michigan's drug-testing program was challenged in a case called *Marchwinski v. Howard* (2000). A federal district court enjoined the testing, ruling that the practice amounted to an illegal search in violation of the Fourth Amendment. In 2002, however, the Sixth Circuit Court of Appeals lifted the district court's injunction, allowing Michigan to proceed with its drug-testing program. The Sixth Circuit extended, some might say stretched, the definition of a "special need" justifying suspicionless searches by grouping a number of social concerns into a special need particular to welfare recipients. These concerns included "the safety of the children of families" receiving aid, "the risk to the public from the crime associated with illicit drug use and trafficking," and the need to ensure that cash assistance was "used by the recipients for their intended purposes and not for procuring controlled substances" ((2002), 336). The Sixth Circuit decision declared that welfare recipients, relative to other citizens, "have a somewhat diminished expectation of privacy" ((2002), 337). The Sixth Circuit opinion stood in stark contrast to the welfare rights cases from the early 1970s, where lawyers argued that the poor do not lose their fundamental rights even when receiving government aid. The majority opinion also expressed the view that the government goal of reducing drug use outweighs both individual privacy rights and the needs of the poor, some of whom might be dissuaded from seeking benefits by the humiliation of urine testing. The case was reheard *en banc;* the Sixth Circuit judges split evenly on the constitutionality of drug testing. By default, the original injunction granted by the district court was reinstated, and the drug-testing program in Michigan ceased (2003).

Since then, however, there have been proposals to modify Michigan's original drug-testing program and give it another try. In addition, over the last decade both members of Congress and state legislators have advanced numerous proposals to require that welfare recipients undergo drug tests. The drug testing of welfare recipients particularly highlights the conflation of poverty and crime and the widespread assumption that poor women of color are the causes of crime. There is some dispute as to whether welfare recipients have higher drug use and dependence than the population at large (Pollack et al. 2002, 259). Drug use among welfare recipients appears to be higher than drug use in the general population, but drug dependence, which interferes with relationships and work, may not be higher (Pollack et al. 2002, 268-69). Further, even if some welfare recipients use drugs, statistics indicate that the vast majority of those who might be subjected to drug testing do not (Jayakody et al. 2004).

Punishing the Poor

In addition to adopting many of the goals of the criminal justice system, the welfare system has its own internal processes of policing the poor. The federal welfare reform legislation instituted a host of new penalties for welfare recipients who did not comply with the welfare rules or, in the case of the family caps, with mainstream mores around sexuality, marriage, and childbearing. Administrative punishments are described and analyzed below.

Administrative Sanctions

During the welfare reform debates of the mid-1990s, politicians and the public repeatedly championed the "carrot and stick" approach to welfare. The numerous people who used this phrase seemed uncritical of the beast-of-burden imagery that the phrase "carrot and stick" evokes with relation to the poor individuals subject to the carrot and the stick. The "carrot and stick" is a phrase with dual meanings: in one meaning, the carrot dangles from a stick as an incentive but is never actually attained as a reward; under the other meaning, the carrot is an incentive while the stick is used to beat an animal too uncooperative and lazy to be lured by the carrot. Use of the metaphor also echoes Louisiana Senator Huey Long's notorious description of welfare recipients as "brood mares" during a 1967 Senate Finance Committee meeting (Orleck 2005, 114). The phrase also conjures up images of coerced, unpaid labor and resonates with images of black servitude under slavery. Martin Gilens (1999) has documented that widespread negative attitudes toward the welfare system are inextricably tied to racism and aversions to providing African Americans with government benefits. In a particularly vivid example of the dehumanization of welfare recipients, John Mica, a Republican congressional representative from Florida, held up a sign during a congressional debate that read, "Don't feed the alligators" (Gallman 1995; Horsburgh 1996, 565-66). On the House floor, Mica argued that providing aid to poor women would do nothing but spur them to reproduce, entice them to return for more free handouts, and threaten the general public safety (141 Cong. Rec. 9194 (1995)).

The federal reforms were supposed to create a new welfare system that included not only incentives but also disincentives, including punishments, even those that would go as far as state violence. The "carrot and stick" approach was designed to coax welfare recipients who were not participating in the formal wage-labor market to seek steady employment and leave the welfare system. There were a few carrots: increased earnings disregards; increased availability of child care subsidies; and the Earned Income Tax Credit. The true underpinning of reform, however, came in the form of sanctions—the reduction or elimination of a family's benefits. They were the big sticks.

Sanctions have become routine. Sanctions may be imposed for failing to comply with welfare-to-work requirements, failing to fulfill the number of work hours required, or merely failing to attend a scheduled meeting at the welfare office. One study of the sanctions imposed in three major cities found that missed appointments were the most common triggers for sanctions (Cherlin et al. 2002). The result of a sanction in California at the time of this study was a reduction of the adult's portion of aid from the grant check—approximately $125 (depending on the family size), a significant penalty for a family living in poverty.

While many people assume that transitions from welfare to work account for dramatic decreases in welfare caseloads, a number of studies indicate that sanctions actually account for the decline. Research by Sanford Schram found evidence that "get-tough policies, especially strict sanctions, have contributed to the roll declines and may have done so in ways that forced people off even while they still needed assistance" (2002, 97).

As troubling as the effects of sanctioning practices are, the sanctions raise other concerns. For example, a study by Yeheskel Hasenfeld and colleagues found that approximately half of the sanctioned adults surveyed did not know they had been sanctioned (Hasenfeld, Ghose, and Hillesland-Larson 2004, 314). For those families, the welfare system became so complex, arbitrary, and mystifying that they could not determine why their benefits were fluctuating. This suggests that rather than creating a set of incentives that would "make work pay," the sanctioning of welfare system recipients simply punished people who could not figure out how the system worked.

Many poor families have suffered as a result of these sanctions. In some states, as many as a third of the welfare cases have been sanctioned (Peterson 2002, 4; Haskins, Sawhill, and Weaver 2001). A group of researchers examining the effects of sanctions concluded: "Sanctions and procedural case closings appeared to ensnare families that were experiencing hardships and possibly to impose more hardships on some of them." They explained: "For low-income individuals with limited education, daily lives filled with personal turmoil, and employment and family responsibilities to balance, meeting all of these demands may be more than many can handle. Being able to turn in forms on time or to follow up with doctors' offices or employers' personnel offices can be a feat in itself. It requires keeping up with the mail; noticing and adhering to deadlines; and reading, interpreting, and responding to questions—all of this by mothers who may have complex and challenging daily lives" (Cherlin et al. 2002, 402). More than half a million families were subject to full-family sanctions from 1997 through 1999 (Goldberg and Schott 2000).

State Family Cap Policies

The family cap policies, welfare rules prohibiting an increase in a family's cash assistance when a new child is born into the family, highlight the ways welfare regulations affect issues of personal and family autonomy. The family cap rules (also known as "child exclusion" or "maximum family grant" rules) were intended by lawmakers to influence women's—and especially poor women of color's—decisions about birth control, abortion, childbearing, and family formation. The policies punish not only women who decide to bear children while on welfare but also their entire families.

Federal welfare reform legislation gave states the option of instituting family cap policies that prohibit welfare offices from offering cash assistance to children born to families receiving welfare. During the 1990s, twenty-one states, including California, adopted the family cap while two others, Idaho and Wisconsin, instituted flat grants for families of any size (Schram 2002, 95). Since 2004, three states—Illinois, Maryland, and Nebraska—have repealed their family cap policies (Romero and Agénor 2009, 356, table 1).

These policies manifest the beliefs that any child born to a family on welfare is illegitimate and unworthy of assistance. The family cap policies effectively deny the existence—the personhood and the economic needs—of children born to mothers who are poor and usually single. They punish mothers for non-normative, meaning nonmarital, sex and childbearing. They also punish not only the mother who has made the decision to become a parent but also the newborn child and any other children in the aid unit. Numerous studies have found that the family cap policies do not seem to have had an effect on birthrates among welfare recipients (Dyer and Fairlie 2004; Joyce et al. 2004; Ryan, Manlove, and Hofferth 2006).

Welfare Fraud Investigations

PRWORA required the states to institute fraud control measures, though it did not specify what those measures should include. In California, the administrative fraud control measures that had been in place under AFDC were expanded. As before reform, California welfare recipients were required to submit monthly forms, known as "CA-7s," by the fifth of every month to remain eligible for welfare. Welfare recipients were required to report any changes in address, income, assets, or household composition on their CA-7s. Aid recipients were also required to record the number of hours they worked. Recipients also had to go through an annual renewal, where they met with a welfare worker and filled out many of the forms again.

The CA-7s were used to determine a family's cash aid eligibility and amount of payment. The first $225 of an adult's earnings was ignored in the calculation of aid; any additional earnings were factored into a complex calculation of cash aid and food stamps based on family size. Families whose earnings varied from month to month therefore faced fluctuations in the cash aid and food stamp grants.

To identify possible sources of fraud, California instituted a system in 1984 called the Income and Eligibility Verification System (IEVS), which continued to be used at the time of these research interviews. Through the verification system, which relied on welfare recipients' Social Security numbers, the welfare offices collected the income and assets data recipients submitted each month and matched this information against records from the Employment Development Division, which tracks employment status and administers Disability and Unemployment Insurance; the Social Security Administration; and the Internal Revenue Service and the California Franchise Tax Bureau, both of which record information about state wage earners. Information exchanges were conducted once every fiscal quarter—every three months. On the basis of these data exchanges, county welfare offices received reports of duplicate Social Security numbers or mismatched earnings reports. Counties then had the burden of investigating the cases that were flagged by the verification system.

Failing to report all of one's income or to report household composition accurately to the welfare department is rule breaking under the welfare rules. Welfare recipients can—and are—pursued either civilly with a claim of intentional program violation or as common criminals charged with welfare fraud.

California county welfare agencies bear responsibility for identifying and reclaiming overpayments from recipients, whether those overpayments are due to recipient error or office error. The federal regulations require welfare offices to notify clients within forty-five days of becoming aware of a likely overpayment, though this notice rule was regularly violated by the research county during the period of data collection. An overpayment to a family still on aid resulted in a 10 percent reduction of the family's future grants until the overpayment was reclaimed by the county. The counties pursued cash repayments from individuals who were no longer receiving aid. When those repayments were not forthcoming, the counties pursued collections, sometimes leading to wage garnishment for newly employed former welfare recipients.

Welfare cheating typically takes one of several forms. The first involves working at a legitimate job but failing to report all of the earnings to the welfare office. The second type involves under-the-table employment for cash that is not reported either to the welfare office or to tax authorities. A third type of fraud occurs when welfare recipients fail to report to welfare officials the presence of wage earners in their households. Other fraudulent activities may include receiving aid for a child no longer in the household or, in rare cases, establishing false identities to collect aid for nonexistent persons.

Welfare offices aggressively investigate fraud before and after welfare recipients receive benefits. In fact, in some California counties at the time of this writing, applicants for public assistance received an unannounced visit and home search by a deputized fraud investigator before receiving any benefits. San Diego's practice of conducting suspicionless searches of welfare applicants' homes was contested in federal court as a violation of Fourth Amendment protections against unreasonable search but was ultimately upheld (*Sanchez v. County of San Diego* (2007)).

Civil Penalties

The line between administrative and criminal penalties for welfare cheating has become increasingly blurry. PRWORA greatly increased administrative penalties, instituting a rule that if an individual loses benefits in any federally funded, means-tested program because of fraud she or he will not only lose benefits under that program but also become ineligible for increased benefits under any other program. In other words, if a welfare recipient is found to be engaged in cash aid fraud by virtue of failing to report all of her income, she will lose cash aid, and her household will see no increase in food stamps or housing assistance to offset the decrease in aid.

As states implemented rules under federal welfare reform, many stiffened their civil and criminal penalties for welfare cheating. Before being criminally charged with welfare fraud, many welfare recipients face administrative penalties for having resources they have not reported. According to the California Welfare and Institutions Code § 11486(c)(1)(B)-(c)(2)(B), an Intentional Program Violation occurs when a welfare recipient is found "(A) Making a false or misleading statement or misrepresenting, concealing, or withholding facts. (B) Committing any act intended to mislead, misrepresent, conceal, or withhold facts or propound a falsity." These violations occur routinely; in fact, they occur whenever a welfare recipient fails to report all income, informal child support, gifts, or new members of the household. Even if a recipient's failure to report income would not change the family's aid calculation, the recipient is still violating the program requirements.

California implemented a "three-strikes-and-you're-out" rule for welfare cheating and the penalties for failing to report required information—even where the reporting failures would not affect aid calculations—are stiff. A finding of one offense in an administrative hearing or in a court disqualifies an individual from aid for six months. A second occasion results in a twelve-month disqualification from aid, and a finding of a third occasion results in permanent—meaning lifelong—disqualification from aid.

Other violations can lead to permanent disqualification from welfare. An individual can be excluded from receiving welfare benefits for life for any of the following violations: (1) "double-dipping," or in other words, making false statements or representations about one's place of resident in order to make simultaneous claims for aid in more than one county or state; (2) submitting documents to receive aid for nonexistent children or for children ineligible for aid; or (3) receiving more than ten thousand dollars in aid as a result of intentionally and willfully making false statements or misrepresenting, concealing, or withholding pertinent facts from welfare administrators.

Disqualification Consent Agreements

California welfare recipients who are identified through Income Eligibility Verification System matches are often called into meetings at the welfare office, where they are asked to sign disqualification consent agreements. These agreements are basically admissions that the recipients did not state all necessary facts in their monthly reporting forms or in their (re)applications for aid. By signing one of these agreements, a welfare recipient waives any available administrative remedies. Before asking an individual to sign a disqualification consent agreement, counties are required to give the individual a notice including the following: (1) "A statement for the accused individual to sign that he/she understands the consequences of consenting to disqualification"; (2) "A statement that consenting to disqualification will result in a reduction in the AU's [assistance unit's] CalWORKs aid payment . . . even though the accused individual was not found guilty of civil/criminal misrepresentation or fraud"; (3) "A warning of the disqualification penalties which could be imposed . . . and a statement of which penalty shall be imposed"; and (4) "A statement that any remaining assistance unit members shall be held responsible for repayment of the resulting overpayment, unless the accused individual has already repaid the overpayment" (California Department of Social Services Manual of Practices and Procedures § 20-352.211, effective July 1, 1998). The procedures do not specify how far in advance the recipient must be given this notice, so it is conceivable that the individual might receive notice only minutes before signing what amounts to a confession. While these consent agreements occur at the administrative level, they are readily used as evidence by prosecutors who may later file criminal charges. It is not at all clear that recipients who sign these agreements are aware that doing so may, instead of resolving their difficulties with the welfare office, initiate their transition from the welfare system to the criminal justice system.

Criminal Prosecutions

In addition to civil penalties, California imposes stiff criminal penalties for welfare fraud, including permanent exclusion from aid. Failing to report all sources of income and support to the welfare office can result in a host of criminal charges. District attorneys may bring not only fraud charges but also perjury charges against welfare recipients who earn income through work but who do not accurately report all of their income on their monthly reporting forms (Calif. Penal Code § 118). Anyone convicted in state or federal court of felony welfare fraud is ineligible for aid for two years if the amount of money in dispute is less than two thousand dollars. A person convicted of fraudulently receiving between two thousand and ten thousand dollars is barred from receiving aid for five years; a person convicted of fraudulently receiving more than ten thousand dollars is prohibited from receiving aid for life.

In 1998, the state of California incentivized welfare prosecutions by the counties by rewarding them 25 percent of any overpayment determined (California Assembly Bill 1542). During this same period, the federal government offered incentives to states for welfare fraud prosecutions. (Congress later passed the Improper Payments Information Act of 2002, requiring states to compile information on overpayments and underpayments of benefits.) At one point, California prosecutors were pursuing welfare fraud so aggressively that in some counties pending criminal welfare fraud investigation caseloads exceeded welfare caseloads. The 2002-3 California budget, however, eliminated the $5.1 million welfare fraud incentive payments that had been provided to counties. Since then, fraud prosecutions have dropped significantly, particularly in those counties where prosecution rates had been unusually high.

The legislative drive to punish welfare cheaters has brought about cozy relationships between welfare providers and fraud investigators. In many California counties the physical boundaries between welfare administration and criminal fraud control efforts have disappeared. Of California's fifty-eight counties, only twenty-eight have the county welfare departments conduct welfare fraud investigations. The remaining counties have moved their fraud investigators to law enforcement, with twenty-one counties housing their fraud investigation units in the offices of the district attorney (DA), nine situating satellite DA's offices in the welfare office, and two placing fraud investigations in the hands of local sheriff's offices. The close relationship between officials who administer aid and those who police cheating raises some troubling issues. Welfare recipients identified as having received overpayments are notified by letter that they must attend a meeting with an official, and many of these officials share office space with caseworkers. Although these officials are criminal fraud investigators or members of the county DA's office, many welfare recipients do not realize that these officials are part of the criminal justice system rather than the welfare system. As a result, they attend the meetings without consulting or bringing legal counsel.

Nationwide Trends in Criminalizing Welfare Cheating

Welfare officials and local prosecutors have the option of either seeking civil remedies or bringing criminal charges against welfare cheats. In California, there has been a push for criminal penalties (Gustafson 2009, 689). In a few states, where welfare recipients do not owe huge sums and where they make restitution, prosecutors typically do not bring criminal charges. In other states—Oklahoma and Wyoming, for example—prosecutors bring criminal charges even when money is repaid to the state. In some states, decisions about investigations and prosecutions are centralized. In Wisconsin, for example, the state has a Model Prosecution Agreement that includes a model diversion recommendation. Wisconsin also apparently attempts to track welfare fraud referrals better than other states. In a greater number of states, however, welfare fraud is left to the discretion of local prosecutors. There appear to be a growing number of state or local welfare fraud diversion programs, efforts to impose suspended sentences, or efforts to address welfare fraud under general pretrial diversion statutes.

The welfare fraud diversion programs share some of the same problems as the drug diversion programs. First, the effects of the welfare fraud diversion programs have undergone even less research than the drug diversion programs. Second, there is some evidence that many of the participants in welfare fraud diversion programs do not or cannot comply with the condition of participation, which is usually repayment. Third, it may be that, as with the drug courts, more individuals are finding themselves under the control of the criminal justice system than if the diversion programs were not available (Miller 2004, 1558-60). This is because weak cases do not get dropped by prosecutors, and those who fail to meet the administrative requirements of the diversion programs—in these cases, repaying the money—find themselves either under the control of the criminal justice system for a longer time than had they been charged or ultimately facing felony charges.

Some states (e.g., Florida) consistently pursue civil remedies first, while others (e.g., Illinois and California) favor criminal prosecutions. Whether criminal charges are brought as felonies depends upon state statutes, which vary significantly from state to state in the dollar amount of overpayment that will trigger a felony charge. In Florida, for example, a loss of state benefits of only two hundred dollars in a twelve-month period is sufficient to establish a third-degree felony (Fl. Stat. 414.39). And while disposition of the cases is left to the discretion of prosecutors in many states, there are other states, such as Illinois, where prosecutors let the cases go to court and have judges determine the appropriate sanctions. In Massachusetts, cases where individuals have not made restitution and are subsequently referred for criminal prosecution typically result in probation.

States devote significant resources to policing welfare fraud. In 2008, California spent twenty-eight million dollars for investigations that screen welfare applicants for possible fraud before a case is opened and thirty-four million dollars for investigations of ongoing welfare cases (California State Auditor 2009, 2). Though devoting more than sixty million dollars to fraud investigations, the state identified only $19.6 million in overpayments—and collected only a fraction of that amount back from recipients (California State Auditor 2009, 2). The costs of policing welfare fraud are so high because the number of welfare fraud investigators has soared in the years since welfare reform. There appear to be two reasons for the rising number of welfare fraud investigators in a period when welfare caseloads are declining. First, much of the welfare money that flows to states and counties is federal money. If that money is not spent, the states and counties lose it. Rather than lay off government employees and lose the stream of federal funding, many counties are transferring former welfare caseworkers and civil fraud investigators into positions as deputized welfare fraud investigators.

Second, the welfare fraud investigators are gaining political leverage. Welfare fraud investigators in many locales are unionizing. In many states (Alabama, Arizona, Colorado, Iowa, Minnesota, Ohio, New York) investigators have formed associations and have even hired lobbyists. These associations urge legislators to step up efforts to investigate and prosecute welfare fraud and to move investigations from the civil to the criminal arena. Whether these efforts to criminalize welfare fraud investigations are in the real interests of the public or merely an example of the power of self-interested bureaucrats remains an open question.

The previous chapter outlines the discursive and political shifts that produced a welfare system that equates poverty with criminality and gives prominence to welfare use and welfare cheating as threats to both society and economy. This chapter has mapped the numerous policies and practices that manifest the criminalization of poverty.

The growth of punitive welfare policies and the policing of welfare fraud represent something more than the policing of crime. There is something fundamentally different about imposing criminal penalties rather than other available penalties. Criminalization serves an expressive function, labeling not only certain behaviors but also certain groups of people as deviant. Welfare policies and practices feed on the view that the poor are latent criminals and that anyone who is not part of the paid labor force is looking for a free handout. In many ways, the policy aspirations to punish nonworking welfare recipients, welfare cheats, and aid recipients who engage in unrelated crimes have overwhelmed any remaining aspirations to help poor children.

The following four chapters focus on individuals who receive welfare—people about whom a lot is assumed but little is actually known. In these chapters, welfare recipients reveal how they experience the welfare system and its punitive policies, how they survive on limited resources, and how they perceive themselves and other welfare recipients within the system.

4

A Glimpse at the Interviewees

The following chapters draw upon in-depth, semistructured interviews with thirty-four welfare recipients in a Northern California county called (for this study) Bayview. Bayview County has a population of just over one million people. The county includes a bustling downtown, Bayview City. More affluent residents live in Bayview Hills, while those who have fewer resources tend to live in South Bayview, which at its southern most edge has a sprawling industrial area. In 1999, twelve adults out of every thousand in the county received TANF benefits. Year 2000 census data demonstrate how racially diverse the county is, with approximately 49 percent of the residents white, 15 percent African American, 20 percent Asian/Pacific Islander, 9 percent other races, and 6 percent more than one race. In 1999, the county's poverty rate was nearly 11 percent. Because the research sample is not representative of the welfare population in the county or even in California, this chapter occasionally highlights the ways that the population of interviewees may reflect the general welfare population and where it may differ. More importantly, the chapter underscores some of the common experiences and backgrounds of the interviewees.

The Backgrounds of the Interviewees
Parenthood

Like many adults who turn to the welfare system for financial assistance, most of the women and men interviewed became parents at an early age. Eleven of the thirty women interviewed gave birth to their first child before the age of eighteen. Nine had their first child between ages nineteen and twenty-one; seven more first gave birth between ages twenty-two and twenty-six. Two other women first gave birth in their early thirties. One interviewee, Nina, never had children but while still in high school found herself stepping in as a substitute parent for her drug-addicted sisters' children. The four men interviewed became parents for the first time when they were somewhat older. Two of them first became fathers at age twenty-two, another at age twenty-seven, and the last at age thirty-four.

The parents interviewed had between one and six minor children in their care (with the startling exception of Aliyah, who had no child in her care). In many cases, the "aid unit"—the number of individuals in the family who were counted for the purposes of calculating aid benefits—was different from the number of individuals living collectively in the household. For example, a couple mothers had children over the age of eighteen who lived in the household but who were excluded under law from the aid unit and therefore excluded from receipt of welfare benefits. Several interviewees—such as Yvonne, Renee, and Crystal—shared cramped quarters with another family but were financially responsible for their own children only. The welfare office does not consider some children in the household members of the aid unit because they receive financial support from some another source, such as child support or Social Security benefits, or because they have aged out of the welfare system.

Of the thirty-four people interviewed, sixteen of them had only one child in the home. Seven interviewees had two children in the care; six parents had three children. Only four interviewees had four or more children in their care. One mother was not looking after any children because a judge had awarded full custody of her child to the child's father. Like most welfare recipients, few of the interviewees had large families.

Substitute Mothering

The interviews included a few women who were engaged in what might be called substitute mothering. While several of the women interviewed would appear to outsiders to look like the mythological welfare queen who has a huge brood of children, this perception would be mistaken. True, these women were caring for a large number of children. The children, however, were not always their own children. These women tended to be the most responsible adults in their extended families and were caring for the children of other relatives who were in jail or prison or otherwise unable to care for their kids.

An easy illustration is Veronica, who at the time of our interview was caring for not only three of her biological children but also a younger brother, a sister, and a cousin. She explained:

The very first time I got on aid was when I was sixteen years old. My mother—not me—had had another child. And she sort of abandoned him with me. So I got on aid with my brother. I was on aid for maybe two years in Los Angeles. And I moved back to Bayview with her and I got off because she was supporting me and him. *[sighs]* Let's see. Then maybe about four or five years later, I had had my first child and I got on aid. And then a year later I had another child. You know, more aid. I had got a job. I got married. He got a job. We both lost our jobs. And then my husband, me, and my three children got on aid. Then I got my brother. Then I got my sister. Then I got one of my auntie's children. So now that's six children on aid.

Veronica was hardly the only interviewee caring for the children of relatives or strangers. Annette, a single parent to her three biological children, was also caring for a ten-year-old niece and a three-year-old foster child.

Another example was Nina, an interviewee I met at the welfare office, who introduced me to some children she described as "my kids." It was only after we were well into our interview that she revealed that not one of the three children in her care was her biological child. Nina's kids were, rather, the children of her two sisters, both of whom were addicted to drugs and had relinquished custody of their children to their mother. After their mother died, Nina, who had been helping her mother out with the kids, found herself the only member of the family capable and willing to raise the children.

Contradicting a stereotype that portrays welfare recipients as irresponsible and self-absorbed, these women took on the responsibilities of other family members, though doing so put quite a burden on them both personally and financially. While adults who receive welfare may be viewed as heading families that are unstable and dysfunctional, they are in some cases the most stable and functional households in extended families.

Marital and Nonmarital History

Like most welfare recipients nationwide, those interviewed for this book were not married and living with spouses. Only ten of them had ever been married. Of those, five were divorced and the other five were legally separated. None of the interviewees had an intact marriage at the time of the interview. Impoverished married couples with children do qualify for TANF cash assistance in California, and many families headed by married parents do receive assistance. In Northern California, however, married-couple welfare households consist mostly of immigrant refugee families, particularly Vietnamese, Cambodian, and Hmong families who often have limited English proficiency. The fact that the interviews in this study were conducted only in English creates a bias in the sample, excluding those potential interviewees most likely to be married.

The Invisible Men

Policy makers engaged in recent debates over welfare reauthorization and leaders of the "fatherhood movement," which arose in the United States in the 1990s, have argued that the welfare system has been responsible for pushing fathers out the door by prompting poor mothers to choose to rely on the welfare system rather than on the fathers of their children for economic support. The participants in this study, however, suggest that the role of fathers is much more complicated.

For example, while many of the fathers appeared to be uninvolved because they were neither listed on the mother's welfare case nor providing child support, many were around and, to varying degrees, involved in their children's lives. While some fathers may have been invisible to the welfare system, they were not invisible to their children. Both Jane and Shanelle explained that they had originally applied for welfare with their low-income male partners. In both cases, the men owned cars valued over the asset limit for welfare receipt and held low-paying jobs, disqualifying the family from aid. Also in both cases, the men earned too little to support the household. In Jane's case, she and her fiancé lied to the welfare office, claiming the fiancé was absent, in order to obtain aid. In Shanelle's case, the boyfriend moved out of the apartment so that Shanelle and her baby could qualify for aid. (After moving out of the apartment, the boyfriend moved in and out of jail.) In both cases, the men remained a part of the lives of their children but became invisible to the welfare office.

Barbara had separated many years earlier from her husband, the father of her two grown sons. They never got around to filing the legal papers for a divorce and maintained contact over the years. Years after the separation, she met Sam, the father of her twelve-year-old daughter. Barbara hoped to marry Sam, but he instead abandoned her and her daughter. Barbara explained:

> He left. And then my husband—the father of my other children—he just thought it was terrible that Sam did that to me, left my little girl. So he didn't live together [with us] but sent her money. If she was supposed to

go to school or something, he'd send her money. You know, in that way. So, uh, I guess without him [my daughter] would not know a father. So he talks to her, you know, communicates with her all the time.

It was true that Barbara's daughter had no contact with and received no support from her biological father. And it may have been a pattern with her daughter's father, according to Barbara, who noted, "You know, he had five kids by three different women." Nevertheless, the daughter received both emotional and financial support from Barbara's not-quite-ex-husband. She was not the pitiable, fatherless child the media commonly portray.

Another mother, Pam, explained that her daughter's father—a man thirty years older than Pam—had abandoned her when she was six months pregnant. Pam said that her daughter's father was routinely in and out of jail. She noted, "He's always been a hustler. He *never* worked." Pam's mother and father took an active role in their granddaughter's life. Pam explained that her daughter held a special place in her grandfather's heart. She recounted a story about her daughter: "She read her birth certificate, she told my mom, 'Grandma, my mommy says my daddy doesn't live with me. But my daddy's name is Granddaddy, okay?'" While the father of Pam's daughter was undeniably absent, her daughter was not lacking a reliable father figure.

Many of the absent fathers who had relationships with the women in this study were unable to care for and support their children, either because they were dead or because they were incarcerated. Tanya, for example, explained that her oldest child's son had been murdered, and Lisa revealed that her oldest child's father had died of cancer. Sharon said that her children's father had "smoked himself to death" using drugs. She did not view his death as a great loss to the family. She complained that when he had been alive "he never helped me with the boys. He popped in every now and then, [to] say hi." She said that the father's erratic behavior had negatively affected their sons until the sons finally lost interest in having contact with him. Sharon explained that the boys "never pushed the issue about going to see him, and I never tried to find him. And half the time I didn't know where he was anyway."

Many more of the fathers were at least temporarily behind bars. The repeated references to fathers who either were in jail at the time of the interview or had recurrent bouts of incarceration were stunning. Yvonne said that although her two-year-old child's father was in and out of jail and had no stable income, the county was determined to pursue him for child support. Renee, the twenty-year-old mother of a four-year-old son, said that his father helped out "when he's not in jail," adding, "But that's not very often, though."

Renee's case was not unusual. It is common for the children of prison inmates to receive welfare. According to research by Amy Hirsch (2003), 55 percent of male state prisoners are fathers. In addition, Hirsch notes about a quarter of inmates have active child support cases while they are incarcerated. "On average, parents owe more than $10,000 in arrears when they go to prison and leave prison owing $23,000 or more. More than half of these arrears are owed to the state to repay welfare costs." Some incarcerated fathers of children on welfare might be supporting their children—either through wage work or through the underground economy—if they were not in jail or prison. If so, then the welfare system is another hidden government cost associated with the high incarceration rate in the United States.

Some of the interviewees expressed that they and their children were better off without contact from the fathers, in most cases because the fathers were abusive. Veronica and the six children in her care left her home and husband after he punched her in the face when she would not give him her last twenty dollars, which he wanted to use to buy drugs. "He decided he wanted to use some cocaine and crank. I couldn't deal with the drugs, the kids, the house, the job, so we left. *[exasperated laugh]* We left." Veronica, in fear of her physical safety, did not want her estranged husband to know where she and the kids were.

Women receiving welfare in California may be sanctioned for failing to participate in the state's efforts to establish paternity and collect child support for children receiving welfare. Yvonne described her experience with one of these sanctions:

> One day they cut my money, 'cause they wanted to know more about her father and all—so much about him. I couldn't tell them something about him, you know, I could only tell them what I knew. Like his home address. I don't know his address. So they were like, if you don't tell us more information, we're gonna cut your check and not give you any food stamps. But I really don't know, you know. And so they cut my check and everything else.

According to Yvonne, she had complied with the second-parent reporting requirements as well as she could but had nonetheless been penalized for her lack of contact with her daughter's father.

Lisa, another interviewee, reported that her younger children's father became physically threatening after the district attorney began pursuing him for child support. While the kids' father was at the time of the interview paying child support to the state, Lisa and her children feared him and had no desire to maintain a relationship with him.

Sarah said that her two boys' father had paid child support only briefly, "until the fool stopped working. To keep from paying child support." When asked if their father kept in touch with his sons, Sarah replied. "No. No. Which don't make no difference anyway. . . . He hates them." While Sarah missed the child support, she claimed that neither she nor her children missed their father.

A couple of the women expressed their desire to raise their children apart from the fathers. Tanya was not living with her oldest child's father when he was murdered. She later had two other children with two other men. She stated with pride, "I'm a single parent. By choice." Tanya said that the middle child's father was devoted to all of the kids, faithfully paid child support, and spent time with the family. According to Tanya, "He's just a really neat person," but, she continued, "He is a *horrible* person to live with because he is so wound up."

The desire to be independent of the men formerly in their lives did not mean the women sought independence from all men. Some of the women could not envision themselves as financially stable without the economic support of a man. Lisa, for example, had her oldest child when she was only twenty-one. The father of her child was twenty years her senior. She joked that she needed to find a wealthy man to get off welfare permanently. Some interviewees expected men they were seeing to support them. For example, when I asked Rhonda whether she was in a relationship, she replied, "No. I wouldn't be in this position if I was." Like several of the interviewees, she expressed the expectation that a boyfriend or husband should support her financially.

The interviews in this study make clear that treating poor children's fathers as an undifferentiated group poses problems. Some of the fathers were present but invisible to the legal system. Others were all too present in the legal system, sitting in jail or prison. Some had abandoned their children and partners, while others had abused their children and partners and had been abandoned by their families. The interviews demonstrate that the existing research on the presence or absence of fathers in low-income households and the relationship dynamics in those households is inadequate and that more intensive and extensive qualitative research would prove valuable.

The Other Invisible Men

Most qualitative studies of welfare recipients are conducted with welfare mothers exclusively. While the overwhelming majority of household heads receiving welfare are women, there are also men heading welfare families. These men have for the most part been invisible to researchers. This study, however, includes interviews with four men who were solo parenting while on welfare. While four men certainly cannot represent all of the men receiving welfare, they can offer a glimpse inside male-headed welfare households. Three of the men had custody of their kids because the mothers of their children had drug problems and could no longer effectively parent their children. In the other case, the mother had been forced to leave her son and boyfriend to serve jail time on a welfare fraud charge.

Dwayne, a twenty-nine-year-old African American father of a two-year-old, took custody of his son when his ex-girlfriend checked into a drug rehab program. Dwayne shared some of the characteristics of the absent fathers described above. For example, he had sold drugs when he was young and had spent several years in prison. He also admitted that he had "laid hands" on his ex-girlfriend while angry, stating that most of their fights had been about her drug use. At the same time, Dwayne had stayed involved with his son's life, both as a caregiver and as a financial provider.

After Dwayne separated from his girlfriend (the mother of his son), his girlfriend began collecting welfare. Dwayne, who after prison enrolled in an apprenticeship program, made decent money in his job as a skilled tradesman. When his girlfriend checked into drug rehab and left her son with Dwayne, Dwayne suddenly could no longer work. He had no one to take care of his son while he worked, and he had no savings to pay for child care. He consequently lost his job. He had not had his son in his sole care for long when we met, and he was wrangling with the welfare office over his immediate needs, especially his need for child care. Dwayne described using the welfare system as "emotional slavery." Part of the emotions he felt, though, might have been his rage at becoming part of a feminized class of low-income parents.

Thomas, a twenty-five-year-old father, was living in a homeless shelter with his three-year-old daughter at the time of our interview. Thomas took custody of his daughter after the girl's mother, who according to Thomas regularly used drugs, continually failed to care for her daughter and routinely failed to submit welfare paperwork. After the mother lost her welfare benefits, she effectively abandoned her child to her grandmother. Thomas sought custody of his daughter not only because of his desire to care for her but also because he was homeless and jobless and knew that if his daughter were in his care he would qualify for welfare benefits and could use the system to bring some financial stability to his life.

Welfare Use
Entry Triggers

For most of the female interviewees, a pregnancy or birth triggered their first application for welfare. Jane, a thirty-one-year-old mother of two, applied for welfare when she was pregnant with her first child. She and her fiancé married and found employment. After Jane and her husband divorced, she got off welfare. "Struggled my butt off" is how she described the experience of supporting herself and her daughter with only fifty dollars a week in child support coming from her ex-husband.

Like several of the interviewees, Jane found herself cycling on and off welfare. She explained: "I got back on welfare when . . . there wasn't help with day care at the time. My daughter was, let's see, I want to say four. I couldn't afford day care." Rather than sending her daughter to kindergarten and looking for work when her daughter turned five, Jane decided to home-school her daughter. Jane then got pregnant again and stayed on welfare.

For other interviewees, the loss of a job led to the welfare office. Kiki, the mother of a ten-year-old daughter, explained that she had briefly received welfare after the birth of her daughter. She then spent eight years holding steady employment. When she was laid off and found herself struggling to pay the bills with her Unemployment Insurance alone, she applied for welfare again.

Still other interviewees turned to welfare when they experienced a change in family circumstances. Barbara turned to the welfare office after her mother died. For years, Barbara had been a housewife, raising two children while her husband worked and provided the sole income to the family. When her husband walked out, Barbara moved in with her mother. Despite suffering from a cognitive disability, Barbara went to a community college and received training as a nurse's assistant. Barbara relied on her mother's help during those years: "My mother, see, when I worked my mother took care of my kids. And she did everything with them. And I was able to work at night. I worked from eleven to seven . . . a forty-hour-a-week job."

Barbara's next pregnancy, the result of a relationship with a man who disappeared after the daughter's birth, exacerbated her disability, impairing her cognitive ability even more and making it more difficult for her to work. Barbara then relied entirely upon her mother's financial support. After her mother died, Barbara received a small inheritance. "And then I lived on it for a little while. And I didn't have welfare. And then when that ran out, I had to get food." That is when Barbara finally turned to welfare.

Tina, a twenty-one-year-old mother of an infant, turned to the welfare office simply because she could not make ends meet despite working as a certified nursing assistant. "I decided because my job wasn't paying that much and I couldn't afford really to buy food and pay my rent. 'Cause my rent here is like $535 a month, and my [bimonthly] check is $600. So, that's it mainly—why I decided to apply for it." Tina earned ten dollars an hour, more than three dollars above the minimum wage. Her job provided health insurance, though it cost her an additional $180 a month to insure her son. With a good half-hour commute between home and work, Tina estimated she spent fifteen dollars every three days to fill up her car's gas tank. When she turned to the welfare office in desperation, she had to wait three months before finding out whether the office could provide any assistance. Because her income was so high, she could not qualify for cash assistance but did qualify for food stamps and WIC (the Women and Infant Children food supplement program for pregnant women and infants). Until the food stamps arrived, Tina had been turning to food pantries.

Another interviewee, Tanya, said that she had applied for government aid initially because she and her oldest child needed medical insurance. She had a young child and no job and was sharing a house with her mother and a friend. "And we just kind of had this communal household, and, uh, I didn't get on aid for a while, and then I decided that I needed to get medical coverage more than anything else—for him, my son, and everything." Another mother, Sarah, also described the need for medical insurance as her reason for going to the welfare office: "I needed MediCal for my son."

Many of the interviewees entered the welfare system more than once. At least eight of the interviewees left the welfare system for extended spells after finding steady jobs. Still, the jobs they found were low-paid, provided few benefits, and offered no means for the interviewees to establish a financial cushion. An illness, a job layoff, or a new birth commonly brought these poor families right back to the welfare office. Though many of the women (but none of the men) I interviewed were working, only one—Patricia, an experienced nurse—had both a job and the job skills likely to offer anything resembling long-term financial stability.

Race, Ethnicity, and Welfare Use

While it may be unusual to identify one's racial and ethnic background as an economic resource or economic impediment, such may be the case. Tanya, who has a multiracial background—Asian American, Native American, and European American—could pass for white, especially while wearing her sunglasses. She spoke of the way people responded when she used food stamps to purchase groceries:

> If you go to the grocery store and you're buying a ton of veggies and fruit for your kids and bread and stuff and you whip out your food stamps, you know. . . . I've had people stand back and go and look me up and down. *[laughs]* And I remember one time—I was just so enraged—this woman was like . . . and I just turned around and looked her up and down and went, "Yes?" and she sort of backed off.

She described the feelings of shame associated with welfare receipt as "like an internalized ghetto invasion that takes place." The word *ghetto* has typically been used to describe the physical segregation of racial or ethnic groups but is also now commonly used as a derogatory label to describe cultural practices and attitudes among poor African Americans and Latinos. Tanya invoked the word to describe her internal processes, suggesting that for her, and perhaps for others, there is a racialized aspect to welfare receipt. For Tanya, welfare receipt was related not only to a loss of economic status but also to a loss of racial privilege. The political scientist Sanford Schram has written that blackness is associated in United States with risk, with economic danger (2000, 42-43). For Tanya, then, having experienced the "ghetto invasion" by welfare may have implications for both racial identity and her future economic possibilities, with the taint of welfare receipt coloring how other people how other people regard her—as a person on the margins rather than part of the mainstream.

Few people talked about race as a social resource, but a couple of the recipients highlighted racial privilege as something that they could transform into social and economic privilege. For example, Jane, a fair-skinned woman with blue eyes and sandy hair, spontaneously talked about how life on welfare was easier for her than for other people. "I don't look like I'm on welfare, you know." Jane elaborated. "In a lot of ways, and I say this ever so humbly, I'm a lot better off than a lot of people. One [reason], obvious, I'm white. Because black women have it even worse." She talked about the frequency with which homeless individuals in her neighborhood streets asked her for money and how they responded with disbelief when she explained that she, too, was struggling and on welfare. She explained:

> Only because I'm able to dress and talk and act like I'm not part of that—whatever that is—I mean, I feel like I'm stereotyping even in my statement—but I'm able to go out in the world and mix and mingle with wealthy people. And I don't have any problems once I've gotten to know 'em.

Jane acknowledged that because she did not look like the stereotypical African American welfare queen, she was able to "pass" as a member of the middle class.

The gendered racism that has informed the stereotypes of welfare recipients affects the experiences of both African American and non-African American welfare recipients. While those welfare recipients who do not look the part of the welfare queen can hide their poverty, once they reveal their economic circumstances their racial identities become tainted. Moreover, African American women who receive welfare are in a position where they fulfill a stereotype, a stereotype that may make it even more difficult for them to leave poverty and welfare.

Family History of Welfare Use

Some of the interviewees—Tina, Shanelle, Carmen, Yvonne, and Rhonda, for example—described growing up in households where their mothers had received welfare for at least parts of their childhoods. These women had no family they could turn to in times of financial need. This suggests that, contrary to the "culture of poverty" theory discussed in chapter 2, certain families may turn to welfare from one generation to the next because they never build up enough financial resources to buffer each other during times of hardship.

Shanelle attributed her use of welfare as an adult to her family's poverty, though not their welfare use, during her childhood and adolescent years. She explained that her family did not have enough money to buy her nice clothes or shoes. As a high school student, Shanelle met men who, she says, "would buy me shoes, they would buy me the things" her family could not afford. She said that after hanging around with these older men for a while she stopped going to high school and never graduated. As a result, she became financially dependent on men who had resources. Shanelle expressed her worry that because of her own economic troubles her adolescent daughter would meet a similar fate: "Some man is going to be easy to entice her, because he can buy her some stuff." Shanelle was pushing her daughter to excel in school so that she would not end up dependent on a man or on welfare.

Just about as many interviewees talked about growing up in families with stable income and the shame they felt in turning to the welfare system. Lisa, for example, grew up with two parents in a household kept financially stable by her father's steady income. She said that she had known little about the welfare system before she applied for aid while pregnant with her first child, except that the system was something her parents had warned her away from.

Length of Time on Welfare

The interviewees varied dramatically in the length of time they had received welfare. Some, such as Tina and Patricia, had been on aid for only a few months, while others had received aid, either continuously or repeatedly, for a decade or more. Annette, for example, had been on aid continuously for almost eighteen years, going back to the time she was pregnant with her oldest child. Several, including Veronica, had cycled between welfare and low-wage employment for many years, never able to raise their families out of poverty. Pam said that her aid had been cut off in 1996 and that she had survived for two years by living in homeless shelters and receiving a small "allowance" from her parents until reapplying for aid in 1998. Pam could not explain what had prevented her from reapplying for so long.

Twenty-one of the thirty-four welfare recipients interviewed had first applied for welfare before the federal welfare reforms were implemented in California. While one might expect more recent first-time aid applicants to be better acquainted with the welfare reforms, there was confusion among both recent welfare applicants and welfare old-timers.

Educational History

There was significant variation in educational attainment by the interviewees in this sample. Five of the interviewees—Carmen, Crystal, Jamilla, Johnetta, and Veronica—had not graduated from high school. In only two of these cases, however, had the women given birth while high school-aged. In both cases, the women not only lacked the education necessary to achieve financial stability but also appeared to lack basic life skills. Jamilla, whose education ended in the tenth grade and who had her first of four children (with the same man) at age sixteen, said that her partner had taken care of all of the financial matters in the household before going to jail three years before our interview. While Jamilla had worked a couple low-skilled jobs, she had never worked a forty-hour week. After our interview, Jamilla also mentioned that she had never had a bank account.

Carmen, whose education also ended in the tenth grade, gave birth at age seventeen, shortly after fleeing her abusive boyfriend. She had never held a job and did not want to be in school while her daughter was young, saying, "When my mom went to college, she paid all her attention to her work and school. I don't want to be like that." Without an education or job experience, Carmen's options other than welfare were virtually nonexistent.

Six interviewees—Annette, Jane, Pam, Sharon, Thomas, Renee, and Sarah—had graduated from high school or received a GED (general education degree certificate, the equivalent of a high school diploma). Lisa and Tanya had never finished high school but had nonetheless successfully completed community college courses. Tanya was taking specialized courses in alternative medicine at the time of our interview. Lisa dropped out of community college because she could not successfully juggle her mandatory work requirement and her class schedule. Shanelle, who also had not finished high school, had taken enough community college credits to receive an associate's degree. Like Lisa and Tanya, however, she needed to take her GED exam. Unfortunately, she did not have the money to pay for the exam and could not receive her community college degree until she passed the GED. So despite her educational efforts, Shanelle appeared to prospective employers like a high school dropout.

A striking fifteen (44 percent) of the interviewees had taken some college courses, which ranged from a few classes at a community college to sustained work at state universities. At the time of our interviews, D'Nay was enrolled in a state university pursuing a degree in nursing, and Renee was taking classes to become an administrative medical assistant. Jill had completed all but the last semester of a bachelor's degree program and planned to complete her credits once she found a steady job. Jill also had a teaching credential. Four of the interviewees had completed a degree or certificate program. (One interviewee did not offer information about educational background.) The interviewees with at least some college education had the strongest employment histories, described below.

Employment History

Most of the welfare recipient interviewees had some job experience. The exceptions were Carmen, a teenaged mother discussed above, and Sarah, a forty-one-year-old mother of two teenage sons—one still in high school and the other too old to receive welfare. For those who had worked, the work histories typically included a list of low-skilled jobs that offered pay too low to support a family. In response to a question about her work history, Veronica explained:

> I've had warehouse jobs. I've had cleaning jobs. I've worked in a liquor store. I've worked in a movie theater. I've been a foster parent. Um . . . I've been . . . child care. Janitorial services. The thing is, I don't have a high school diploma. Which I guess is not really my fault because I was too busy taking care of other people to, I guess, take care of myself. And that's really bad in this day and age when you have to leave school to take care of your family.

Jane provided a similar laundry list of low-paying jobs: movie theater manager; bank worker; projectionist for a cable access channel; manager at a fast food restaurant; salesperson of newspapers, Christian videos, and air purifiers; house cleaner; attendant for elderly and disabled clients; and housing discrimination investigator. She noted, "Three to five jobs [at a time] is not uncommon for me." Like most of the other interviewees who lacked a high school diploma, Jane and Veronica had little hope of securing stable, sustaining employment.

Shawnique, a twenty-two-year-old mother of two, had held a number of low-paid jobs—café employee, stockroom clerk, and security guard—before landing a couple jobs that paid better. Unfortunate circumstances put an end to both of them. She left her fifteen-dollar-an-hour job as a medical assistant when the physical abuse by her husband began to interfere with her ability to work. She had previously left a job that paid more than twenty dollars an hour because of sexual harassment. Shawnique explained:

> I was also doing carpentry, because I'm an apprentice carpenter. I went to trade school for that for one year, and got certified, and I was making some pretty good money. I was making some really decent money, like twenty-something an hour. And I was only twenty years old, and I thought I was just all that. But, I just got tired of the sexual harassment and, um, the splin-

ters and being all dusty and dirty every day. *[sighs]* I just couldn't take it any more. It was mainly the sexual harassment. The guys, you know. I would have to hear comments every single day, about something. You know, I wear my pants baggy. I had my overalls. I was real baggy, nothing tight-fitting, form fitting, because I would be drawing attention to myself. And I didn't want to do that. And I was, um, strictly there to do what I had to do and then get my check and go about my business. But I had to deal with the comments all day—about women and working and guys talking about sex all day. It just really discourages women from getting into that field, 'cause we're still not treated as equal to them. So that didn't work. But the money was good. It was really hard to let it go. But I tried two or three different sites, and every site, sure enough, there was some guy there, all he could think about was sex or saying something derogatory. And I'm not really a petty person. I don't believe in snitching or tattle-telling. I can pretty much hold my own. And I would, like, take them to the side and say, "You need to quit this or else." And just break it down to them. They were just laughing at me like it's just a joke, like, yeah right, what are you going to do? So I just quit. I didn't want to go to the supervisor, to the boss, and get them in trouble because of their weird personalities. So, it's best if I just leave.

Shawnique willingly left a job that paid well enough to allow her economic independence because of the hostile work environment. Though her next job paid more than twice the minimum wage, she still relied upon her partner's wages to support herself and her two kids. When she could no longer take his abuse, she turned to the welfare system, which included a substantial loss of financial security.

A few of the interviewees had extensive and strong work histories. Millie began her career in food service at age fourteen, working a series of jobs in fast food. While working in a pizza chain after she attended college, she received a series of promotions. She left that job and became a cook in a downtown hotel, earning twenty-three dollars an hour. She then worked four years as head cook at a large corporate plant that offered its employees meals. She left that job after her active participation in the union produced continual tension with her manager. Millie then worked for a hospital and a grocery store, while running a catering business on the side. Persistent and increasing back pain, which she traced back to a serious car accident in college, slowly impinged on her ability to work and eventually sidelined her career. Her pain, the effects of the drugs she took for the pain, and the clinical depression fostered by both pain and unemployment rendered her unable to work. After receiving TANF benefits for a while, Millie eventually had her Social Security benefits approved. Two of her three children received TANF benefits, and Millie was exempted from the work requirements under CalWORKs.

Another interviewee with substantial work experience was Jill. Jill had worked for a number of years as a kindergarten teacher. Feeling burned out from teaching, she took an office job in a start-up company during the dot.com boom. When the company flopped, Jill found herself receiving unemployment benefits. For months, while receiving unemployment benefits, Jill searched for employment. She described herself as independent and said it was difficult for her to apply for welfare when her unemployment benefits ran out. "I'd passed by the office many times. *[laughs]* And said I always hope I never have to go in there. But I did." The morning of our interview, Jill had been offered a permanent position as a preschool teacher. While she said she preferred other work, she said she would take the job if she had no other employment option. She was waiting for a response to a job application and several rounds of interviews she had had for a government office job. She was hoping she would receive the government job offer before she had to respond to the job offer from the preschool.

The work skills and work experiences of the interviewees varied dramatically. Those who had limited work skills complained that the services offered by the welfare office did little to improve their skills or employability. The interviewees with substantial work backgrounds found the employment services offered by the welfare office useless, time consuming, and patronizing. Further, the welfare office discouraged the very thing that would have made many of the interviewees more employable: additional education.

Questioning Some Assumptions behind Welfare's Work Requirements

The lawmakers who implemented welfare reform apparently assumed that most welfare recipients were work-ready. The welfare reform rules were designed for poor individuals who could work if they wanted to but needed some motivation to actually do it. Not all welfare recipients, however, can easily access employment.

Like a number of other studies, the interviews in this study revealed a number of barriers to employment. One of these barriers is disability. A number of the interviewees were hampered not only in finding and holding jobs but also in their day-to-day lives by their physical and mental limitations. Barbara, a mother of two grown sons and a school-age daughter, suffered a head injury when she was a young woman. As a result, she suffered cognitive impairment, particularly affecting her short-term memory, and was prone to seizures. While she had taken great care to attend all of her meetings, trainings, and work assignments as directed by the welfare office, she had not been able to keep a job because of her memory problems. Her application for SSI, a cash aid program for low-income individuals who are too disabled to work, was denied.

Despite her mental and physical limitations, Barbara was eager to have a job.

> BARBARA: I've worked! It's not that I'm a person who has not worked. Even with my disability, I've worked. And then the one time—two times—I've tried out for Disability [benefits], they've turned me down.
> INTERVIEWER: Why is that?
> BARBARA: Well, because I hadn't worked. I hadn't worked before. *[pause]* I've never worked on a real full-time job. All my jobs have been part time. Because I get really, really tired and all, then. And then I thought, well, maybe I should try Disability again now that I'm more mature. And then that's like welfare too. You know what I mean?

Barbara was trapped between the separate aid categories the state has created for workers and for the disabled. The Social Security system was designed as a safety net for full-time workers with established work histories. Under the system, once a worker becomes totally disabled, the government steps in to provide support. But people like Barbara, who are disabled but who have only worked part time, fall between the cracks.

A disability was also the source of economic struggles for Millie. As mentioned above, for years Millie made good money working as a head cook for an upscale hotel and running a catering business on the side. When a back injury worsened, she could no longer work. She ultimately applied for and was approved Social Security Disability Insurance (SSDI) benefits, but not until her savings had run out, she had lost her apartment, and she had moved her family into a homeless shelter. In addition, though Millie was exempted from the welfare work requirements because of her disability and because only her children technically received TANF benefits, she still received letter after letter from the welfare office saying that she was not complying with her work requirements and requiring her to travel by bus to the welfare office to resolve the administrative problems.

Some of the interviewees, if they sought employment, probably had difficulty finding jobs simply because they looked ill. Sarah, a mother who had never held a job, told me she suffered from asthma and a knee problem that made it difficult for her to walk. By her looks, though, she also suffered other ailments. Sarah was very, very thin, and on both occasions I saw her, the whites of her eyes were tinged dark orange, suggesting perhaps problems with her liver.

Other interviewees described difficulties with mental illness. Kiki described slipping into a deep depression after she was laid off from her job: "I couldn't take . . . my little brain just couldn't take any more, and I just shut, I just shut down." She provided details of her battle with severe depression, which lasted a year: "I just flipped. I just got in my little cocoon, and I wouldn't see [my daughter] after school, I wouldn't, you know, wake her up, see her [off to school], you know to make sure that she got through, you know, give her breakfast, all this." Kiki said she relied on the routine and the meaningfulness of work, saying "It keeps me mentally sane." Far from fulfilling the stereotype of the welfare queen who avoids the wage labor market, Kiki craved a steady job.

While some of the interviewees had disabilities themselves, others were caring for children with disabilities. In these cases, the adults not only had their work routines undermined by health emergencies but also had to take children to regular therapy or counseling appointments between the hours of nine and five. Veronica, for example, was caring for three children who had been born to drug-addicted relatives and who therefore suffered from the effects of their mothers' drug use. One of the boys saw three different therapists a week. Another interviewee, Yvonne, described her daughter as having "special needs"—a term used by the welfare office—and had to take her daughter by bus to weekly sessions with both a psychiatrist and a speech therapist. At the same time, Yvonne suffered chronic conditions—a back problem and asthma—that limited her physical capacity as well.

Annette, who had not held a full-time job since her oldest teenaged daughter, who was deaf, was born, feared leaving her daughter and her two younger children home alone while working. She said she lived in a neighborhood controlled by teenaged Asian gangs. She described a frightening experience of leaving her daughter home alone one night.

> She can't hear things at night. Well I mean, period, but I mean it's just . . .
> at night. Her not having on her hearing aid, she doesn't hear. And, like,
> earlier this year, I left her at home 'cause she doesn't like to hang with me

and the [younger] girls all the time. And it wasn't late. It was like, about . . . between eight and ten . . . and I left. And when I came back, um, she was telling me that someone had been in the backyard. And she didn't hear it, but she looked out the blinds and seen somebody standing there. And she was at home by herself, you know.

Annette feared that her children would come to harm if she left them home alone.

In some of these households, the disabled children qualified for Social Security benefits, which are higher than benefits under TANF. In some cases this left the family better off financially than those with welfare benefits alone. In other cases, the Social Security payments simply covered the additional costs associated with the additional care the disabled children required, leaving the families struggling. This was true for Veronica's boy and for Annette's daughter.

Other common barriers to work among the interviewees concerned the needs of the children in the households. Mothers particularly described the difficulties of coordinating the children's school schedules with their own work schedules. Tammy explained that her three oldest children had three different school schedules and that, in a neighborhood like hers, she had to pick up and drop off each child.

Some parents described the difficulty—or near-impossibility—of finding safe, affordable child care for their children. Still others feared putting their young children in child care. When I asked Tammy if any of her four children had been with babysitters or in child care, she said:

> No, 'cause, you know, some of that stuff happening at day cares . . . that makes you scared, you know, you don't know what people [do], you know? Just because they have a certificate, that don't mean, you know, sometimes you feel uncomfortable, you know? I feel at least they should wait for your baby get at least about two or three. You know what I'm saying? And then you'll feel more comfortable when they're at a talking stage. 'Cause some of them babies, they let sit in dirty diapers all day, you know, they can't . . . they doing the best they can. They can't keep going to this baby. You know, 'cause it's crying or whatever.

Not only was Tammy distrustful of day care providers, but she also had a premature infant in her care. With long local wait lists for infant care, at an average cost of more than $1,100 a month, and few child care providers able to care for children with extraordinary needs, Tammy was resigned to an extended sanction of her welfare check for failing to meet her work requirements.

Transportation also posed a barrier to employment for these families. For families who relied on public transportation, getting young children to and from school safely was sometimes a major endeavor. The transportation barriers faced by welfare recipients, particularly urban welfare recipients who do not own cars, are well documented by policy researchers (Coulton 2003; Ong 1996). But these are not the only barriers to employment.

Criminal records may also hinder welfare recipients from finding jobs (Pager 2003). Shanelle, a mother of three, had a felony record for shooting her abusive boyfriend. According to her account, she shot him in self-defense after he came to her apartment in disregard of a restraining order and began beating her. Thomas and Jerome also had criminal convictions in their backgrounds that impaired their abilities to find wage work.

Some interviewees described welfare receipt itself as a barrier to employment. Lisa, a thirty-seven-year-old mother of three who had been on welfare for sixteen years at the time of our interview, said, "A lot of employers . . . they already have it in their minds . . . she's got lower mentality or whatever because . . . she's on CalWORKs." The stigma of welfare receipt may impede employability both by discouraging employees from hiring welfare recipients and by discouraging recipients from applying for jobs.

Certainly one of the biggest barriers to employment for a number of these families was homelessness. Eleven of the thirty-four interviewees were homeless at the time of the interview. Four of the interviewees were staying in homeless shelters, one in transitional housing, and one at a hotel. The others were straining relationships with friends or family by staying temporarily in their homes. The constant crisis of securing the family's most immediate need—shelter—absorbed the time and energy of many of the mothers and fathers. Several of the other interviewees who were not homeless had been homeless in the past. Looking back on her experience with homelessness, Shanelle explained, "It's all-consuming being homeless, and not having nowhere to stay, not having no kind of help at all." Being homeless absorbed a lot of time and energy.

The welfare system had inadequate resources to address the multiple barriers to employment many of these families faced. While the welfare office sometimes provided bus passes to poor mothers, it could not fully relieve the stress that these mothers endured in transporting children from a homeless shelter on one side of town to an elementary school on the other side of town by bus. Moreover, the paperwork, lines, and appointments required for homeless parents just to get on a waiting list for subsidized housing could constitute a part-time job. While some of the homeless interviewees received both additional homeless benefits and exemptions from the work requirements, others apparently received no benefits and were being sanctioned for failing to meet their work requirements. A couple recipients, Pam and Thomas, were working despite being homeless.

Annette described the simple emotional difficulty of finding full-time employment after years of being out of the full-time, formal labor market:

> I have seen nothing that says they're helping you with your self-confidence, or the emotional side of this stuff. Nobody's talking about that. Who cares about how it feels? Okay, yeah, you've been in the house for X amount of years, you've put on a hundred pounds, you don't have clothes, you don't feel good about yourself, your self-esteem is low, we don't care about that. Just do something and get out.

It was this fear of the labor market that welfare reformers hoped to overcome through the welfare-to-work programs. Some of the interviewees complained, however, that the welfare system provided few resources to help them become work-ready. This was particularly true for welfare recipients with low skills and multiple work barriers.

In the end, the families who relied on the welfare system were unable to secure economic stability for their families through sheer determination. And it seemed that many of the interviewees would remain in desperate circumstances unless or until they could change their lot. The welfare reforms enacted in 1996 seemed to rest on the belief that welfare recipients were making simple choices to receive welfare rather than work. They also rested on the belief that making welfare receipt more onerous would prompt welfare recipients to choose employment over welfare. The interviews revealed, however, that multiple barriers—including low skills and education, disabilities, caretaking responsibilities, domestic violence, and housing insecurity—stood in the way of employment. As a result, most of the interviewees relied on public benefits to meet their basic needs.

But even with irregular employment and the help of public benefits, most of the interviewees had difficulty meeting their basic needs. The following chapter describes the vast gulf between these families' needs and the resources they received through regular wage work and government assistance.

5

Living within and without the Rules

The welfare recipient interviewees led their economic and family lives wandering a maze of welfare rules and regulations. They also lived within a maze of family needs—both economic and otherwise. Sometimes the interviewees lived within the rules, both specific and abstract, of welfare. At other times, however, they lived without the rules—sometimes because they did not know the rules, sometimes because their economic or family needs outweighed their compliance with the rules, sometimes because they were simply flouting the rules.

The discussion that follows makes clear that in some cases, or at least to some extent, the interviewees complied with many of the welfare rules, fulfilling work requirements and reporting earnings to the welfare office. In other cases, however, the interviewees survived by going outside the rules—taking "side jobs" that paid cash and that they did not report to the welfare office, or receiving undeclared support from friends or family. The first two sections of this chapter describe the financial needs that went unmet in interviewee households and how the interviewees attempted to meet their needs. The next sections describe interviewees' difficulties with the rules—difficulties understanding the rules and difficulties seeing the rules as logical.

The Gap between Needs and Resources

The economic, and one may even say the existential, instability of welfare recipients is frighteningly real. Bayview County had a high cost of living at the time of these interviews. Between the time of the first interview in late 1998 and the last interview in early 2002, the fair market rent for a two-bedroom apartment in Bayview County (as calculated by the U.S. Department of Housing and Urban Development) rose from $812 per month to $1,155 per month.

Many of the interviewees had suffered at least one bout of homelessness. Moving out of homelessness proved difficult for them. Veronica explained that when she and her six children had fled her abusive husband they had all stayed in a shelter. She estimated that she had submitted applications and credit checks at hundreds of dwellings, but none had offered to let her move in. "And it wasn't because I have bad credit, it's because I had six children." She eventually found an apartment for $950 a month.

Two others, Shanelle and Lisa, had also been homeless in the past. Lisa explained that even when she was approved for Section 8, a government program providing housing subsidies in the form of rental vouchers, she had difficulty finding landlords who would accept Section 8 renters. Both said that the experiences of homelessness made paying rent their number one priority. Shanelle said "the fact that we've already gone through that homelessness. . . I guess, that's why, I, regardless of whatever, my rent is paid." Lisa said, "Once you been homeless with kids, out there, you going to make sure that . . . your rent is paid." Shanelle and Lisa both described going hungry and sometimes having to provide their children with inadequate meals in order to have enough money to cover the rent. Shanelle, who had worked as a prostitute to support her drug habit before she quit drugs and got into recovery years earlier, said that if she could no longer receive welfare she would "probably, you know, prostitute in order to pay the rent." Sarah, a forty-one-year-old mother with a teenaged son at home, echoed Shanelle's statement, saying that in the case her welfare benefits and housing subsidy ended, "I'm going to have to try to find me a job or . . . go to the oldest profession or something. Because I would be homeless again." Many of the interviewees who had housing expressed fears that they would soon lose it and would not be able to find new housing.

Most of the interviewees who described their housing situations as stable received support through the Section 8 program, which subsidizes low-income tenants in the private rental market. Of the thirty-four interviewees, only seven received housing subsidies through the Section 8 program. The high costs of housing in the research county made it difficult for the interviewees to survive financially, even when employed.

The interviewees in this study generally devoted most if not all of their welfare grants to their housing costs. Even those interviewees living in homeless shelters or transitional housing had to contribute their welfare grants to cover housing expenses. Simple details of life were complicated for welfare recipients. While the interviewees received food stamps, the food stamp benefits were often not enough to provide food for the entire month. In addition, the food stamp benefits could be used only for food. Interviewees discussed the problem of providing enough food, especially toward the end of the month. They routinely struggled to find money for day-to-day needs such as clothing, shoes, laundry detergent, household cleaning products, and feminine hygiene products. One woman, Pam, talked about the frustration of running out of toilet paper and having no money to buy more.

Veronica, a twenty-eight-year-old mother of two children and caretaker of three (sometimes four) others, told me that she had occasionally not had enough money to buy toothpaste, bath soap, or laundry detergent. She told me that when she had no laundry detergent she filled the bathtub with water, poured in some dishwashing detergent, threw in the children's school uniforms, and told the kids to strip down and dance on their clothing. Veronica worried that the children in her care, most of whom were relatives she had spared from the foster care system, would "get tore apart" because of her poverty. She worried, she said, "because they don't have all of their needs. They have most of their needs, but not all their needs. And they probably have none of their wants right now. You know, 'cause I'm struggling, I really am."

Tanya, a mother of three who had more income flowing into the household than many of the other interviewees, spoke vividly about the difficulties of living with very little income:

> Because living off the amount we have to live off is . . . it's, you know, there's nothing more devastating than being, than having to turn around to your kids and say, "You know what? I can't afford to get meat tonight." Or, you know, "Can, you know, can you handle eating just pasta? Cause I bought two hundred pounds of pasta at the canned food store and some tomato sauce. Is that cool?" You know? And if we can get some change together, we get some lettuce. You know, I mean, it hurts! It's really hurts! And I went through that last year. It was really bad; it was really, really bad. 'Cause I had to pay for car insurance. And I decided not to pay my electric bill last month, all right, so I could pay the phone bill and the car insurance. And it's like this juggling act. So this month I paid the electric bill and it was $180. And I just kind of went, *[sighing laugh]* what could I cut out this month?

Like the other participants, Tanya struggled with the very basics of subsistence.

Shanelle, who admitted to taking occasional sides jobs such as braiding hair, said that the money from those jobs went for household basics:

And it was like, okay, we got an extra roll of toilet paper for the month 'cause I done worked a little. . . . You know what I'm saying? Or, you know what, kids, instead of us having to eat chicken livers, we going to eat a chicken today, I mean, you know what I'm saying? It's not like, oh, well we about to go out and buy us some cars.

Like other mothers in urban areas, Shanelle worried about her inability to buy burial insurance or life insurance for her kids, stating, "Lord, Lord, please, if any[thing]—forbid—happens to my kids, I wouldn't have no money to bury them."

The welfare system prioritizes fraud prevention over poverty alleviation. To prevent fraud, the welfare office collects vast amounts of information about welfare recipients and their families. Those who want to receive welfare have to fill out extensive paperwork at the time of their initial application and again yearly for their annual renewal of aid. In addition, they have to submit the monthly CA-7 forms describing any changes in their income or household circumstances. Paperwork problems routinely tied up recipients' assistance payments. Annette described the frustrating experience she was having at the time of our interview:

ANNETTE: This month, I didn't get my food stamps, and I still ain't got them. You know why they didn't? Because they sent my renewal papers or the paper that asks about the absent parent. That paper say, "Do you know any relatives of the father." So, I left it blank. They sent it back. So that's the reason they cut my food stamps off, right. 'Cause I left it blank. There are no other relatives. Now, I got his name on there and everything. That's what they ask. And because . . .

INTERVIEWER: So, one line.

ANNETTE: Yeah. Well, and because they ask whether he has any scars or tattoos. I didn't put that down there. I kid you not, that's why they did that.

Annette explained that her failure to write "Don't Know" on the blanks in her renewal papers was not the only problem with her paperwork that month.

And another thing . . . they wanted to know why my phone is in my mother's name. Well, I had her to write out a statement last year, so it's in the file. We was told at the time, it's been eleven years ago, because I was pregnant with [my daughter], when she first came. So, at the time, I was eight months pregnant, and my sister had ran up the other apartment bill accepting for collect calls from her man in jail, so they had it turned off. At the time, I was pregnant, was getting ready to move, and needed a phone. So my mom had the phone turned on in her name. She had credit, 'cause, you know, if you don't have credit you gotta pay a deposit and all that kinda stuff, so she got it turned on. Well, it's been, like I said, almost eleven years and, so what! I pay the bill, it's no big deal. But that's why I haven't gotten any food stamps this month, because of that. They did send a check. It was late, but they did send a check. They didn't send the food stamps. And as of . . . the last time I went in there was Tuesday of this week, and as of Tuesday they still have not released my food stamps.

To receive aid, Annette had to document the small details of her life, such as the misrepresentation she was making to the phone company.

Jane refused to fill out paperwork even when she knew it would hurt her not to do so. She simply described the paperwork as a nuisance. For example, she owned a car of such low value that owning it would not put her above the assets limit for welfare receipt. She did not report ownership of her car, she said, because of

all the crap that I would have to go through—like all the proof and the paperwork and all the extra, extra stuff that I would have to do just to have them say it's okay to have my car. I just filled out my renewal papers two days ago. And this whole thing went through my head. And it was just like, hell no.

In other words, Jane avoided following rules when compliance was inconvenient.

The documentation of daily life is a form of state surveillance to which welfare recipients submit but also a form of surveillance they resist, sometimes to their detriment. It was this routine documentation that the interviewees described as invasive and oppressive.

Bridging the Gap between Financial Need and the Welfare Grant

There were a number of ways that welfare recipients bridged the gap between their welfare benefits and their financial needs. The following sections describe the strategies interviewees discussed.

Legitimate Employment

Employment is not necessarily a way out of poverty, or even a way off welfare. The dividing line between the welfare poor and the working poor is a blurry one. While the lawmakers who instituted welfare reform hoped that increased employment among welfare recipients would make them economically self-sufficient, most of the welfare recipients who took jobs and subsequently left welfare earned too little to bring economic stability to their households. A University of Wisconsin study summarizing a number of earlier studies on adults who had left the welfare system after reform found that "about two-thirds of leavers [nationwide] work in the first years after exiting and that they earn between $6.50 and $7.50 per hour. Poverty rates are quite high, more than 50 percent in the early years after leaving" (Cancian et al. 2002, 606).

Many parents participated in the wage labor force while receiving welfare. Kiki, one of these parents, was laid off from the administrative job she had held for five years and applied for welfare while still receiving Unemployment Insurance payments. During her two years on aid, she had managed to find a series of part-time jobs, but nothing stable, well paid, or full time. She described welfare as "a little bit of supplement." Despite working, Kiki was homeless.

Work and education do not necessarily provide stable routines for families. Welfare recipients often have temporary jobs or rotating shifts. Since the jobs they can obtain are marginal, they do not have control over what their schedules will be. Policy makers' assumptions that work will provide stability to otherwise chaotic families do not bear themselves out. Jade, a mother of two, provided in-home health services as needed, but the needs varied. Veronica had a "temp" job at a warehouse an hour away from her home. She usually worked the late shift, from 3:30 p.m. to 2:00 a.m., returning home around three or four o'clock in the morning. She had to rouse her kids at 6:30 a.m. to get them off to school. Sometimes she learned only in the afternoon that she would be working that evening. Veronica then had to contact a friend to take care of her kids. She relied on two buses for each leg of her journey to and from work. In chatting with me after her interview, Veronica said that because she was often on the streets in the wee hours of the morning as she returned from work, she was routinely offered money for sex by men who assumed she was a prostitute and was also hassled by police who made the same assumption.

Natalie, a thirty-four-year-old mother caring for a nine-year-old and a thirteen-year-old, was grateful for the fact that she could work and receive welfare, saying, "It's pretty good! I like the program. I *love* the program. I think it's really great." Natalie enjoyed working, enjoyed getting out of the house. Still, she admitted that her ten-dollar-an-hour job as a security guard did put a strain on her and her family. She worked nights, leaving her two children home alone.

> NATALIE: By the time I'm at work, the kids are asleep. They're fed, they're in bed. And then I go home from work—that's a school, school night—I'm home in time for them to get off to school. So that kind of works out. But it's a killer though, eleven to seven. That graveyard shift.
> INTERVIEWER: When do you sleep?
> NATALIE: Never. *[laughing]* Never! There's always something in the house that has to be done.

Natalie's odd working hours were not unusual for wage-earning welfare recipients. A study of welfare recipients participating in post-reform programs in three different states found that almost half "worked irregular hours, including evening and weekend shifts" (B. Fuller, Kagan, and Loeb 2002, 3).

Because she worked, Natalie received a welfare check adjusted down to reflect her earnings. While Natalie's cash grant from the welfare office was small, she and her children relied on that money to stay afloat financially. In fact, at the time of our interview Natalie was trying to figure out why she had not received her welfare check on the first of the month. The delay had prevented her from paying her rent in full, and she was anxious to resolve the problem because she had already received a thirty-day-notice from her landlord. While Natalie found work personally fulfilling, her job was not financially fulfilling.

Workers with few skills have little weight to bear in negotiating the terms of their employment. The work requirements under CalWORKs, which sanction individuals who do not meet their work requirements, put additional pressure on poor families to accept low-paid, dangerous jobs with no hope of advancement. Veronica described one of her experiences as an employee:

> VERONICA: Last year I worked at a job where . . . I worked there for nine months. I worked hard, because I was supposed to be working eight hours. But I was working ten to twelve hours a day, six to seven days a week. And they kept saying, "We're going to make you permanent." You know, so I'm like, yes, I know I got me a permanent job. So after ten months of me work-

ing there, ten months of me working there, I found out that they were playing with my emotions and they let everybody go. So I had to start all over
again, which is hard because they're doing a lot of people like this, where
they're saying they're going to make the person permanent. You know, getting their hopes up. "Okay, I'm gonna have me a job."

INTERVIEWER: So they won't leave and go somewhere else?

VERONICA: Right. So around Christmas they said, "Bye." And they did a
lot of people like this. And they had [said] to all these people, "We're gonna
make you permanent." And they didn't. Which is wrong. Because I coulda
been looking for a different job.

I: What job was it?

VERONICA: This was a warehouse job in, uh, South Bayview. And it's a step
up from slave labor, um, because it's supposed to be after forty hours you
don't have to come to work. This place, if you don't come on the Saturdays
or Sundays, you get fired. And, um, they had gave me a raise 'cause I really
worked hard. Everybody else was getting paid $5.75. Doing a job where they
should have at least been making nine dollars. But I guess that's . . . well,
that's to me what welfare reform does. If you could pay someone five dollars
what usually you could pay them to do for ten . . . . You know, that's what
they're doing. They're giving everybody who doesn't have a lot of experience
of working or doesn't have a GED, they're giving them jobs that are really
jobs for a lot less money. I mean, these are half-assed jobs.

According to Veronica, on-the-job injuries occurred frequently at the work
site. She said these injuries included employees passing out from chemi-
cal fumes in unventilated areas. She said, "If someone's mean to me and or
something goes wrong on the job and I complain and they're permanent, I'll
get fired. So it's kinda hard for CalWORKs workers."

Veronica also described applying for a job at the warehouse for a big
department store. Veronica said that applicants were asked if they were
receiving welfare and, if so, were asked to fill out additional forms. The job
was advertised as paying $6.75 an hour. She said, "When they hired me, it
wasn't that much. It was $6.00." She attributed the pay differential to her sta-
tus as a welfare recipient.

A number of the interviewees described their need for medical insurance
as one reason they remained on welfare. Many explained that the low-wage
jobs available to them offered no medical insurance. Many, especially those
who had health problems or whose children had chronic health problems
such as asthma, said that they were better off using welfare and receiving

MediCal than they would be working without insurance and finding themselves facing a family medical emergency. Kiki, for example, described her family's need for medical benefits as her biggest barrier to employment. These interviewees were weighing and benefits and disadvantages of working and determining that the risks of uninsured employment were too high.

While it was certainly not the case that most of the interviewees wanted to remain on welfare, there was little evidence that welfare reform succeeded in its promise to "make work pay" or that there were substantial incentives for welfare recipients to take employment. For the most part, the jobs available to them would not only leave them in poverty but also provide them no benefits. Unlike the jobs held by those in the upper-middle class, the jobs welfare recipients worked offered little opportunity for advancement, no personal satisfaction or prestige, and even more stress than home life.

Side Jobs: The Underground Labor Market

To earn extra money, a lot of the interviewees explained that they took jobs that paid in cash and that they did not report the earnings to the welfare office or on any tax forms. These jobs were generally low-paid service jobs and were irregularly available. Braiding hair, cooking, babysitting, and doing household chores for others were typical examples of these jobs. Jamilla, a mother with four children and little education or work experience, stated: "I was doing hair from the time that I got fired up until now." She continued, "I braid hair so I can pay my rent, you know, and buy food or, you know pay [utilities] and water." These little bits of income were important to someone with such desperate financial needs.

Many of these side jobs were done for other low-income people who would have difficulty paying the market rate for the services they received. For example, Barbara, who had received some training as a nursing assistant, took side jobs caring for the ill and elderly poor.

> Oh, well, you know, I do the nursing, the home help, and I go help older people. You know take care of themselves. And then I have one lady that I went to, she have . . . she was very ill. . . . This lady was just eighty-two. And she had had several strokes so she couldn't get up and around. And she kept her arm like this *[gesturing]* because her body wouldn't move. So that's why she sleeps in one spot and gets those ulcers, decubitis. So, uh, but she's in the hospital now. So I don't know if she's gonna get out or what. But, um, I took care of her. And you know, when someone needs a nurse's assistant and they know about me, then they call me and I help. Morning care, you know, the aid and stuff.

Barbara's role in the underground economy was important not only to her economic survival but also to the survival—physical and economic—of the persons she cared for. Her cash aid from the welfare office was only $505 per month, while her rent alone was $750. Without the money from side jobs, as well as help from her estranged husband, her adult children, and members of her church, Barbara would not have been able to stay afloat financially.

It appeared that members of the community were aware that welfare recipients had trouble making ends meet. D'Nay explained that she had done a number of odd jobs for cash. They included babysitting and cleaning houses. She mentioned that her pastor, perhaps as an act of charity, had offered many of the odd jobs. He paid her to clean his house, iron his shirts, and clean the church. She never reported this income to the welfare office.

In some cases, individuals were working multiple side jobs. Veronica, the sole caretaker for five—sometimes six—children, not only worked nights in warehouse jobs and went to school in the mornings to get her GED but also held a number of side jobs.

> I struggle here, I struggle there. See there's, um, an elderly man that I clean his house. Three times a week. There's another elderly lady that I cook dinner for. Say I might make five meals in a row for her and put it in the freezer. That way she can take it out and put it in the microwave.

Veronica's landlord also reduced her rent a little bit each month in return for her work on the property.

Annette sometimes did hair and helped in her girlfriend's cleaning business. She said that her work in the cleaning business allowed her to make it through the holidays the year before but that it required her to work at night, leaving her children home alone. When I asked Annette if she reported these earnings to the welfare office she said:

> Of course not! *[laughs]* Of course not! Every nickel . . . they want to have that, you know. Um-um. And you see, the thing about reporting things like that is, it's never consistent. You know what I'm saying? You might have something this month. You might not have nothing for . . . like, I've been working for my girlfriend maybe about a couple times this whole year. Now, if I reported that I worked like the end of last year—end of last year I worked with her a lot. You know what I'm saying. But they'll still be going off of what you did a long way—months ago.

She added, "You can't make it. And that is the only part that's consistent, basically. Other than that, there's nothing consistent, you know."

Side jobs offered none of the protections that aboveboard employment provided, including means of enforcing the employment contract itself. Shanelle said, "They worry about people . . . doing the welfare fraud" but explained:

> You know . . . I've held, I had a couple of jobs but you know what. They don't give you nothing to say about [pay]. You know what I'm saying. I had a job, it was under the table; because it was under the table, they [shorted] me. You know what I'm saying, when it came time to getting paid.

Thus even attempts by welfare recipients to avoid the reporting rules by taking side jobs sometimes backfired. By working outside the formal labor market, recipients who took side jobs had no way to ensure that their labor was compensated fairly, or even at all.

Some of the unreported wage earning was quite entrepreneurial. Tammy, a mother of four with very little experience in the paid labor force, admitted that she sold cupcakes to pay the bills. Through cupcake sales she had saved enough money to buy an old car. None of this money had she reported as income to the welfare office. She said that this underground economy was part of the normal landscape of her neighborhood. "Some people like to sell the little Icees and stuff. That be helping with the money during the month." Without the cupcake money, it is unclear how Tammy would have made it through the month. She had four children, and the youngest, subject to the family cap, received no cash welfare benefits. In addition, Tammy's welfare check was reduced as a result of the sanction she received for her noncompliance with the welfare-to-work rules. Working outside the home for the mandatory work hours would have allowed her to receive her full benefit and an additional $225 in earnings, at the most. Tammy did not say how much money she made by selling cupcakes, but if she made more than $330 a month or so, she was coming out ahead. And by working at home she saved the work-related expenses of transportation and clothing. For Tammy, cheating the welfare system by baking and selling cupcakes made more economic sense than participating in the welfare system's welfare-to-work program.

Child Support: Formal and Informal

Many of the interviewees relied on the strength of their ties to other people and financial help from family and friends to pay for their basic needs. Financial support from children's parents, usually fathers, came in two different streams: (1) formal child support, paid to and distributed through the state child support collection system; and (2) informal child support, meaning cash or goods provided to the caretaking parent without the state acting as intermediary. Several of the women interviewed received regular and sizable financial support from the noncohabiting fathers of their children.

There were significant financial incentives for parents to avoid the formal child support system. If a court found a father liable for support, the money got funneled into the county coffers while the parent (usually the mother) on welfare saw only an extra fifty dollars added to the cash grant (known as a "child support disregard"). The rest of the money went to "repay" the state for the welfare benefits provided to the children. Thus child support payments did not provide substantial benefits to children on welfare. In addition, court-ordered child support sometimes resulted in a father having his paycheck garnished for the funds, leaving him with little control over his earnings. In those cases where the fathers were paying child support through the formal child support system, the mothers described the way the welfare system discouraged men from paying, and women from seeking, child support through the system. Jane, whose ex-husband paid child support through the formal system, complained:

[The governor] says they have to go after the deadbeat dads, to benefit the mothers. That's a bunch of crap. My ex-husband makes $11.75. They take one hundred dollars a week out of his paycheck and we get something called a disregard, which I think the terminology sucks. It needs to be changed. My child is not a disregard. Any money for her is not a disregard. But that's what they call it, so. I get fifty bucks a month, but I'm in a statistic that says that they give me five hundred and something a month, when in actuality they only give me a hundred and something because my ex-husband pays four hundred dollars a month in child support that I don't see. And in the paperwork they tell me that my basic need is much higher than my allotted grant. So now my ex-husband only makes $11.75 an hour, forking out a hundred dollars a week. If I go to him and say, you know, I need shoes for her, I need a little extra money for this or, you know, her school pictures were due—that's another thirty bucks—he doesn't have it. So, helping the mothers . . . it doesn't help the mothers, it helps the state.

According to the interviewees, the policy of passing only fifty dollars of a father's child support through to a child on welfare discouraged both fathers and mothers from complying with efforts to participate in the formal child support system.

The father of Tanya's middle child paid child support both through the formal system and informally: "He pays the [district attorney] $350 a month. And he also gives me, um, basically slips me $250 a month to pay for clothes for the kids and incidental stuff." Under this system, Tanya and her children were able to add three hundred dollars a month to their welfare benefits. This money helped considerably given that her aid payments were $732 at their peak and only $611 a month while she was being sanctioned.

With informal child support, the women sometimes got more money and the men were free from state regulation and the inflexibility of standardized payments. The women, however, put themselves at risk of penalties from welfare investigators. They also put themselves at the mercy of the fathers, who, if they had provided cash under the table, could, at their whim, report the mothers for welfare fraud.

Patricia, a woman in her late forties, moved from the Midwest to California to be closer to her adult son and his wife around the time the young couple became new parents. She brought along her twelve-year-old daughter. When I first met Patricia outside the welfare office and explained that I was interviewing aid recipients about the welfare system, she said, "The system here is great!" While I heard many comments about the welfare system every day, I had never heard one this positive. Her interview revealed why she thought the system was great.

While Patricia and her daughter received only "$493 or something" in cash per month, Patricia was also earning money as a nurse and receiving one hundred dollars per week in child support from her ex-husband, who lived in the state she had left. Though the child support payments were done formally through the court system, Patricia did not report these payments to the welfare office, and the office had not yet caught on, apparently because the payments were coming from another state.

Others, too, received support from former partners—sometimes regularly, sometimes sporadically. Yvonne faced a welfare fraud charge at just about the same time she was expecting her second child. When the welfare office stopped her check because of her failure to report past earnings, Yvonne's boyfriend set her up in an apartment for a while and paid for everything. That support, however, did not last long—apparently because of the objections of the boyfriend's other girlfriend, with whom he lived.

Natalie, separated from her husband and receiving welfare under the claim that she received no support from her co-parent, noted that her disaffected husband provided a "great deal" of financial support. According to Natalie, the kids' father—who held two jobs—still paid for most of the clothing and groceries in her household. While Natalie reported none of this to the welfare office, she prided herself on her unfailing efforts to submit her check stubs to the welfare office every month, proudly stating, "I follow the rules."

While welfare reform policies were intended to encourage welfare moms to work and to hold "deadbeat dads" accountable, the reforms may have unintentionally discouraged absent dads from working in the formal labor market. Shanelle reported that once the child support system caught up with the father of her three children, the state started garnishing his monthly paychecks almost five hundred dollars a month. Only fifty dollars of that money flowed to the children. Shanelle said that the kids' father "came up with a master plan. Now he works under the table, so it's not like, we're not even receiving the fifty dollars anymore." Shanelle's story, like others, suggests that the child support system may be working at odds with itself in efforts to have fathers support their children who are receiving welfare.

One of the few women who received regular child support through the formal child support system was Millie. Her two oldest children had the same father; her youngest, a child excluded from TANF benefits because he was born while Millie received welfare, had another father. Millie's Cal-WORKs grant was soon to end because the support provided by the two fathers exceeded her maximum CalWORKs grant. She said, "I'm getting four hundred dollars from one father and three hundred dollars from the other guy. And no matter what, I'm only going to get fifty dollars, so I might as well and go ahead and just get the child support." She said one of the fathers had consistently provided support without protest. The other started paying once he was contacted by the District Attorney's Office. The welfare reforms of 1996 increased government efforts to pursue absent fathers for child support in an effort to shift the burden of support from the state to the fathers. Millie was fortunate to have had children with men who were economically secure.

Support and Encumbrance from Other Family Members

Many of the interviewees received substantial economic support from close family and, occasionally, friends. Natalie, a thirty-four-year-old mother with two kids at home, stated that her estranged husband provided routine help with clothing and food.

He buys them school clothes. I don't have to worry about that. Summer clothes. I mean, if we're low in the house on food or something like that, he'll, you know, give me money and I'll go to grocery store. He'll take me to the store, stuff like that. Financially, he helps me out a great deal. And I can say that more than I can say about some parents. Some dads are just not in the home, don't do anything.

Jamilla, a young mother of four, admitted that her mother had been paying her rent and utilities.

Other interviewees received support from members of their extended families. Renee, a twenty-year-old mother with a toddler, was living in her uncle's two-bedroom apartment with his wife and two children. She had moved in with her relatives when she was pregnant. She contributed only fifty to one hundred dollars per month to rent and utilities. Her uncle and aunt provided child care at the times she worked and attended school. Without these supports, it is unclear how Renee and her child would have survived.

While some of the interviewees had extended families that could provide economic assistance, some had extended families that proved more burdensome than helpful. Annette explained that not only had she never received any child support from her children's father, but also that she could not rely on her siblings for support. She said, "I have two sisters and two brothers. All of which have children. Three of which have had substance abuse problems. You can't really depend on people who have had substance abuse problems because you never know what they on." She was caring not only for a niece but also for a foster child who was a distant relative.

Shanelle, supporting her three children on her welfare check and sporadic temporary employment, also provided what financial assistance she could to her mother, who had quit her job. Shanelle noted, "We all family, 'cause it's like, well, mama, I'm not going to let you starve." Rather than relying on help from her family, Shanelle found herself providing for family members in circumstances even more dire than her own.

Use of Other Government Aid Programs

Many of the interviewees lived not only under the rules of CalWORKs and the food stamp program but also under the rules of other government aid programs. A number of the interviewees had household income that came from sources of government aid other than TANF cash aid, food stamps, and MediCal. Some also received subsidized housing in the form of Section 8 vouchers; some received SSI benefits. With different streams of government aid flowing to families, not all families receiving government assistance were suffering from the same levels of deprivation.

Families with a member who qualified for SSI received more income than families who relied only on CalWORKs cash benefits. Annette noted that her disabled daughter's "SSI [check] is more, or almost, as the welfare check. And that, I can't understand. Three people! How that happened, I don't understand. How do you expect three people—*three people*—to make it on almost the same amount as SSI gives to one person." Annette explained that if it were not for her daughter's SSI check and her Section 8 housing voucher, she and her family would not have been able to make it. Because of her Section 8 voucher, Annette had to pay only $320 a month for her apartment. "And then another thing that helps is the baby's WIC. I know it's for the baby, but we all use it. Shoot, we all use it. So, the WIC, that really helps, you know the cereal and stuff." Because Annette had a three-year-old foster child in her care, she also received money from the foster system. Annette and the five children in her care relied on a complicated mix of government aid programs to pay the bills.

The interviewees who received government housing subsidies described them as crucial to their survival in an area with such high housing costs. Through the Section 8 program, Jane was able to rent an apartment that was listed at $875 per month and pay only $128. She described herself as unconcerned about the five-year limit on welfare cash aid so long as she remained eligible for her Section 8 voucher. She said, "Without Section 8, I'd be just as screwed as the next person. But because I have Section 8, I'm not really worried about it. Now, if something happens with that [the Section 8 program] . . . oh my goodness. I don't know."

Lisa, a mother of three, received CalWORKs cash assistance for her two youngest children only. The oldest child, whose father was twenty years older than Lisa and who died of cancer, received Social Security Disability Survivor's Insurance. This income was a reliable source of income, unlike the CalWORKs cash aid and food stamps, which varied dramatically on the basis of Lisa's earnings, and unlike the fifty-dollar child support pass-through from the father of the younger children. The daughter's Social Security income, though intended solely for the oldest child's benefit, provided the entire family with some stability.

Systems of Credit

Interviewees turned to different strategies when money got extremely tight. Some families had more resources in the form of credit than others. Discussions with welfare recipients who had credit, however, revealed the processes through which credit histories become tarnished. For example,

Patricia had a strong work history as a nurse and, thanks to years of stable employment, had been able to secure credit cards. But her recent move to California, the resulting financial strain, and her inability to pay her bills on time were catching up with her.

> INTERVIEWER: Um . . . if you were to come up short of money, what would you do?
> PATRICIA: I'd just tell you—no, I can't pay you. No, you just have to wait. I can't pay! *[laughs]* I can't do anything! But I really did need to pay a credit card. I'm forgetting them. I'm going to have to put them off. Because now, they'll just take it out of my checking account. But even when they do that they still charge you a little charge. So, I'll put them off. Besides, it's my money. And that's so weird to me. I already paid for what I charged. So why are you bugging me?!?
> I: So you juggle . . .
> PATRICIA: No. I just don't . . . some people I just . . . they're gonna have to wait. *[laughs]*

Patricia was actually short of money at the time we met. She had forgotten to turn in her CA-7 form on time, an omission that put her welfare check on hold. Twice during the interview, conducted in Patricia's home, our conversation was interrupted by people phoning to demand money that Patricia owed—one call from a credit card company and one from the landlord reminding her that the rent was overdue. She told them both that they would have to wait, that when she received a check they would see money from her.

Illegal Activity

The interviewees who did not have credit had fewer options for making it through rough financial times. Several of the women said that, whatever happened, they would never go so far as to sell drugs or engage in prostitution to provide for their kids. Other welfare recipients, however, were a bit more equivocal about their willingness to engage in vice. When I asked Jane what she would do if she were to come up short of money in the following month, she replied:

> Call my friends. And, again, I am fortunate enough to have friends that do have money—that I could go to for help. And worst-case scenario, I have some clothes—not a ton—I have a few pieces, so I could get dressed

up and I could go out and meet somebody wealthy in Silicon Valley and we could have a nice dinner and get a few bucks. But I'm not that kind of person, so . . . *[laughs]* But don't think it hasn't crossed my mind. *[laughs]* It has.

A few interviewees—including Shannelle and Rhonda—acknowledged that they sometimes turned to prostitution when faced with financial crises. They did so not because it was a thrill or because they were inherently corrupt. They turned tricks only when they desperately needed to provide the essentials of food and shelter for their families. When asked what she would do if her welfare stopped (a looming prospect given that her youngest child was approaching age eighteen), Sarah forthrightly said, "I'm going to have to try to find me a job or . . . go to the oldest profession or something."

Welfare Rationality and Unmeasured Information Costs

The welfare reforms of 1996 were intended to create incentives for welfare recipients to work, to create disincentives for welfare recipients to remain on aid for extended periods, and to punish welfare recipients who failed to satisfy the requirements of the welfare system or who failed to follow the rules. The reformers assumed that welfare recipients would have enough information about the incentives, deterrents, and penalties to make informed, rational decisions that would lead them away from reliance on government aid. Welfare researchers, however, have not gone far in finding out how welfare recipients obtain information about welfare rules or in examining what factors facilitate or hamper recipients' access to accurate information. Some of the interviewees, however, provided some insights into the question of information access.

Many of the interviewees described the application, renewal, and orientation processes as so overloaded with written forms that there was no way they could absorb all of the information. Tina, who had applied for welfare for the first time less than six months before the interview (and well after welfare reform had been implemented) said, "I don't really know the regulations—the regulations or the rules." When I asked her how the welfare office informed clients of the rules, she responded, "Well, they give you a, um . . . the reason why I don't know is I didn't read the book." The book to which she referred was the one-hundred-plus pages of paper an applicant receives when requesting aid in Bayview County.

When asked how she was informed of the welfare rules, Kiki, a laid-off administrative assistant with a ten-year-old daughter, said:

> They just give you a whole bunch of papers and they tell you to read through them. And they get [a] little group thing. And then they "Start here, sign here, sign here, sign here, sign here." They never have you really go over with you, go over this policy and procedures, in detail. You know what I'm saying? So they don't go over, in great detail, about the different things that you know, the different policies and procedures.

Kiki felt that because many individuals who were attending the group information meeting for welfare applicants were so desperate to "deal with their money" they did not take the time to find out the details of the welfare rules or spend time asking questions of the welfare workers.

Some of the interviewees talked about the time costs involved in getting information. For example, Veronica, a woman parenting six children, received no assistance with child care from the welfare system. She lacked the information she needed to apply for child care assistance and lacked the time to obtain the information because of her efforts to meet her work requirements. She explained, "I keep making appointments, and then I get called in for work. Or when I was doing a day shift, when I get off work they're closed. So it's . . . and the jobs I'm getting, ask for a day off and they fire you." Because Veronica could not afford to pay for child care, her children, who ranged in age from five to twelve, spent a lot of time at home without adult supervision. And Veronica spent a lot of time worrying about their safety.

Kiki said that merely asking questions about benefits could take a significant investment of time.

> You can call them at four. And sometimes you're on the phone for forty-five minutes, sometimes longer, and you still, well about that time, I guess they want you to [inaudible]. You hang up the phone. Because there's other things that you need to be doing. So sometimes you get better results if you go down there.

Kiki then explained that visits to the office always required a long wait in line. She said that even when she finally reached her turn to talk with a caseworker, she often had to then ask for the supervisor to clear up a question the worker could not answer.

Tina, who waited three months for a response to her initial welfare application, did not press the issue of her wait with the office. Once she received notice that her application for cash aid had been denied and her application for food stamps had been approved, she assumed that her food stamps would be retroactive to the time of her application:

> TINA: I called, as soon as I received my first notice saying how much I was gonna get, I called them and I asked them, Well, am I gonna be getting all the way back from . . . three months back. And, um, he told me yeah. And when I picked them up, they only had gave me $209. . . . I was grateful for that. I hate for to look crazy arguing on the phone. It's a trip. I was grateful for what I had, so . . . I just took that.
> INTERVIEWER: That's too bad.
> TINA: I know. I want to question it, but I know I'll probably have to fill out another form, a load of paper.

Thus the time consumed by paperwork and dealing with the bureaucracy deterred Tina from seeking information, even information that might have increased her benefits.

Yvonne complained that the workers in the welfare office "don't really tell you all the rules." She described the application process as less than fully informative and talked about how difficult it was to get in touch with a welfare caseworker, much less have an extended discussion with one. She said she learned about the welfare rules from other friends on welfare.

Some of the interviewees stated that they received information about the welfare system from people who did not work in the welfare office. Renee, a young mother, explained that she had turned to the sister of her son's father when her son was two-and-a-half and she found herself in financial straits. Renee said, "Oh, it was my son's aunt on his father's side. She took me down there and helped me fill it [the application] out. So, I mean, she was pretty familiar with the system."

Renee's quasi-sister-in-law, however, was less than objective. The advice she gave Renee was, it appears, intentionally provided to get her brother off the hook for child support. When I asked Renee what advice the woman had given, she said, "And it's basically to leave out the father, you know. To just, like, [write] 'Oh, I don't know where he's at.' Because if I do [give his information], then they won't give me any money." In either case, however, Renee's consequent failure to provide information about her son's father not only caused her hassles with the welfare office but also prevented her son from receiving any child support through the state's child support system.

Gaps in Knowledge of the Essential Elements of Welfare Reform

The federal welfare legislation Congress passed in 1996 imposed a strict sixty-month lifetime limit on receipt of cash aid for all adult TANF recipients in the country. States were given the option to establish even shorter time limits. California initially instituted an eighteen-month time limit for adults already receiving cash benefits and a twenty-four-month time limit for those who opened new cases. Initially, adults were ineligible for aid once they reached these time limits. The regulations, however, were modified in 2002 to allow recipients who reached their eighteen- or twenty-four-month time limits to remain eligible for aid so long as they fulfilled their mandatory work requirements (California Department of Social Services All-County Letter No. 02-33, May 1, 2002).

Knowledge of the time limits varied dramatically among the interviewees. For example, Patricia, who had applied for welfare at the county office in the fall of 1998, did not know about the time limits during our interview in the early summer of 1999. On the other hand, Annette, a long-term welfare recipient who was well aware of the time limits, described herself as "pretty scared" about her time running out.

Knowledge of the work requirements also varied. Annette, who had three children and was the foster parent of an infant, had heard about the work requirements well before she received a letter from the welfare office telling her to show up to an orientation. She prepared herself for the work requirements by signing up for cosmetology classes at Bayview Community College. Once she was there, she learned of a program the college had for welfare recipients. The next semester she dropped her cosmetology classes and signed up for the special classes the community college offered for welfare recipients:

It's your basic math, reading, writing. It's, um, six or eight weeks of computers. The other thing is sociology and career development. So, see, this is working on you, not the career. This is working on *you* right now, your basic skills, brushing up on your math, showing you the basics of the computer. I think the computer part of it was too short for me, because I don't know anything about computers, but it gave you a little bit of, you know, like . . . they tell you what icons are and different little things, showing you how to use the mouse. Because at first I was real upset trying to do that because when I moved that thing, it moved. You know, the cursor going all over the place, and I was trying to control that. I started using some strategies and whatnot, so, that's what I'm doing right now.

Annette was not necessarily pursuing the rational path welfare reformers had hoped—getting off aid as soon as possible. Instead, she was pursuing an economically rational path that would maximize her skills in the workforce and ultimately her wage-earning capacity.

Many of the interviewees, however, treated the work requirements nonchalantly, approaching them not as a first step in leaving the welfare system but instead as a mere hoop to jump through to receive aid. The interviewees who possessed basic knowledge of the work requirements generally knew about the sanctions. Still, for these individuals, the influence of the sanctions on their employment decisions was unclear. A couple women, including Tammy, who were aware of the sanctions and knew that only the parent's portion of the grant would be cut under sanction said that the amount cut from the grant—roughly $125—was simply not enough of an incentive or deterrent to make them change their actions.

For parents who were complying with the work requirements, cash grants varied from month to month depending upon recent earnings. As a result, most of the interviewees with jobs had a hard time predicting what their future checks would look like. As a result, some may not have been aware when they were being sanctioned. Those interviewees who were unaware of the work requirements were unaware of the sanctions.

For welfare recipients, there were costs—both real and perceived—to obtaining accurate and detailed information about the welfare rules, regulations, and available programs. While some of the interviewees were willing to pay the costs of obtaining information, others would not or could not. In still other instances, individuals did not pursue more accurate information about rules or programs because they had no idea that the rules or programs existed.

Rules and Arbitrariness

The interviewees frequently commented on how they perceived the rules as arbitrary and the application of rules as unpredictable. For example, they complained they could not predict how large or small their next aid check would be because of the office's accounting procedures.

Some of the interviewees described the welfare office's rules and procedures as senseless or counterproductive. Shanelle, a twenty-nine-year-old mother of three, attended her CalWORKs orientation midway through her final semester of community college, completion of which would lead to an associate's degree. She had planned to pursue a degree in social work and bring her past experiences as a drug abuser, prostitute, and domestic violence survivor to her vocation. Shanelle explained, however, that the welfare office's "employment counselor told me, she was like, you cannot go to school. If this is what you're going to school for, you can't go to school." The CalWORKs employment counselor, according to Shanelle, said, "Well, maybe you need to repair TVs." Shanelle was told that completing a liberal arts degree was not considered an approved work activity and that she would have to drop out of school right before midterms, which she did. A year later, she had still not found a regular job. If she had spent two or three more months in school, she would have been on the job market with an associate's degree. Instead, she was on the job market with an eleventh-grade education.

Shanelle also talked about a frustrating encounter she had recently had with the welfare office. Welfare recipients were required not only to submit proof of earnings with their monthly CA-7s but also to submit it at their annual recertification meetings for aid. Shanelle submitted her original pay stub with her recertification papers but did not submit a copy with her CA-7 form the same month, assuming that one copy in her file would be sufficient. Shannelle explained:

> So I get a letter saying that my CA-7 form was incomplete because I failed to give [it to] them. . . . I said, well, look. I called them up, saying, "My check stubs are there. I just had a renewal, all you have to do is go look in my file. It might be in with my CA-7." "Well, it needs to be in with your CA-7 so you're going to have redo." "Okay, well, you send me back my check stubs. I can make some copies, and I'll send them back." I just got my check stubs in the mail, along with a letter saying that my cash aid will be discontinued [for failing to submit the check stubs]. *[laughs]*

Shanelle offered this experience as an example of the way that the welfare system mechanically applied rules without regard for either efficiency or financial need.

Numerous interviewees described the frustrations of submitting their monthly CA-7 forms and then receiving either a threat of discontinuance or an actual discontinuance of aid for failing to submit their forms. These situations not only required the interviewees to spend a significant amount of time and energy resolving the problems but also drove the already strapped families into financial panic. Interviewees described a sense of unfairness about their suffering when they had complied with the rules and when the problems were the result of administrative errors in the welfare office.

Pam, the persistently homeless mother of a ten-year-old daughter, described the intricate system of government programs as irrational and arbitrary. She found it unfair that her former partner, a drug user with little employment history, could receive much more generous benefits under SSI than she and her daughter could receive under CalWORKs. She also complained about the workers, saying, "They can do anything they want." In her opinion, all they wanted to do was shovel paper all day. She believed they had no interest in either applying rules uniformly or helping individual welfare recipients.

The Moral Catch: You Can't Live on It, You Can't Live without It

At least for the participants in this study, economic need, not greed, fueled welfare cheating. The interviewees themselves realized they were in a moral trap. When I asked her what should happen if welfare recipients got caught cheating, Aliyah, who was lying to the welfare office in a desperate attempt to regain custody of her son, talked about the need to take risks. She said, "Well, I think that they should cut them off, you know. You know, people who have to take that risk and that chance to get on, they have to lie or get on. But I think that you have to try." Hedging, then, on her support of cheating, she continued, "But it take away money from other people too." Many of the welfare recipients knew they were cheating but also knew that they sometimes had to cheat.

Renee, who had been able to find only temporary jobs despite persistent efforts to find work, admitted that she had knowingly failed to report the earnings from her last spell of employment, claiming that she could not risk a cut in benefits. Both Aliyah and Renee knew they were caught in a moral quandary, taking risks they would rather not take and hiding information they felt they were obligated to provide to the welfare office. Compliance was something they negotiated on a daily basis.

Welfare recipients' interactions with the welfare rules were varied and complex because their individual circumstances were varied and complex. Most of the interviewees relied not only on a mix of public benefits but also on a combination of formal employment, underground employment, and help from friends and relatives to survive. None of these provided a reliable source of income—not even the welfare benefits because of the frequent administrative problems. As a result, all of the interviewees were extremely insecure financially.

But getting a job and getting off welfare were not straightforward tasks for the interviewees. Most interviewees, if they could find wage work at all, lacked the skills to find jobs that paid well and provided family-friendly work schedules. For many, employment created other types of insecurities for their families. Many had to leave their children home alone, sometimes at night, while they worked.

In some cases, they believed it made economic sense for them to stay on welfare while working on their employment skills. Some considered it a better deal to accept sanctions for failing to comply with the welfare-to-work requirements, to work sporadically in the underground labor market, and to risk getting caught for failing to report income to the welfare office. Many believed that hiding sources of income from the welfare office was not only in their interest but necessary to their economic survival.

Welfare recipients are rational actors. They are pursuing financial self-interest. But they are also trying to take care of their families—and caretaking requires time. Working full time, or even part time, was not the most rational choice for some of the interviewees. In the context of welfare, economic rationality is gendered; it gives value to goals other than wage earning. Cooking, cleaning, walking children to school, taking children to medical appointments, and maintaining relationships with family members and church members are all tasks important to the long-term well-being of families.

Moreover, rationality is bounded, with the boundaries often so close that they act as blinders to risk. Few people are able to obtain full and perfect information about the rules and regulations that govern them, but welfare recipients rarely have perfect information when getting a question answered may require a bus ride and a full day's wait in a welfare waiting room. Choices of action are limited when the struggles of managing a family on inadequate financial resources absorb time and emotion. Simple rational actor models do not fit well for welfare recipients. Researchers should be careful, perhaps through qualitative research, to test their assumptions about how knowledge of rules and policies filters through written regulations and welfare officials to welfare recipients themselves.

The individuals in this study made their decisions about working or not working, seeking other sources of income, and reporting their income on the basis of their knowledge of the rules, their perceptions of the risks of getting caught breaking the rules, and their assessments of the consequences of their choices. The following chapter examines the interviewees' engagement with the rules, regulations, and risks more closely.

6

Engaging with Rules and Negotiating Compliance

If the interviewees in this study are at all indicative of general trends among welfare recipients, then breaking the welfare rules is the norm. Other studies have found that welfare recipients are often inadequately informed of welfare rules and programs and possess only superficial knowledge of sanctions (Fragile Families Research Brief 2002; Meyers, Glaser, and MacDonald 1998; Hasenfeld, Ghose, and Hillesland-Larson 2004; Kidwell and Gottlober 1999). But ignorance of the rules and penalties is not the only factor. The families in this study generally could not survive on their welfare benefits alone or by following the welfare regulations and requirements. This finding is nothing new: a number of researchers have found that welfare recipients find it impossible to make ends meet on welfare (Edin and Lein 1997; Gilliom 2001; Seccombe 1999). The maximum aid payment available to a single parent who had two children, who lived in Bayview, and who was subject to the work requirements was $626 in 1999, a figure that rose to $645 in 2000 and $679 in 2001. This money was too little to sustain a family. Almost everyone interviewed overstepped the rules to feed, clothe, and shelter themselves and their children. The data in this study suggest, however, that rule breaking by adult heads of households varied, with a number of factors influencing the type of rule breaking that occurred. These factors included

- Knowledge of the system—including knowledge of the rules and regulations, knowledge of the sanctions for noncompliance, knowledge of welfare surveillance systems, and knowledge of the various benefits available
- The availability of financial support from resources other than the welfare system
- Human capital—including education, paid labor skills and experience, self-confidence, age, and race
- Attitudes about fairness of the rules
- Degree of financial desperation

Some interviewees were willing to accept the economic sanctions that accompanied noncompliance with the welfare-to-work requirements, while others feared sanctions. Some were willing to take risks with their welfare benefits if they believed the long-term benefits would outweigh the short-term costs. At the same time, many of the interviewees did not accurately assess the risks of their noncompliance, unaware of the methods the welfare office used to detect cheating and the severity of penalties for breaking the rules.

The term *rule engagement*, as used here, includes an individual's knowledge of the rules; ability to obtain information about the rules; and willingness and effort to comply with the rules. From the data, several categories of rule engagement emerged. While the boundaries between the categories are not precisely clear, especially given that some individuals appeared to possess detailed knowledge about some welfare rules and regulations and less about others, the categories nevertheless effectively describe some of the significant differences between—and similarities among—the interviewees. The first three sections that follow describe the three labels that generally describe recipients—the Informed/Knowing Recipients; the Misinformed Recipients; and the Preoccupied/Disengaged Recipients. The later section of the chapter turns to how recipients understand the normative pull of complex rules.

Informed/Knowing Welfare Recipients

The Informed/Knowing welfare recipients interviewed knew the ins and outs of the welfare rules. They knew about the sixty-month lifetime limits on cash aid and knew when their limits hit. They generally possessed detailed knowledge about the reporting requirements, the consequences of failing to report income, and the methods the welfare system employed to catch cheats. Most of the Informed also regarded the system as a sham. Because they understood the rules and how the system worked, they also knew how to use the system to their advantage and avoid the pitfalls that might put them at risk of getting caught for their unreported sources of income.

Informed recipients knew how changes in their compliance with the rules and regulations would affect their benefits and could therefore make decisions that took into account the economic effects of noncompliance. Some of these recipients were willing to accept the economic sanctions that accompanied noncompliance with the work or education requirements. For example, Tanya, a mother of three, was consciously risking a welfare sanction in order to pursue an educational program in alternative medicine, which she hoped would ultimately end both her reliance on welfare and her poverty. (California was a "work-first" state, where getting every recipient into a job, any job, was the top priority, and where welfare offices, with few exceptions, would not count educational programs toward work requirement hours.) Tanya was willing to accept the sanction against her welfare check because she believed the long-term benefits would outweigh the short-term loss of cash assistance.

Unlike many of the welfare recipients interviewed, Tanya considered herself knowledgeable enough about the rules and self-assured enough about her own choices to file an administrative appeal challenging her sanction. At the time we spoke, Tanya, through the help of an attorney at a legal aid office, was trying to have her education plan approved as an SIP, which would allow her to have her classroom and study hours count toward her work requirement hours. She hoped not only to curtail future sanctions and continue to attend school but also to recover the money that had been withheld from recent welfare checks because of her noncompliance with the formal work requirement.

While Tanya was struggling economically and described the frustrations of regularly trying to explain to her kids why there was nothing to eat but pasta, her knowledge of how to get around the rules put her in much better circumstances than most of the welfare recipients interviewed. Tanya knew that taking a regular job would mean a reduction in her welfare benefits. She also knew that she would receive no more than fifty dollars of any child support that her children's fathers might pay through the formal child support system. To avoid these reductions in aid payments, Tanya made ends meet by taking several hundred dollars a month in under-the-table child support. None of this did Tanya report to the welfare office.

Jane, a mother of two, was similarly informed of the essential elements of welfare reform and was being sanctioned by the welfare office for non-compliance with the work and training requirements. Jane, however, was not certain her strategies would pay off in financial security for her family in the end. To the contrary. She wanted to pursue a creative arts program. The welfare money she was sanctioned—about $125 a month—was not enough to prompt a change for Jane. Her cash grant was so small that, with or without that $125, she had to make money under the table anyway. Jane seemed to feel that following the welfare rules held no benefit to her. Whether or not Jane followed the formal rules, she and her family would be struggling. Because Jane had no high school diploma, her opportunities in the workforce and her ability to support herself and her two children were limited. Resisting the welfare rules—which she did in a number of different ways—appeared to be her only way to exert some resistance to a social and economic status she found oppressive.

Jane did not view the welfare system as a set of policies designed to help her enter the economic mainstream. Rather, she described her experiences with the welfare office as lessons in learning how to lie. The first time she applied for welfare, she and her fiancé owned a car they had bought only a year earlier when their financial situation had been more stable. They had taken out a twelve-thousand-dollar loan on the car and still had eight or nine thousand dollars to repay on it when they applied for welfare. According to Jane:

> Well, we hadn't learned yet to lie in order to get help, so we didn't. We put down that we had a car. Welfare wouldn't give us any assistance—not even food stamps—because we had to sell that vehicle first and live off that money first. Which means we would have gotten two thousand dollars for the car—maybe—and still had five thousand dollars in debt.

Jane and her fiancé soon moved to another county, where her fiancé found a job. Jane applied for aid in the new county.

> I ended up duping welfare. I didn't tell them about the car. I didn't tell them about bank accounts. I didn't tell them we were married—'cause I think he was only making like seven, eight bucks an hour. So . . . I got welfare and we were married and he worked. You do what you have to do.

The way Jane described welfare, it was a system of financial incentives and disincentives. For her, however, it did not serve as a system of incentives prompting her to leave the welfare system and seek employment. Instead, she viewed it as a system of incentives to lie and disincentives to tell the truth.

Jane's deceptions did not end with the hidden car and the hidden husband. Jane also found a way to work and hide her earnings from the welfare office:

> I even went so far . . . somebody had sent me . . . somebody had inadvertently sent me . . . 'cause there's somebody with my same name—my same married name, not my maiden name—who lived in Bayview. And they sent me her information—the bank. So I used her Social Security number and went to work. So we [my husband and I] both had paychecks and collected welfare, lived in a studio—one room—so we weren't living fat. Yeah, we were working. Yeah, I was using welfare. But we were still just getting by.

Jane was aware that the welfare office used Social Security numbers to track earnings. With this knowledge, she was able to avoid having her earnings tracked. (She seemed unconcerned with the effect that using another woman's Social Security number would have on the other woman's dealings with the state and federal tax authorities.)

Jane not only transgressed the authority of the welfare system by circumventing the rules but also resisted the system through formal avenues. Jane was being sanctioned because she was not meeting her work requirement hours. Instead, she attended school full time, something she had been doing a year and a half before the welfare office notified her that it was time for her to sign her welfare-to-work plan. Though Jane had submitted paperwork to the welfare office to have her educational plan approved as a SIP, her request had been denied. Jane nevertheless continued to go to school and refused to sign a welfare-to-work plan. Her welfare check was sanctioned and she received no ancillary benefits from the welfare office to help her with books, transportation, or child care. Not easily dissuaded, Jane sought help from a law office. She appealed her sanction and the denial of her SIP request.

Jane seemed to have no fear of getting caught for the cheating in which she had engaged. When I asked her what she thought would happen if she got caught, she said:

> I would use it as a platform to address the real issues in a court of law. Um, I don't think anything I've done would ever warrant me being put in jail. So I wouldn't really stress on that. And if I was, I have wealthy friends who could get me out.

While Jane was savvy about the rules and how to skirt them, it was not clear that she was fully aware of the penalties for breaking the rules. In misperceiving the risks of criminal prosecution, Jane was not engaged in a truly rational analysis in making her decisions.

Like Jane and Tanya, others who fell under the category of "The Informed" were not necessarily eager to leave the welfare system. They knew exactly how long their time limits ran and had no plans to leave until the moment their time was up. Some of the Informed even had plans to remain on aid after they reached their time limits. When interviewed, Viola, a forty-two-year-old mother with two adolescent children at home, was enrolled in both a substance abuse program and a computer class. Because of her participation in these programs, the welfare office was temporarily exempting Viola from the work requirements that normally applied to welfare recipients in the county. While the substance abuse and computer training programs were intended to prepare Viola to be a self-sufficient member of the paid labor force, Viola had other plans.

Viola had worked as a caseworker in a social service office before her alcoholism cost her the job and led her to apply for welfare. Because of her experiences as a caseworker, Viola was well informed of the details of the welfare time limits, the family cap, the work requirements, and the exceptions to both. Rather than planning for life after welfare, Viola was gearing up a strategy to extend her work exemptions and to exempt herself from the time limits. She was also trying to appeal her previously denied Social Security Disability Insurance claim, hoping to receive even more generous federal benefits.

For the Informed, the intricate rules and regulations created by the 1996 round of welfare reforms did not necessarily create incentives to leave the welfare system. The changes merely created more obstacles for these welfare recipients to negotiate, more rules to contest. The ironic twist lies in the fact that the Informed were the most likely to be successful in their efforts to live without the support of the welfare system. They tended to be better educated and to be entrepreneurial. Moreover, they had used their time on welfare to improve their potential for economic self-sufficiency. In addition, their knowledge of the welfare rules and the welfare system's methods of identifying sources of unreported income allowed them to successfully skirt the rules and avoid entanglement with welfare fraud investigations.

While some of the Informed recipients may have had some initial inclinations to resist the welfare system, they also had help in learning about their rights. Both Tanya and Jane discovered welfare rights organizations at some point while on welfare. Jane found out about a welfare rights organization through a flier that was included with her monthly form mailed from the welfare office (known as a CA-7 form). She attended a meeting the group held and ended up volunteering for them for a while. Tanya hooked up with a welfare rights organization at about the time the 1996 welfare reforms were being implemented in the state and county. She was taking classes at Bayview Community College and attended an informational session held at the college by a local welfare rights organization.

In Tanya's case, the welfare rights organization prepared people for the work requirements and had a strategy in place to organize students to demand that the welfare office allow them to continue going to school. As a result, when Tanya received notice of her CalWORKs orientation, she was well informed of her legal rights and ready for a fight. She was also prepared to organize other welfare recipients.

Tanya explained that CalWORKs orientations were "big mass meetings, big cattle calls" involving a number of welfare recipients at one time. She said that one of the welfare workers had told all of the recipients who were in school to go into one room. She said that once she had gotten into the room with a welfare caseworker and the seven other student-recipients, she had told the caseworker she was going to refuse to sign a welfare-to-work plan and that she wanted the paperwork necessary to approve an SIP. As she describes it, the worker was taken aback and left the room to find the forms. Then, according to Tanya:

> When he left, I turned around and addressed the women, and they were kind of freaked out. And I just said, look, I don't work for the county. I am here to tell you that you should not sign this form, you know. What you should do is tell them that you are a SIP, get all the stuff you can from your school, you know, get the support you can, get everything you can. 'Cause you have until December—you can push it 'til December and get as much schooling as you can.

Not only was Tanya well informed of the welfare reform rules, but she was also doing her best to share her knowledge with other welfare recipients.

Knowledge Gaps

Even those interviewees who were relatively well informed of basic incentives and disincentives associated with welfare reform policies had significant gaps in knowledge. For example, Lisa and Shanelle, two women who had been on welfare long before welfare reform, believed they understood the welfare reform rules quite well. They were aware of the time limits and knew exactly when their time limits ran; they knew about the sanctions for failing to meet the required work hours and knew that only their portion of the grant check would be cut; they knew that they had to report all earnings and that their earnings in one month would lower their cash aid in future months. They did not, however, know about the exemptions to the work requirements or about the availability of SIPs, knowledge that would have been of great benefit to them.

At the time of our interview, Lisa was being sanctioned. Because of her earnings during an earlier month and because of her sanction, she had received a cash grant of only four dollars the month before. Lisa was working part time at her daughter's school and taking classes. For her class time to count toward her work requirement hours, she had to submit a progress and attendance report to the welfare office. Lisa's daughter, however, had spent three days in a hospital the month earlier. Lisa had missed classes while she stayed at the hospital with her daughter. She explained:

> Okay, so I had like doctors' forms, you know, saying that I wasn't going to leave my kid in the hospital. She's nine. She's, you know, never been in a hospital before, so I stayed there. And so it was like on my record, okay, that I missed three days, but I was getting threatened because I didn't fulfill the hours that week. So I couldn't understand that, okay, I, you know, I read and studied while I was there at the hospital but for me to leave the hospital, that's really asking a little bit too much and if you want to cut me off because I decided to stay with my daughter while she was in the hospital, then go ahead because you would do the same if it was yours, so you have to worry about that, too. It's like a lot of threatening if you don't do this, we're going to do this, you know, and it's a process.

On the basis of her need to care for her sick daughter, Lisa should have been exempted from her work requirement activities that month. Lisa, however, had no knowledge that any exceptions to the mandatory work requirements existed. Her knowledge of the rules was incomplete. And given her less-than-perfect knowledge of the detailed rules and exceptions to the welfare rules, her decisions were rational. Her decision to care for her sick-enough-to-be-hospitalized child and miss three days of work to do so clearly came out of Lisa's weighing of the costs and benefits of her limited options.

Lisa explained that she had learned about the thirty-two-hour work requirement from someone in the welfare office. She learned of her sanction by letter:

> They wrote a letter. Yeah and it's a[n] ultimatum—either you do it, or you get cut off, and that's it, there's really no explanation. They don't say nothing. They set it down there, if you're not completing your thirty-two hours, you're getting off and that's it. There's no explanation, no excuse; you can't tell them that, they say.

There is no way of knowing from Lisa's description whether the information about California's exemptions to the work requirements was provided to her or not. Instructions about how to file an administrative appeal appear (or should appear) on the back of all sanction notices. Without any knowledge that she had a basis for appeal, however, Lisa would have no reason to file an appeal offering the excuse that she was caring for a sick child, a situation that is almost inevitable for any parent.

Shanelle, a mother of three, was finishing up her coursework for an associate's degree at the local community college when she received notice that her participation in the CalWORKs work requirements was to begin. Shanelle, who had suffered abuse from her father as a child and from her male partners as a young woman, had spent her time in the community college taking classes with the goal of becoming a social worker. As someone who had suffered domestic violence, spent time in jail, and recovered from drug dependency, she felt she could draw upon her experiences to counsel troubled girls. The welfare caseworker, known as her employment specialist, told her otherwise. As Shanelle explained it, she was told she could not continue taking classes unless they were part of a brief vocational training program. Shanelle said that the caseworker suggested TV repair. Feeling defeated, Shanelle dropped out of school shortly before exams.

By dropping out of school, Shanelle reduced her chances of achieving economic self-sufficiency. Shanelle knew nothing about the SIPs available by petition (though applying was certainly no assurance that the welfare office would approve the plan). Shanelle had been unable to find employment, no doubt because of her lack of employment experience and her felony record for shooting her batterer. In Shanelle's case, the strict application of the "work-first" policy backfired, leaving Shanelle and her family even farther from economic stability than they had been before the welfare reform rules were imposed.

General knowledge of the goals of welfare reform combined with imperfect knowledge of the detailed rules and regulations undermined the goals of welfare reform, particularly the goals of transitioning welfare recipients into economic self-sufficiency.

Rule Knowledge, Compliance, and Resistance among the Informed

The Informed generally possessed detailed knowledge about the welfare rules to which they were subject, as well as accurate knowledge of the consequences of rule breaking. With this knowledge, they carefully assessed the costs and benefits of compliance and accepted short-term sanctions of their benefits when they thought their time and energies were better invested elsewhere. The Informed made use of the ancillary benefits available to welfare recipients, including child care assistance, transportation assistance, and educational opportunities. For example, Lavetta, a twenty-four-year-old mother of a first grader, used her time on welfare to get a license as a real estate agent. She took advantage of the child care assistance from the welfare office to find the time to work on her career skills. She met her work requirements but also tried to pursue a more lucrative profession, a profession requiring an early investment of time.

Lavetta described her use of the welfare system as temporary and transitional. "You know, it's supposed to be there for a stepping-stone, and that's exactly what I have used it for." She viewed her time on welfare as an opportunity to gain sufficient skills and work experience to become financially self-sufficient—independent of both the welfare system and a male partner. In many ways, she was one of the ideal welfare recipients, responding to the incentives created under welfare reform. In other ways, however, she was not the ideal candidate. She had experienced many problems after returning forms to the welfare office late.

She also had no ill feelings toward those who tried "to get over on" the welfare office. She knew that a lot of people were in jail for welfare fraud. And she said that unless individuals were involved in the underground labor market—"doing something on the side, under the table, you know, where they're not getting a check stub, they just get cash"—then the welfare office was sure to track down cheating. She said, "They will always find ways to get you." Lavetta said that if she knew how to find side jobs like braiding hair, she would have done that for extra money as other women did. And Lavetta did do some rule breaking of her own. Lavetta's boyfriend had recently moved into her government-subsidized apartment and was helping her cover the housing expenses. Lavetta, however, was keeping that information from the housing and welfare agencies.

Lavetta herself suggested that the lines between honesty and cheating were blurry within the welfare system, saying, "I don't know what's right and what's wrong anymore, you know?" She said "Welfare is not stability, I mean, how can you pay your rent steadily for years on end with four hundred dollars, plus buy clothes, plus . . . pay your utilities? You know what I'm saying?" She was critical of the welfare system and criminal justice system for penalizing welfare recipients who "made a little bit of extra cash, on the side." She said the message the welfare office conveyed to welfare recipients was not to get a legitimate job but rather to get a side job and keep it quiet. "They want you to do it [work for pay] but they want you to sneak and do it, and then they say go ahead and do it, but don't get caught doing so." For Lavetta, the economic incentives to enter the mainstream labor force, not to mention the incentives to report all income, seemed less than convincing.

Many of the interviewees who were generally well informed of the components of welfare reform were even more critical of the welfare reforms policies than Lavetta. For example, many were critical of the five-year time limits as indifferent to the sometimes unexpected needs of family and as ineffective at pushing people to find jobs that could support their families. Shanelle complained:

> They're just telling you, look, this is what you have to do, this is your time limits, so regardless if you do it or not, this is it, this is all, you know, and that's not fair because a lot of people that are on CalWORKs have been on welfare for years.

Many of the Informed interviewees also described the welfare reform measures as being unfair because the rules—especially the work requirements and the related limits on pursuit of higher education—circumscribed their choices in pursuing their interests and in pursuing the routes they believed offered the best promise of long-term economic well-being for their families.

A couple of the Informed, however, thought that the push for employment and the work supports were good. Lavetta described the CalWORKs system—particularly the child care supports and the expectation that welfare recipients work—as "good" and "healthy." She was well aware of computerized data checks that allowed the welfare office to detect wage earning and was aware that a welfare fraud charge could lead to jail time. She also knew, however, that her friends who worked under the table never got caught. For Lavetta, the welfare system was good because she knew how to work with, and around, the rules.

Jill, the only interviewee who seemed both to have a good working knowledge of the rules and to comply with them fully, also believed the rules were good. Jill was fortunate to have a mother who could cushion her through rough economic times. Because of her mother's support, Jill was in no immediate threat of hunger or homelessness. She stated, "The rules are pretty simple. I mean . . . just comply." Jill took advantage of the child care subsidies, transportation subsidies, and services at the work training center to continue what had been for her a long job search. Her home was centrally located in Bayview, so she faced no transportation barriers. She contributed a small portion of her welfare check to help her mother pay the mortgage and turned to her mother every month for help covering the costs of groceries. She had no disabilities, was relatively well educated, and, because of many years of stable work experience, had a work-ready wardrobe. Jill explained that because she understood and had complied with all of the paperwork, she had not had one-on-one interactions with anyone in the welfare office since she had applied for aid. Unlike many other interviewees, Jill could comprehend the system of incentives and could easily comply with the welfare rules and requirements while still keeping her child fed, clothed, and schooled.

In many ways, the Informed recipients were the rational actors that policy makers had envisioned when they went about planning the welfare reforms. At the same time, they were a minority of the welfare recipients encountered. These recipients were reasonably educated about the rules, the incentives, and the sanctions built into the welfare system. They were also knowledgeable about the benefits available to them to help them prepare for life after welfare. Moreover, they were the ones with the most human capital and the most available resources to help them become self-sufficient members of the wage labor market, with or without the welfare system. Most of those who possessed a strong working knowledge of the rules had enough job skills and experience to find and hold a full-time job. While most of the Informed cheated, they were familiar enough with the rules to know how to skirt them without getting caught. Their noncompliance and their criticisms of the welfare rules never registered with anyone in authority.

Misinformed Welfare Recipients

The majority of welfare recipients interviewed fell under the category of the Misinformed. Their understandings of some rules were fuzzy and of others were clear. For example, many did not understand the time limits and did not know who to ask to have them clarified. At the same time, they worried about what would happen when their welfare clocks ran out and their time limits hit. Carmen, an eighteen-year-old woman who had been on aid for only three months, was not even aware that there were time limits or work requirements.

With only a vague understanding of the rules and requirements, the Misinformed knew little about what the consequences would be for either failing to comply with the rules (such as the work requirements) or breaking the rules (for example, by failing to report earnings). They were unaware of the methods the welfare office used to detect cheating or the severity of penalties for breaking the rules. As a result, many interviewees could not accurately assess the risks of their noncompliance or rule breaking.

Pam, for example, was aware that the welfare office obtained employment and earnings information through the tracking of Social Security numbers. She was, however, earning money as an administrative assistant at her daughter's school and was not reporting her earned income, assuming that by the time the welfare office realized she had income she would have saved enough money to be self-sufficient. She believed that if her ten-dollar-an-hour earnings were discovered by the welfare office, the office would merely ask for the welfare money back. She was unaware that the monthly reports she had submitted to the welfare office stating that she had no income put her in jeopardy of being charged with criminal perjury and welfare fraud and being excluded from welfare receipt for the rest of her life. She also mistakenly believed that once she saved up enough money and ended her cash payments she would leave the reach of the welfare system. Pam did not know that in an effort to recoup aid overpayments the Department of Social Services' Welfare Fraud Investigations Unit tracked down recipients long after they left the system.

Another example of someone properly labeled Misinformed was Renee. Renee had first given birth at age sixteen and had a four-year-old son at the time of our interview. She had dropped out of school in twelfth grade. Until she applied for welfare when her son was two-and-a-half, her only self-generated income had come from babysitting and braiding hair for cash. At about the time she applied for welfare, Renee also gave up the apartment she could ill afford and moved, with her toddler son, into the living room of her aunt and uncle's apartment. She and her son shared the two-bedroom apartment with not only her aunt and uncle but also their two children. Renee had been on welfare for two years at the time we spoke. Still, she knew little about the measures that had been instituted under welfare reform. Renee's experience belied that promise of welfare reform to "make work pay."

Renee mistakenly believed—perhaps because she had received some of her information about the welfare rules from her sister-in-law—that the welfare office gave stiff penalties to welfare recipients who reported that they were working. Renee had worked at a bakery in another city for a while but had left the job and never reported her wages to the welfare office. She quit because the bakery called her in and kept her only as long as they needed her help, but that ended up being only four to six hours a week. Renee explained that the job was not worth the effort, that just taking public transportation to and from the work site cost her six to seven dollars. Renee had no idea that the welfare office could provide help with transportation to welfare recipients who were working.

Renee also had no idea that the welfare calculations included an "earnings disregard," meaning that her meager earnings would probably have had no effect on her cash grant. Renee knew she was breaking the rules by not reporting her earnings. She said:

> I didn't report to 'em, and . . . basically because I wasn't making a lot of money, I didn't feel like I shoulda reported to them. They would have took that money out of my check. And that, that was something that I couldn't afford, you know, for them to do. So. I will admit to that. *[laughs]*

Renee did not seem to have the slightest idea that her failing to report her earnings on her monthly CA-7 form was, under California law, an act of perjury.

Renee had a vague knowledge that the welfare office went after welfare recipients for their unreported earnings, but she seemed unconcerned:

> INTERVIEWER: What do you think happens if somebody breaks the rules, doesn't report something?
> RENEE: They'll have the penalties on them.
> INTERVIEWER: Do you know what . . . what would happen?
> RENEE: I think they'll try to charge you with welfare fraud. I'm not sure, though. But I think in most cases, if you don't report or aren't reporting a certain amount of time, based on that report, then they'll try to get you for welfare fraud.
> INTERVIEWER: And how do they find out?
> RENEE: That I don't know! *[laughs]* They find that out. I guess they must investigate on you sometimes.

Renee had a friend whom, she said, had been charged with welfare fraud and could no longer receive aid. Renee took her friend's example neither as a warning nor as a lesson to learn the rules. She described her friend's case as "a setup." While it would be unlikely for Renee to face a criminal fraud charge based on one month of low, unreported earnings, a series of months of unreported earnings could well lead to criminal charges. And at the very least the unreported earnings would eventually show up in a governmental data exchange report and cause her hassles with her future welfare checks. (It was possible that her wage earning had already been flagged by welfare fraud investigators but that the long backlog of cases had to that point delayed any further action.) Reporting her earnings would have taken little of Renee's time and cost her little or nothing of her welfare grant. Renee's confusion over the rules, however, led her take an uninformed and potentially costly risk.

Renee was at another disadvantage because of her lack of rule knowledge. Renee, aware that her lack of education left her with few options in the workforce, had decided to start a training program to be a medical assistant. Had she obtained approval for this from an employment specialist in the welfare department, she could have received assistance with school-related expenses, transportation costs, and child care. Instead, she was taking out student loans to cover all of her costs and relying on her aunt and uncle for child care during her school hours.

Like Renee, many of the Misinformed welfare recipients were ignorant of, or at least misunderstood, some of the very basic workings of the welfare system. The retrospective calculation system in use at the time served as a prime example. Under the retrospective calculation system, welfare recipients submitted a monthly statement of all their outside economic resources and their household composition. On the basis of their reporting, their future aid payments were adjusted to account for their resources and household size. However, the lag between the time of their reporting and the time that their benefits were adjusted could be up to three months. This lag was widely misunderstood and misinterpreted, to the detriment of many welfare recipients.

A number of welfare recipients interviewed believed either (1) that the welfare system gave recipients a three-month grace period to report earnings; (2) that recipients did not have to report earnings during the first three months of a job; or (3) that no one was required to report earnings for a job they held for less than three months. On the basis of these mistaken beliefs, many were not reporting their wages.

In fact, some of the interviewees were taking and leaving jobs every couple months, believing that these earnings were not subject to the reporting requirements and would go unnoticed by the welfare system. The welfare reform goals of transitioning parents from welfare to work were undermined by these mistaken beliefs. For example, Sharon, a forty-year-old mother with an eight-year-old at home, misunderstood the reporting requirements, even though the welfare office had pursued her earlier for failing to report her income from wages. According to Sharon's interpretation of the rules, "At the end of the three months, if you decide you want to stay [at a job], you report it. You tell them. I'm going to stay in the job. I like it. But you just continue work—working four, five, six, seven, eight months, then . . . then there's a problem." Sharon was confused about not only the income-reporting rules but also the requirement that she report her household composition. When asked during the interview if she had informed the welfare office that she had a roommate who was contributing to the costs of rent and food, Sharon replied, "No, no, no, no. That's something you don't have to do." Sharon also occasionally worked for cash as a truck driver. Her misunderstanding of the reporting rules put her at risk of being investigated for overpayment of welfare. But even a minimal investigation of her case would reveal the roommate and her side job, putting her at great risk for a criminal perjury or felony fraud charge.

Viola was a former case manager who was well versed in many of the changes instituted under welfare reform, yet she similarly misunderstood the income-reporting requirements. She said:

> They give you a three-month grace period. The first three months you usually don't have to report the checks. But after three months, you're supposed to report your checks. I don't see where that's a problem. Because I think that should give you enough time, to at least build up a bank account or something. And, you know, get you on your feet at least, you know. With the money they're giving you and from your job. You know, I think they're pretty fair.

Viola mistakenly believed that the welfare office offered a three-month grace period during which welfare recipients could build a financial cushion. Such a rule might have some merit, particularly if the financial buffer could help an individual transition from welfare into stable employment. But no such rule exists. Johnetta, another working mother, believed she had six months to report her earnings to the welfare office. Many of the Misinformed interviewees were unaware that underreporting of income could result not only in an administrative claim from the welfare office demanding repayment but also in criminal fraud charges and lifelong exclusion from the welfare system.

The fluctuations in benefits also befuddled the Misinformed. The fact that the cash benefits were calculated retrospectively meant that the amount of aid a family received in a particular month might be frightfully out of line with their actual needs that month. Most of the welfare recipients interviewed could not predict what their next welfare check would look like. President Bill Clinton claimed that welfare reform would "make work pay," and the reforms did indeed increase the earnings disregards for working families receiving welfare. The particulars of the reforms, however, were lost on welfare recipients themselves. Most of the recipients interviewed knew that reported earnings would affect their checks but did not know how much earned income the system disregarded or how much money they could earn without being excluded from the welfare rolls. Rather than creating a system of incentives and disincentives appealing to rational and calculated wage earning, the welfare system appeared arbitrary to those who were engaged in the legitimate labor market.

To complicate matters, the county fraud investigators were months—and sometimes years—behind schedule in investigating the welfare cases flagged by the data exchange reports that were generated quarterly. While state and federal regulations mandated the counties to investigate inconsistencies in wage reporting within forty-five days after a computer match flagged a case, during the period of these interviews some California counties were *years* behind in addressing the backlog of incidents. As a result, welfare recipients' misunderstandings and failures to report were not quickly addressed and corrected, leaving them vulnerable to increasingly harsh penalties.

Incentives and disincentives—those "carrots and sticks" so often described in the debates over welfare reform—only work if they are known. The Misinformed respondents were only vaguely aware of the rules and policies designed as the incentives to make welfare recipients leave the welfare system under the 1996 reforms. Many, though certainly not all, of the Misinformed knew of the two-year and five-year limits on cash welfare receipt. If they did know about the limits, however, they commonly did not know when their own limits would hit or what would actually happen to their welfare benefits once the limits did hit. The available exemptions to the time limits also seemed to be unknown. Barbara, who, on the basis of her disability, should have qualified for an exemption to both the work requirements and time limits under state rules, knew nothing about them and was being sanctioned. She knew about the time limits but had no idea what would happen to her once they came around:

> I'm hoping and praying that I'll have a job. And I won't be cut off. I don't know what they do. I'll have to ask my job counselor what they do after you've been on it for two years. I don't know. I really don't know. I don't know if they have, uh, exceptions or something.

Barbara's incomplete knowledge of the rules was working to her disadvantage. And her disability, a brain injury that affected her cognitive skills, almost guaranteed that she would not be able to make use of the rules without guidance from someone either inside or outside the welfare system. It is unlikely that lawmakers envisioned a mother like Barbara when they instituted punitive welfare reform measures.

Most, though not all, of the Misinformed were aware of the work requirements; however, those who were meeting their work requirements were unaware of what would happen if they ever failed to meet their minimum required hours—between twenty hours and thirty-two hours for a single parent, depending on the date of the interview and child's age, and thirty-five hours for a two-parent household. Lisa, who was working and attending school, had worked the prior week but had failed to complete her full twenty hours because her child was sick and because her boss rescheduled her job. She presumed that the welfare office would punish her with some reduction of aid but had no idea how much that penalty would be. She also had no idea if the office could or would excuse her missed hours. Further, she was not sure whether making the effort to reach a live person at the welfare office and trying to get these questions answered was worth the expenditure of time and energy. The Misinformed commonly viewed the work requirements as an annoyance in their own lives, especially because of the documentation involved with the requirement. Nonetheless, many of them viewed the requirements as a good mandate for other welfare recipients, whom they viewed as lazy.

Under California's family cap rule, the household's cash welfare benefits are capped to the number of children in the household when the parent applies for welfare. If a woman gives birth to another child, her cash benefits will not rise. Recent studies have found that most state welfare agencies did not provide clients with information about family caps (Romero and Agénor 2009, 357) and that welfare recipients subject to the family cap either were unaware of the policy or misunderstood it (Romero et al. 2007). Similarly, the Bayview County interviewees who had given birth under the family cap rule were unaware of the rule when they got pregnant. Four of those six women were homeless at the time of our interview. While legislators argue that welfare recipients must be responsible for their own decisions and actions, the denials of additional aid to mothers who have additional children strains entire families, including children.

After CalWORKs was implemented in Bayview County, several women, with the help of the local legal aid office, appealed the exclusion of their newborn children from their cash aid grants. They brought due process claims, arguing that they had not been informed of the family cap (or maximum family grant, as it is also known) until their children were born. The women succeeded in their appeals, and cash assistance for the newborns was added to their family grants. These successful appeals prompted changes in the welfare office and in the county welfare application. To fend off future family cap appeals, the county began attaching a cover sheet to the welfare application. New applicants for aid were thereafter required to sign the cover sheet, a recipient acknowledgment of the family cap, before completing an application for welfare. In other words, government disapproval of childbearing and sexuality became the first written statement that a poor parent received when applying for aid.

Despite the notice requirement, the family cap rule was largely unknown to the Misinformed. Six of the interviewees had conceived and given birth after the family cap rules were instituted. Two of them learned of the family cap rules only after their children were born and they attempted to add the babies to the welfare case. One interviewee, Yvonne, discovered that the family cap rule was the reason her infant was not receiving cash benefits only after I explained the rule after our interview. Another interviewee, Kiki, had gone to the hospital for a fetal ultrasound the morning of our interview and did not learn until our interview of California's family cap on welfare payments, a policy that would prevent her from receiving any additional cash assistance for her new child. Kiki was not inattentive to the welfare rules: she was relatively well informed of the time limits, the work requirements and sanctions, and the possibility of criminal conviction for underreporting income to the welfare office. The family cap rule, however, was news to her.

The public perception seems to be that childbearing by welfare recipients is devastating to families and society. Kiki, pregnant with her second child, had quite a different view. Though her pregnancy was unintended, Kiki planned to keep the baby and was joyful to be pregnant despite her economic difficulties. She explained:

> Things were really prosperous for me when [my daughter] was small and I'm looking forward to it happening again for me, but double this time. I don't know how but I just . . . just . . . I'm looking forward to that, you know what I'm saying? So, you know, I think about having a baby, it'll just make me either strive harder, you know what I'm saying, 'cause I have another person that I have to, you know, take care of.

While Kiki understood the new baby to be an impediment to her short-term economic well-being and readily acknowledged that it would be unlikely she could satisfy the welfare department's work requirements during the baby's infancy, she saw the additional family member as a long-term benefit.

All of the women who got pregnant after the family cap rule was instituted said that prior knowledge of the family cap rules would not have affected their choices to bear another child. The common sentiment was that they would be poor with or without another child. They all found laughable the idea that anyone would have a child to receive more welfare.

The formal income- and asset-reporting rules were generally understood, but some of those rules were treated more formally than others. Most of the Misinformed knew that they were supposed to report all resources to the welfare office on a monthly basis. Most of them did report their earnings that came from long-term and legitimate jobs where they were paid by check. As described above, small earnings from short-term or temporary jobs were often not reported. Many recipients simply said that providing the documentation was not worth the effort. Nobody reported the financial help they received from family, friends, boyfriends, or the other parent(s). When I asked why they did not report this income, many, referring to the welfare office, replied, "It's none of their business." Natalie said, "You know, every little thing, that, you know, they want to know whether you had this or somebody's giving you money to help you, or . . . My God! I think that's just a little too personal! You know what I mean?" Many of the interviewees also noted that they needed extra money to survive. Still, the first response was often along the lines of privacy, suggesting that the Misinformed had some sense that there were justifiable limits on the welfare system's reach into their daily lives. They did not view this omission of information as cheating; instead, they viewed help from friends as personal exchanges, unrelated to their interactions with the public welfare system.

Most of the Misinformed knew that the welfare system employed mechanisms to track legitimate wage earning. However, they did not know the scope or regularity of the tracking. Many assumed that most fraud investigations were triggered by calls to the welfare fraud hotline. In general, the Misinformed were unaware of the full consequences of violating the welfare rules, especially the criminal consequences of failing to report income. Because the Misinformed, unlike the Informed and the Preoccupied/Disengaged, were often participating in the formal labor market, their failures to report income were those actions most likely to be caught and penalized by the welfare system.

Patricia, for example, seemed unenlightened and unconcerned about California's system used to conduct quarterly income matches and seemed equally unconcerned about the consequences for failing to report income she earned working in health care.

PATRICIA: You're supposed to send in the CA-7 [monthly reporting form] every month. And, um, declare anything important like, um, any money. I didn't declare everything all the time because I wouldn't have been able to pay rent. *[laughs]*
INTERVIEWER: So what do you declare and what don't you?
PATRICIA: Um, first I was like, if I was working for the agencies—the pool—then it wasn't consistent because you can't really get booked all the time, get anything consistent. And so until I found something consistent, I didn't see any sense in reporting it. It was gonna mess up the way they do that and my food stamps and then I really can't pay anything, so . . . Until it was consistent. Sometimes I would be booked to go at General Hospital and then somebody might say, well, go to Hillsburg, and I go out there and then they cancel. And then they might say, oh, I was canceled or I was booked wrong. And then I go over there and all I get is "show pay"—you get two hours just for showing up when you work. And so it's not anything that I would report, I guess. So . . . until now . . . that's when I told them I started working for decent health services. And so, hopefully they'll give me a check this month and some food stamps. 'Cause I don't get paid until the twenty-first. I said, "That's a long time to go without getting my check." So . . . *[laughs]* So, hopefully.

Patricia perceived no great risk for not reporting small amounts of earned income she received from occasional nursing jobs. She did, however, perceive a great financial risk of reporting her income and having her cash aid reduced or eliminated.

The Misinformed generally did not question the actions of the welfare office. They did not resist the formal rules by filing administrative appeals. While the actions of the welfare office sometimes appeared arbitrary to them, the Misinformed accepted the actions, assuming the system to be beyond their comprehension and control. They took little or no action when their aid was reduced. Nor did they seek advice or assistance from community organizations or from lawyers.

Because the Misinformed tended to have stronger and more extensive social networks than the Preoccupied and Disengaged, they were likely to have better access to financial help from friends and better opportunities to engage in under-the-table labor such as doing hair, housecleaning, cooking, and caring for the elderly or disabled. At the same time, these extensive social networks and opportunities for informal labor made them particularly vulnerable to exploitation and blackmail. A sad example of this vulnerability was Veronica (discussed more extensively in the previous chapter), who in addition to meeting her work requirement hours did a number of odd jobs for neighbors and her landlord to stay afloat financially. At the time of our interview, Veronica mentioned that her landlord was pressuring her to enter into an intimate relationship with him even though she had no desire to be involved with him. Given that she and her children had suffered a long bout of homelessness before this landlord offered to accept her housing voucher, Veronica worried that repeated refusals for sex might soon lead her family back to homelessness. She also had to worry that angering her landlord might cause him to report her under-the-table earnings to the welfare office in retaliation. Veronica's reliance on the state put her at the mercy of a man who held her future in limbo.

The Misinformed recipients lacked full understanding of many of the critical elements of welfare reform: the income-reporting rules and the increased income disregards that allowed them to keep more of their earned wages; the lifetime limits designed to spur them to seek employment; and the increased surveillance and stiff penalties to police hidden sources of income and support. Traveling in a fog, the Misinformed tried to make their way as best they could but in the process took unknown risks with unforeseen consequences.

Preoccupied/Disengaged Recipients

A few of the welfare recipients interviewed offered quite a contrast to those earlier described as the Informed. Those welfare recipients falling into the category of the Preoccupied and Disengaged were in the midst of long-term crises with no foreseeable end. They were too preoccupied by their desperate efforts to live day to day to engage in any meaningful way with a welfare system, especially with rules and policies built on expectations of shared commitments between the state and the welfare recipient. The Preoccupied/ Disengaged shared several general characteristics. First, they were socially isolated, with few or no friends or family members to turn to for assistance. Second, most were homeless, sometimes living in shelters, sometimes scraping together enough money to spend time in cheap hotels, and sometimes crashing on the floors of the few similarly situated people who made up their limited social networks. Their appearances and behaviors suggested that they might have had substance abuse problems. Some admittedly relied on prostitution, or "hustling" more generally, to come up with cash. Some had already lost custody of their children; some were in peril of losing the children in their care.

For the Preoccupied and Disengaged, the welfare time limits, the work requirements, the welfare office's electronic income verification system, and the other details of the welfare system were hardly relevant. Finding the next meal or finding a room for the night posed far more pressing concerns than the welfare rules.

A clear example of one of the Preoccupied and Disengaged was Rhonda, a thirty-six-year-old mother of five children, ranging in age from eighteen months to seventeen years. She had been on and off the welfare system for seventeen years, applying for the first time when she was pregnant with her oldest child. I met her outside the welfare office. Though it was a week after the first of the month, she still had not received her welfare check and had no money to pay for another night at the cheap hotel where she and her children had slept the night before. She eagerly accepted the offer of a free lunch for her family in exchange for an interview. Rhonda explained with pride that she had graduated from high school and taken two years of computer classes. At the time of our interview, however, she was disheveled and missing her front teeth (a common sight at the welfare office).

Rhonda's desperate circumstances at the time of the interview were generally related to her lack of adequate housing. Rhonda had become homeless almost eleven months earlier when her apartment burned down:

> I had a three-bedroom that I was paying six hundred for a month. That's the one that burned down. Anyway, AFDC said they were going to pay for me—that's what they used to call it, AFDC, but CalWORKs [now] was supposed to pay for me to move into another place. I've been trying to find a place in my price range. They haven't helped me far as . . . anything. All they could do was recommend me to shelters and stuff, like. I would just get the runaround from them all the time. So, finally I found me a one-bedroom place that we were gonna move into. I was supposed to get a check within twenty-four hours, a permanent housing check. I put the application in for a permanent housing check and the rental agreement in last week. This is the third time they say they've lost my fire papers. They claim they lost the papers again. I gotta go back down today and get the fire report from the Red Cross and everything else. And it's just been back and forth, back and forth every day. I've been staying in motels. Now they have me staying in motels. They're all screwing my whole check up, plus some. And I've had to sell food stamps here and there to keep going.

Rhonda told me that she normally received a monthly welfare check of $767 for her and her five children. The maximum aid payment potentially available to her as a homeless parent with five children was $1,064. Her approximation of her benefits, though, suggested both that she was being sanctioned and that her youngest child was excluded from aid under the family cap.

Rhonda estimated that the aid she received was only about half of what she needed to survive each month.

> INTERVIEWER: How much do you think you would need to really be okay?
> RHONDA: I'd say about $1,500—you know what I'm saying, to survive. Considering that the rent I'm gonna have to be paying, if I really want a nice place, is gonna be about seven, eight, ten hundred dollars. Then there's [utilities], telephone, all sorts of expenses for the kids. Transportation, feeding, all that. About $1,500 a month to make it.

There was a significant gap between Rhonda's economic need and the assistance she received from the welfare office. She was ill equipped to maximize her welfare grant, much less to seek and hold a job.

Rhonda could rely on little or no help from friends or family. In addition, she received no child support, through the formal system or informally, from the fathers of her children.

> My kids have three different fathers. They all have houses, they have cars, they have jobs. They all know the situation I've been in. They all know my house burned down. None of them have offered to help me do anything.

While Rhonda's sister let her and the children stay at her place from time to time, her sister's assistance to this six-person family was (understandably) limited.

In addition, all of Rhonda's children had chickenpox at the time of the interview. Rhonda's sister was unwilling to put her own children at risk of illness by letting the family stay with her. For the same reason, Rhonda's family was at the time being excluded from housing shelters. A motel was Rhonda's only option for housing.

Rhonda relied on a host of desperate measures to scrape up enough money to pay for a motel room for her family, measures that included prostitution and selling food stamps for cash. When asked how she made ends meet, Rhonda described her strategies:

RHONDA: I'm real lucky. I belittle myself to go out there and turn dates. Uh, other than that, I just depend on the Lord. Somebody always helps me, like you just did. It happens every day.

INTERVIEWER: Do you get help from family or friends?

RHONDA: No, I don't. My family hasn't helped me, hasn't given me a dime since my house burned down.

INTERVIEWER: You said that sometimes you have to sell your food stamps?

RHONDA: To get a room, yeah.

INTERVIEWER: How much can you get?

RHONDA: When you sell $40 worth of food stamps, you get $20. You can sell them right in front of the check-cashing place. But I do sell food stamps. I do have to get a roof over my head. That's what I do.

While Rhonda was aware that selling food stamps violated the rules and did note that she had to "belittle" herself to turn tricks, she was very matter-of-fact about her need to provide her children a place to sleep. When I bumped into Rhonda a week after our interview while recruiting other interviewees, she still had not received her welfare check or found a place to stay. She said, "I don't want to have to sell myself, but if that's what I have to do, that's what I have to do."

When I asked Rhonda whether she reported everything—all of her economic resources and the composition of her household—on the form the welfare office requires recipients to submit monthly, she replied, "Yeah, I do!" She made no suggestion, however, that she reported her money from "dates" or food stamp sales on her monthly reporting form.

Though Rhonda had experienced the welfare system before and after implementation of the 1996 welfare reforms, she was oblivious to most of the substantive changes to the system and uncritical of the system itself. Rhonda was unaware of the two-year or five-year time limits on cash aid that applied to welfare recipients. She seemed unfazed when I informed her of the limits. I asked her several questions to see if she had any criticisms of the welfare system, if she thought the system was fair. Her only criticism of the welfare system was the less-than-friendly attitudes of the workers in the welfare office.

INTERVIEWER: Do you think all the rules are fair—like the reporting rules or . . . ?

RHONDA: Yeah! It's not too much the system; it's the people.

Like others who fell into the category of the Preoccupied/Disengaged, Rhonda was surprisingly uncritical of the welfare system or welfare regulations and requirements. For Rhonda and the others described as Preoccupied/Disengaged, making it from one day to the next was so difficult that any new requirements and regulations were merely new annoyances. Missing welfare checks or being excluded from the system from time to time neither disrupted a pattern nor prompted the Preoccupied/Disengaged to challenge the problems. Economic life was chaos, and there was little hope of bringing order to the chaos in the near future. The Preoccupied/Disengaged were too busy trying to survive to invest any time in learning how the system worked, what benefits they might be missing, or what pitfalls they might face in the future. The realm of free choice was so narrow that the introduction of new incentives and disincentives was irrelevant.

Another example of someone who fell into the category of the Preoccupied and Disengaged was Crystal, a twenty-three-year-old woman who was caring for her baby, about six months old, at the time of our interview. Crystal was also the parent of an older child who, she said, "got took away from me." She did not want to discuss the details of her separation from the child, who was at the time in the custody of Crystal's aunt. Crystal described her mother as a drug addict who had been convicted of welfare fraud and explained that she herself had grown up in foster care for most of her childhood.

Crystal also explained that she had spent most of the previous two years incarcerated for participating in a violent felony as a teenager. She had apparently conceived and given birth to her infant while incarcerated. Crystal was released about a month after her child was born. At the time of our meeting, Crystal was relying on the financial help of her grandmother and three older siblings who lived outside the state. She also received help from her lover, a woman about ten years older than Crystal. While she had spent most of the time since her incarceration homeless, she and her baby were living with three other women and another child in a ramshackle house at the time of our interview. She said she paid two hundred dollars a month to stay there.

When Crystal was released from her incarceration, she had no place to stay but hotels. After applying for welfare, she received emergency cash aid, a housing allowance, and food stamps. Crystal explained, "They gave me one check and then—the check that they gave me couldn't afford a week. Like they expect to pay like $210.58. And the room is like $230 [a week], $240 at the most. And I couldn't rent anything with that rent." Though she did not say so explicitly, Crystal apparently turned to prostitution to cover her hotel costs. When I asked how she covered the hotel expenses, she said, "Hope men would help me pay for it. Help me pay some of that."

Crystal knew nothing about the welfare time limits, the work requirements, or the income-reporting requirements. She said she wanted to work, but her work experience was limited to a part-time job she had held as a teenager. In addition, Crystal said she would trust no one other than her grandmother, who lived on the other side of town, to care for her baby while she worked. Crystal said that if she got a job she had no plans to report her earnings to the welfare office. "The welfare is for my son," she insisted. "That money is for him. What I make is for me."

After our interview, Crystal left her house without checking on where her baby was or who was caring for him until another young woman ran out of the house and yelled, "Where's your baby?" Until then, Crystal apparently had not given the child a thought. Crystal also showed signs of alcohol abuse. When I turned off my tape recorder after our interview, Crystal immediately said, "You can tell I've been drinking, can't you." I actually had not picked up on any drinking. What I did understand was that she had multiple barriers to moving into the workforce and mainstream society—from a lack of skills and job experience, to child care responsibilities for an infant, to a history of incarceration. The welfare system is not well equipped to help Crystal—or other women who are Preoccupied and Disengaged—overcome any of these barriers.

Members of the Preoccupied and Disengaged category typically fall below the radar of the welfare system's quality control and fraud investigation efforts. Because they tend not to engage in legitimate employment, where the multiagency exchange of information through the use of Social Security numbers allows the welfare system to track earnings, the outside—and perhaps illicit—income they generate goes unnoticed by officials.

Yvonne, another member of the Preoccupied and Disengaged, had not avoided a fraud investigation (as described in more detail in chapter 8). Yvonne, who looked much younger than her twenty-eight years, was bone thin when we met. I scheduled five interviews with her before she finally showed up, and even on the fifth scheduled attempt she showed up forty-five minutes late. At the time of our interview, Yvonne and her two children were homeless and temporarily staying in a room at a friend's apartment. Yvonne had been approved for Section 8 housing assistance but, despite a constant search over the previous eight months, had not yet been able to find an apartment where the landlord was willing to rent to her.

Yvonne appeared to be so engrossed in her efforts to find housing that everything else fell by the wayside, including a working knowledge of the welfare rules and regulations. Yvonne knew exactly what the maximum aid grant was for a family of two—$505. She knew the county withheld part of her monthly check to offset an earlier overpayment. Still, Yvonne's knowledge of most of the welfare reform rules was slight. She mistakenly believed that signing a welfare-to-work plan was optional and that the work requirement rules did not apply to anyone who did not sign the plan. She believed that if a welfare recipient took a job and lost it she could not reapply for aid. In addition, she had no clue about the family cap rules, even though she had given birth almost a year earlier to a child excluded from cash benefits. Yvonne knew she was receiving cash aid for a family of two instead of three but did not know why an increase in aid for her baby had not begun. Surprisingly, Yvonne possessed specific knowledge of the rule excluding drug offenders from government aid programs. In general, however, the welfare rules and regulations were elusive to Yvonne.

Another interviewee falling into the category of the Preoccupied and Disengaged was Sarah. Sarah said she had never held a job and had been on welfare for ten years. At the time of our interview she had lived in a government-subsidized Section 8 apartment for several years. She told, however, of her past experiences as a homeless mother, dragging her kids from shelter to shelter. It was lucky for Sarah that she had subsidized housing because she lacked a reasonable understanding of the market cost of housing. She said that if she lost her apartment she would be in big trouble because "right now, a studio, it's like three [hundred] something, four [hundred] something. A one bedroom is like five hundred or six hundred dollars." In actuality, the market rate for studio apartments in her neighborhood was running close to one thousand dollars at the time of our interview. Detached from most market interactions, Sarah possessed no knowledge of local housing costs.

Sarah had no telephone of her own but was on good terms with her neighbors, who allowed her to use their phone when she needed to make calls. She was a regular visitor to food pantries. While Sarah had been on welfare during the system's transition under welfare reform, the changes occurred without much notice from Sarah. Sarah had a vague understanding of the CalWORKs program. She had attended an orientation, which she described as "fun." She was also happy to have received a free bus pass as part of her participation in the program. At the same time, she had no plans to participate in work activities under the program. According to Sarah, she had been in the CalWORKs program for a year at the time of our interview without participating in work activities. She was unclear how much her monthly welfare check was and, given her confusion, may have been being sanctioned without her knowledge. She had no idea what would happen when the welfare time limit hit but seemed unconcerned, saying, "I was told that they're not going to just cut you off, unless . . . you're not doing what you're told." Sarah was apparently unclear that through the CalWORKs program she was being told to find a job.

In fact, Sarah fundamentally misunderstood the welfare system's rules about work. According to Sarah, the people in the welfare office "said you could work, like . . . I think they said it was like a month. Yeah, work like a month." Sarah believed that anyone who worked longer than a month was breaking the rules.

I asked Sarah what she thought of welfare recipients who broke the rules. Her response: "If they're breaking the rules, um, they shouldn't have been breaking them. And they shouldn't have got caught! *[laughs]*" Sarah said she had known several people who had been caught for breaking the rules by working while receiving aid and had been required to repay the money to the welfare office. When asked how she thought they got caught for cheating, Sarah said, "Someone got jealous and reported them."

Like Rhonda, Sarah felt that the welfare rules, and the CalWORKs rules specifically, were fair. Why? "Because," she said, "it's expecting a certain amount of something out of somewhere, assistance or something, and so it's only applicable for them to expect something out of you. You gotta give to receive. That's basically how I look at it." According to Sarah's understanding, however, giving something back merely meant attending meetings at the welfare office. Sarah missed the deeper message of welfare reform: get a job and leave the welfare system.

The only rules Sarah considered unfair were the sanctions imposed against parents when their kids failed to attend school. She said she had faced this sanction in the past and it had brought financial hardship to the family at a time when her son was "going through a phase." She considered it unfair because she suffered as a result of her son's truancy.

The Preoccupied/Disengaged interviewees had virtually no knowledge of the central elements of welfare reform. The were unaware of the time limits, the work requirement rules they would need to follow to receive the maximum benefits, or the sanctions applied against welfare recipients who failed to follow the rules and requirements. The Preoccupied/Disengaged were in no way complying with the spirit of welfare reform by seeking work. At the same time, these individuals demonstrated no active resistance to the authority of the welfare system or the law. Their failure to seek work was in many ways reasonable given that they had few skills and little hope of finding jobs that would sustain them. Any time they invested in futile attempts to find work would have taken away from the time they needed to secure food and shelter, if only temporarily.

How Recipients Define Rule Fairness and Noncompliance

Tom Tyler has argued that individuals will follow rules they believe are fair (Tyler 1990; Tyler and Darley 2000). One goal of this study was to examine welfare recipients' assessments of the fairness of the rules instituted under welfare reform and to see if those assessments correlated with compliance. Noncompliance with the rules was ubiquitous among my interviewees. Still, one cannot understand the nature of noncompliance without examining an individual's engagement with the rules. Noncompliance may flow from (1) difficulties complying with the rules, an issue examined in the previous chapter's discussion of the gap between needs and resources; (2) a misunderstanding of the rules and the consequences of rule breaking, discussed earlier in this chapter; or (3) a view that the rules are illegitimate and need not be followed. Anyone subject to rules difficult to understand or difficult to follow might, one would assume, lose faith in those rules over time. But while the interviewees described some erosion in their perceptions of the welfare rules' legitimacy, the erosion was not so great as to undermine the system as a whole.

Many of the interviewees spontaneously discussed their views of the fairness of the welfare rules or their faith in the legitimacy of the welfare system generally. When interviewees did not bring up the issue of fairness themselves, I raised it with them. I asked the interviewees whether they thought the welfare rules were fair. I specifically asked them if they thought the reporting rules were fair, since these were probably the rules most commonly broken. I asked them about the fairness of the time limits and the work requirements because these were an essential part of the welfare reforms of 1996. And I asked them about the fairness of the family cap, also known as the maximum family grant rule, because this rule limiting aid to newborn children was not only a key piece of the welfare reform legislation but also the rule affecting what many people consider the personal realm of family formation and sexuality.

Perceptions of the Welfare System's Fairness

For the most part, despite their own difficulties complying with the rules, the welfare recipients I interviewed expressed support for the existing rules. For example, Barbara, who knowingly omitted her earnings from side jobs and who, despite her disability, was being sanctioned for failing to meet the hourly work requirements, criticized neither herself nor the welfare system but rather other welfare recipients. "So, ah, they've given me a rough time. Because I know there are so many people that try to trick them, you know."

A small number of the welfare recipients interviewed, and almost exclusively those described earlier as the Informed, felt that the welfare rules were generally unfair. Jane, who circumvented the reporting rules in a number of ways, argued:

> People are forced to being dishonest. As I told you at the beginning, it wasn't my first inclination. My first inclination was I'm grateful to have the help. I'll tell you whatever you want to know. You learn real quick—real quick—that's not how you get help. So forget that! You know. If lying is what it's gonna take, then all right.

Jane criticized lawmakers as being out of touch with the circumstances of poor families.

> I would love to see these silver spoon-fed bureaucrats in their ivory palaces live off what we get. I would like to see them stretch the dollars. They say we're lazy. They say we're uneducated. I beg to differ. Yeah, there might be a few, but it's not the norm. The norm are really smart, know what's going on, have really high moral values and family values, and are resourceful as hell, and hardworking. Whether that means it's under the table, whatever, they're working.

While acknowledging the rule breaking that she engaged in, Jane stressed the fact that she and other poor parents were not lazy, that they had to work as hard as, and sometimes harder than, people who were well off. Her views, however, stood apart from the vast majority of the interviewees.

Kiki admitted that she resented other welfare recipients, especially those who received aid for a long time. Still, Kiki did not support the federal five-year time limit on cash assistance.

But then I don't think it's really fair either. That now that they passed the new laws saying, okay, five years, *boom*, you're out. You know what I'm saying, you know, you still need—no matter what kind of situation people are in—sometimes they need, maybe they need mental or physical healing. You never know. Sometimes they might need a little bit more than five years, but who are you to say that we're going to put a time limit on the time that we're going to help you.

In other words, Kiki felt that the five-year time limits were unfair to people who suffered from physical or mental problems and could not find or keep work because of their problems. It was, however, not just individual circumstances that made the time limits unfair but also the broader and collective issue of economic uncertainty. She went on:

'Cause what happen if you use up your five years and then you go to work, and then, say, they have a mass layoff at your company. Or you get fired. Well, if you have a mass layoff, of course you automatically get your unemployment benefits. Well, if you get terminated, what are you going to do? You can't find another job the next day. You know, job hunting is a job by itself. So I think there should be type of program to assist people. And that's how I feel about it.

In short, Kiki, like many other interviewees, felt that the sixty-month lifetime limit on cash benefits was unfairly indifferent to circumstances outside the control of individuals. At the same time, Kiki, like others, said that she did not think welfare recipients should receive welfare for a long time without being expected to improve themselves, both personally and financially. Kiki said, "I mean, you know, if you are able, if you are able, you should do stuff. A little something to help yourself."

In discussing their views of the five-year time limits, many of the interviewees expressed their fears that their neighborhoods would experience increases in crime once poor families began reaching their time limits. Still, because these interviews were conducted within the first sixty months after the time limits were instituted, most of the interviewees found it unfathomable that time limits would actually be imposed.

Most of the interviewees, even the ones who were not working, felt it was fair for the welfare system to ask welfare recipients to work. D'Nay, a twenty-year-old mother of two, said, "If you're going to take their money, you need to be doing something. You know, just not lousing around the house, abusing it." At least among the Informed and Misinformed, there was a widely shared work ethic and belief that low-income parents should work.

The interviewees did not feel it was fair to ask welfare recipients to report financial support they received from friends or families. Here the interviewees invoked legally imbued language, describing help from friends and family as "private." D'Nay, Jamilla, and Johnetta all spoke of the private nature of financial exchanges between close friends and family. For the most part, the interviewees did not complain that the reporting requirements—or at least the requirements to report wage-earning income—were unfair. This sentiment was inconsistent with the widespread underreporting of earnings. In short, there was a significant gap between individuals' assessments of the formal rules and individuals' actions under those rules.

Most of the interviewees shared the view that welfare recipients should face penalties for failing to report income, though they believed that the penalties should be much less severe than they actually were. While some perceived the threat of welfare fraud investigations or criminal charges—usually because of a personal experience or a friend's experience with investigation—the Preoccupied/Disengaged and the Misinformed generally, and mistakenly, believed that failing to report resources would merely result in a readjustment of aid or the county's effort to recoup any overpayments from future welfare checks. Shawnique, who was not reporting the ample support she received from her father, believed that if someone got caught cheating, the welfare system simply cut off her aid and required her to reapply, thereby causing a delay in the cash grant. Along the same lines, Jamilla, a mother of four, assumed that anyone caught cheating would simply have her check reduced until the overpayment was recouped by the welfare office.

A few interviewees did feel that the welfare office overemphasized the problem of welfare cheating. When I asked Patricia, a health care worker employed by a temporary agency, what she thought about people who broke the welfare rules, she responded: "I don't know why people are making such a big deal. It's really not a lot of money that you're jacking off *[laughs]*, that you're misusing. You know, I can see if you're getting aid and you're not feeding your children or something like that." For Patricia, cheating meant misusing the money from the state, not misrepresenting one's resources to maximize the welfare check.

Like the interviewees in Karen Seccombe's study (1999), some interviewees viewed the family cap as unfair, while others considered it a needed deterrent to childbearing among welfare recipients. Often interviewee complaints of unfairness were related to recipients bearing the brunt of administrative errors in the office. In the end, most of the recipients supported the over-all structure of rules and regulations under welfare reform, particularly the work incentives—the carrots. At the same time few knew of all of the benefits available and almost no one possessed full knowledge of the penalties of noncompliance—the sticks. The punitive components of welfare reform designed to deter cheating could not serve their deterrent purpose because they were largely unknown.

A Normative Framework for Rule Breaking: Dissing the Welfare Queen

Tom Tyler's (1990) study of obedience to the law, while illuminating the relationship between rule compliance and legitimacy, avoided both complex rules and the people at the margins. Welfare recipients must carry on their daily lives even where the boundaries of rule compliance and rule breaking are unclear. Tyler's study on compliance with the legal rules examined contexts (for example, stopping at stop signs) where compliance was easy, where the rules aligned with both the dominant morality and with individual self-interest.

What, though, emerges when law's commands are ambiguous or in conflict with physical needs or the moral demands of parenthood? Among welfare recipients, a new moral code develops. While nearly all welfare recipient interviewees denounced welfare cheating, they carried a largely consistent normative view of what welfare cheating might involve—a view inconsistent with formal law's description of welfare cheating. I asked respondents what behavior should be considered against the rules and what should be punished. For the most part, interviewees tended to share common views of what noncompliance entailed. Everyone dismissed as an issue of noncompliance any unreported financial assistance from family and friends, which for most recipients tended to be small and sporadic anyway. They considered these loans "private"—personal efforts to fill the gap left by the market and the state.

Interviewees, however, consistently considered it a welfare "violation" to spend welfare money wastefully or to spend it on oneself rather than on one's children. There was a shared norm about how the money should be spent. According to a number of welfare recipients who responded to the question about cheating, a mother who spent her welfare money on herself rather than her kids should no longer be able to receive aid.

There was also a shared norm when it came to justifications for lying to the welfare office. Jane, for example, clearly expressed that lying to maximize one's welfare check was justified when the family truly needed the money. Still, she felt there were at least three circumstances where welfare receipt constituted misuse. The first misuse of welfare occurred when someone received "a whole bunch of different welfare checks in a whole bunch of different cities." The second misuse of welfare in her mind occurred in situations where "the man live[s] at home and doesn't work and just lays up on the mother's welfare check." The third misuse she identified occurred when mothers spent their welfare benefits on themselves rather than their children:

> So . . . what's out of bounds? I see some women in Bayview City who have got the really long fake nails. They got two gold rings on every finger. And they've got about fifteen gold chains around their neck. Their hair is in one of those seventy-five-dollar styles. They've got a Gucci bag and Fila shoes. They're wearing leather coats. And they're kids are in some dirty, scummy, holey, nonmatching, nappy-hair, broken-up beads, runny noses. That's sick to me.

So even for someone who was admittedly a welfare cheat—who lied about her marital status, lied about owning a car, and even used someone else's Social Security number to hide earnings—there were normative limits on the cheating. And in her mind, using welfare for greed, vanity, or sloth rather than need went beyond the pale.

Jane's response leads to one of the surprising findings during the interviews, which was that, aside from the Informed interviewees like Jane, welfare recipients both accepted and redeployed the stigmatized stereotype of the welfare queen. The individuals interviewed seemed acutely aware of the negative public opinion of welfare recipients. The welfare queen—or allusions to the welfare queen—were frequent in the interviews. The power of the welfare queen as a cultural symbol manifested itself in the language of those very women whom many would describe as welfare queens.

During our conversations, the women frequently resisted this stereotype, to which they were subject, by asserting their positive roles as mothers. (The four fathers interviewed did the same, though they seemed aware that as single fathers they were already entitled to some social esteem for stepping up to the plate and looking after their children.) All of the women stated that they were good mothers, or at least doing the best that they could. Several of the women said that caring for their children during working hours (and schooling hours) was more important to them than working. Without diminishing the value they placed on parenting, it should be noted that the work opportunities available to these women offered little reward in terms of financial gain, job autonomy and satisfaction, or social status.

Rather than using their own experiences and frustrations with the welfare system to critique or attack broader views of the welfare queen, many of the women and men I interviewed merely sought to exempt themselves, and only themselves, from the negative stereotypes about welfare recipients that pervade popular culture. Many granted legitimacy to the stereotype itself and simply attacked other welfare recipients as welfare queens.

Several of the women made a point of distancing themselves from other welfare recipients. Austin Sarat has reported similar criticisms in his interviews with welfare recipients in a legal services office. "Such criticism," Sarat writes, "puts distance between the individual welfare recipient seeking legal assistance and the class of recipients as a whole. It gives voice to the shame and stigma associated with receiving welfare and, in so doing, ratifies and reinforces the images that produce such shame and stigma" (1990, 354). My interviews suggest that this distancing occurs not only among welfare recipients who feel empowered enough to seek legal advice (those who would fall into my category of the Informed) but also among those who do not. Many of the interviewees described other welfare recipients as lazy, selfish, and uncaring toward their own children. Several of the Misinformed also made strong points that, whatever their strategies of economic survival, those strategies would never include selling drugs or prostitution; they thereby declared their moral superiority to welfare recipients who did engage in those activities.

Only a few of the interviewees were critical of the pervasive negative stereotypes about welfare recipients. Annette, who began receiving welfare when pregnant with her first child and who had given birth to two others while on aid, was one of them. She said, "Everybody's not shiftless and lazy!" She explained that she was stuck because she could not see how she could adequately care for the five children in her care, some with special needs, and work forty hours a week. She said that she could manage a thirty-hour-a-week job but did not see how she could support her family on the meager income she could make working less than full time, especially with her limited skills and job experience.

And yet, in the gap between the welfare system's requirements and welfare recipients' abilities, there seemed to emerge an alternative normative framework for complying with the rules. Some of the Misinformed interviewees in particular seemed to interpret "following the rules" as behaving the way that welfare workers considered compliant. Following the rules for them meant submitting all required forms, answering all questions (even those they considered intrusive), and showing up for meetings. They believed that doing this would keep them safe. They believed that keeping their heads down—both in the sense of kowtowing to welfare officials and in the sense of not making themselves obvious to welfare workers—was the best way to ensure that cash assistance appeared every month. The strategy of keeping their heads down, however, meant that they did not ask questions about the rules, missed out on some of the additional benefits or work training or educational programs that might have been be available to them, and often unknowingly overstepped rules in a journey that held the potential to lead them to felony convictions.

From looking at the welfare reforms rule by rule, this study suggests that it was not critical views of the welfare system or rejection of the welfare rules that prompted welfare recipients to violate the rules. While there were certainly critics of each element of welfare reform, most of the interviewees lent their overall legitimacy to the reforms. And as the following chapter discusses, this personal investment of legitimacy in the welfare system leaves all three categories of welfare recipients—the Informed, the Preoccupied/Disengaged, and the Misinformed—struggling within an increasingly punitive system of welfare rules.

7

Contextualizing Criminality, Noncompliance, and Resistance

The recipients of largess themselves add to the powers of government by their uncertainty over their rights, and their efforts to please. Unsure of their ground, they are often unwilling to contest a decision. The penalties for being wrong, in terms of possible loss of largess in the future, are very severe. Instead of contesting, recipients are likely to be overzealous in their acceptance of government authority.
—Charles Reich, "The New Property"

Just as the network of power relations end by forming a dense web that passes through apparatuses and institutions, without being exactly localized in them, so too the swarm of points of resistance traverses social stratifications and individual unities.
—Michel Foucault, *The History of Sexuality*

Welfare reformers of the 1990s hoped to create a new welfare system that would appeal to individuals' economic self-interest, a system that would spur the poor to leave the welfare system and assume the risks of the labor market. The simplistic model of welfare reform excluded a number of important factors. First, the economic needs of welfare recipients exceeded either the money they received from welfare or the money they would be likely to earn in the low-wage labor market. For many welfare recipients, making the transition from welfare to work simply meant making the transition from a consistent source of inadequate income to an inconsistent source of inadequate income. This was not a risk that some were willing to take.

Second, most welfare recipients already had unreported sources of income. Entering the full-time wage labor market would limit the time they could devote to side jobs such as housecleaning, cooking, and doing hair. Earning wages, even if low, would also diminish their chances of calling on the sympathies of family and friends for additional economic support.

Third, family obligations made it difficult for many welfare recipients I interviewed to meet their thirty-two-hour-a week work requirements, much less work a full-time job. The time required for caring for young children, a widespread distrust of child care providers, and the high costs of child care diminished the willingness and ability of many recipients to seek wage work. Further, many of the interviewees were caring for children with disabilities or had disabilities themselves; still others were in substance abuse recovery programs. While the interviewees saw working as creating physical and mental risks for themselves and their children, this was not a risk generally recognized by policy makers who instituted welfare reform. Indeed, many interviewees were willing to take these risks, for example, sometimes leaving their children home alone at nights. Still, the risks of such actions were high, and many were unwilling to assume them. Fourth, many welfare recipients were so far from employable that an expectation for them to enter the workforce without intensive intervention was unreasonable. Homelessness, lack of job experience, and lack of job skills rendered self-support through employment nearly impossible for many of the interviewees.

In sum, for many welfare recipients the risks of working outweighed the risks—and punishments—they faced under the reformed welfare system. Many of the interviewees were complying with the CalWORKs requirement by meeting or at least trying to meet their work requirements. Nonetheless, the larger welfare reform goal of having parents endure the risks of the wage labor market without the welfare safety net was not a shared goal, or at least an immediate goal, for most of the interviewees.

This chapter examines welfare recipients' resistance to and investment in law's legitimacy when their formal compliance with the law was often tenuous.

On Being the Object of the Criminalization of Poverty

Bayview County spent three million dollars on its CalWORKs and food stamp fraud investigation units in 2002-3. Thousands of California welfare recipients were swept up in welfare fraud investigations and prosecutions in the first five years after federal welfare reform. The aggregate numbers, however, fail to reveal how individuals become entangled in welfare fraud and welfare fraud investigations and prosecutions.

Fraud Investigations

Many low-income mothers find themselves the targets of welfare investigations. While welfare fraud has not been a cause for feminist advocates or an area of inquiry for feminist social scientists, it is becoming a growing women's issue. In Bayview County, hundreds of women each year have their lives opened up and disrupted through fraud investigations and prosecutions. While the state of California does have some statewide fraud control measures such as the fingerprint-imaging program, investigations of welfare fraud are left to the counties. At the time of the interviews and at the time of this writing, California counties varied dramatically in their methods of investigation, their administrative systems for pursuing fraud cases, and their rates of prosecution.

Like many other California counties, Bayview County had shifted much of the responsibility for investigating welfare fraud from the county Social Services Agency to the District Attorney's Office. In the mid-1990s, the District Attorney's Welfare Fraud Division physically resettled, moving its attorneys and investigators into a building they shared with welfare caseworkers. Fraud investigations, once handled by personnel in the Social Service Agency, were transferred to district attorney's fraud investigators, who were peace officers enabled to engage in criminal searches, seizures, and arrests. The move was intended to create a seamless process for investigating and prosecuting cases of welfare fraud. The integration of space and practices, however, also blurred the boundaries between what were once two distinct arms of the government—one beneficent, the other punitive.

Bayview County, like other California counties, conducted what is known as early fraud prevention by screening welfare applicants for possible fraud before a case is even opened and a check issued. Bayview County, however, engaged in less intrusive early fraud prevention measures than some other California counties. San Diego County, for example, employs an early fraud control process that includes an unannounced home visit to every applicant for welfare. Bayview County has avoided early fraud control efforts as aggressive as those taken in San Diego. The Social Services Agency nonetheless has investigated a significant number of new welfare applicants. The Bayview County Social Services Agency tracks the number of early fraud prevention referrals received and the number of investigations completed. The data compiled between March 2000 and March 2002 show that the county typically received between 150 and 225 early fraud referrals each month.

Welfare fraud investigations occurring once a welfare case is open can be triggered in one of several ways. First, an investigation may be triggered when a data exchange based on a recipient's Social Security number identifies an inconsistency in information about income, assets, or household composition. Second, an investigation may be initiated by a welfare caseworker who suspects a problem in a case. Third, an investigation may be triggered by an anonymous call to one of the state or county welfare fraud hotline numbers or by any other form of tip provided to the welfare office. While overstepping the welfare rules is a common practice among welfare recipients, welfare fraud investigators cast their nets broadly, routinely investigating welfare recipients who are not engaged in fraud. A 1999 Los Angeles Grand Jury Report found that "the statewide rate for the number of completed investigations with allegations unfounded or insufficient evidence was 52.3 percent" (Los Angeles Grand Jury 1999, 4).

It is rare for researchers to examine investigations from the perspectives of the criminal suspects, but the interviews in this study allow just such an examination. Barbara had gone though an unannounced home search, ostensibly by the fraud investigation unit, about a year before our interview. She explained:

BARBARA: They came to my house and . . . I thought they like bombarded my house. And [my daughter] was having a Bible Study. They came by and thought [the youngsters] were evading school. You know, it was an adult home, I can't leave her by herself. [But] I wasn't there when they came. So my friends, the male, you know, the Bible friend, said, "Well, do you stop by people['s] houses without an announcement?" The other guy said, "Yes, we do." They do that! Got up, walked all around my house, through the bathroom and all through my room, through the kitchen, and came back and told the girl, "Well, I think this is okay. She doesn't have a man." They thought I . . . ! They said that! This was, uh, last year. You know. Must have been around September. It was a male and female.
INTERVIEWER: And they just came by unannounced?
BARBARA: Uh, yeah. 'Cause I guess, they say, "We wanna see! We wanna see who you're related to. And we do this all the time." So. So anyway, they could see I had no men there. [laughs] I wouldn't do that. I'm not, you know, that kind of person.

Despite this search, Barbara did not use any language of rights or privacy but instead talked about governmental need for the search. While complaining about the welfare office asking all about her business in one breath, in the next she said: "I'm trying to look at in a more governmental vein. 'Cause they can't give me money without asking all that stuff. You know, I know they can't. So I just try to think of it in that way." For Barbara, the government interest in deterring or catching fraud outweighed any interests she might have in keeping "her business" to herself.

Kiki described her experience of being investigated after turning in the check stub for a new job. "And this one lady, I don't know what was wrong with her. . . . I went down there to turn in my check stub. By the end of the day, she had contacted investigative services on me. And they had people out, in, um, investigators out looking for me." She described the investigation:

> We're homeless, we're using [a friend's] address and Social Security number to get into school. And so what happened was [my friend] called and she was like, "I got the message and, um, call them back." [My friend] called and said, "The investigators are looking for you." "For what?" She said, "Oh yeah, these men in black suits came by, to my mama's house, looking for you." And I'm like, for what? And, and, and, you know, then my cousin, says, "Oh yeah, the sheriff's department came over here looking for you." I'm like . . . I tried to say, "For what?" She says, "I don't know."

Kiki then explained what happened when she contacted the investigator to find out what was going on:

> And then finally I got a hold to somebody out of the office, or whatever, one of the men, the investigators. . . . I said, "What, people are looking for me and I'm surprised." . . . And he was like, "Oh, we just wanted to know if you was, like, really, you know, living here, in the county, and if you were collecting benefits from somewhere else." I said, "So you had to go send out an investigator? You couldn't have just, you know, asked me that?" I was so mad about that! And plus I was scared because, I was like, "What did I do?" I'm doing everything that they tell me to do. What? And that's all it was. That I . . . it was my check. So . . . that was the most horrible experience I've ever, ever had. With the county.

Kiki was so humiliated and frightened by the experience, and by the investigator's comment that they had been heading over to her workplace to question her employer when she called, that she left the job she had just begun. "I got scared! So I quit the job. I wouldn't go back to work." Rather than making sure a welfare recipient followed the routines of law-abiding and employed life, the investigation in this situation prompted Kiki to leave her aboveboard job.

The Fourth Amendment of the U.S. Constitution provides citizens protections from government searches by government officials. For most of us, a government investigator cannot walk into our home without either our consent, a strong indication that there are exigent circumstances involving peril to life or a crime in progress, or a warrant based on probable cause and issued by a neutral and detached magistrate. Those protections from government intrusion are not, at least in practice, in effect for welfare recipients. By virtue of their poverty, their rights are impoverished.

Criminal Prosecutions

In 1997 Erik Luna, then a deputy district attorney in San Diego, one of the country's local governments most aggressive in the pursuit of welfare fraud cases, wrote a law review article proclaiming, "Welfare fraud is an epidemic" (1997, 1235). Indeed, welfare fraud is rampant. As chapters 5 and 6 make clear, families in the CalWORKs system cannot live on their cash aid alone. Yet the meager benefits provided by the welfare office are important to families living on the edge. Many families, if not most, therefore conceal some of their earnings or other income on the monthly reporting forms they submit to the welfare office. All but four of the thirty-four interviewees in this study admitted concealing income from the welfare office. In three of the four cases where families were not hiding resources, someone in the household received a relatively generous Social Security benefit. In the remaining case, a mother provided the recipient almost-free housing.

The disjuncture between the government goals of welfare fraud investigations and prosecutions and the actual effects of these investigations and prosecutions highlights the irrationality of the policies and practices. According to welfare officials, welfare fraud measures are designed to achieve several goals: to catch and punish welfare cheats; to deter would-be welfare cheats; to reduce the government expenses associated with the welfare system. The first goal, punishment, is one that the system is certainly achieving. The problem, however, is that the vast majority of welfare recipients are technically welfare cheats. If they were not, they would be unable to survive. Thus welfare fraud is a symptom of various problems, not the underlying social ill.

The goal of deterrence is going unmet. As the interviews reveal, the criminal penalties for welfare fraud were largely unknown by welfare recipients. Unless welfare recipients are aware of the severe consequences for rule breaking, those penalties can have no deterrent effects on welfare recipients' actions. Cesare Beccaria, who wrote *On Crimes and Punishment* in the mid-eighteenth century, called for a rational system of criminal punishment. Under this system, individuals must be informed of both the rules and the consequences of the rules (1963, 17-18). With this knowledge, Beccaria theorized, individuals would be able to weigh the costs of rule breaking and opt to follow the rules rather than risk the long-term consequences of pursuing short-term gain. This system, however, cannot function where neither the rules nor the consequences of rule breaking are known by individuals (94). The system also cannot function where immediate needs actually do outweigh the risks of long-term suffering.

Criminal punishment does not necessarily make sense when lawbreakers do not know they are breaking the law and when they do not understand the penalties. One mother offers a vivid example of this illogic. Yvonne, a twenty-eight-year-old mother of two children under the age of three, described her experience with fraud prosecution. Around the time her daughter was six months old, Yvonne worked in the cafeteria in ValueMart. She said, "I was making below minimum wage." She continued, "I was getting like, $4.25. . . . The law was in effect that was getting five dollars an hour. ValueMart wasn't giving it." (It should be noted that federal law, though not California law, allows employers to pay food service workers who receive tips less than minimum wage. It was not clear whether Yvonne was being underpaid or whether she was confused about the distinction between gross pay and net pay.)

When I asked Yvonne if she reported her income, she said, "They knew I was working." Yvonne seemed to be unclear about the importance of submitting written information and pay stubs, stating, "They tell you, just put it on your CA-7 that you're working." Yvonne also seemed unclear about how the computer system kept track of recipients. She asked, "Why I gotta tell the clerk my Social Security number? I mean you could put it on your CA-7, but you still have to go in there and tell them that." While Yvonne did not report her income on her monthly CA-7 form, she believed that telling a welfare caseworker and including a note about her earnings in a note in her annual renewal form was sufficient documentation for the welfare office.

Two years after quitting her job at ValueMart, Yvonne received a letter telling her that officials wanted to ask her some questions. Though Yvonne could not explain exactly who the man was, her description strongly suggests that the man who met with her in the office was an investigator with the district attorney's Welfare Fraud Investigation Unit and that she was not asked questions but rather subjected to accusations. Yvonne was told that she had failed to report her earnings to the Welfare Department and consequently owed nine hundred dollars, a figure that was later reduced to about seven hundred dollars. Yvonne described the experience she had with the court and her public defender:

> They have this thing, they call the self-surrender program. They make it sound like it's real nice, real good, all you do is go to court, go home. No, all you do is be a criminal for a whole day, *then* go home. You don't even get a public defender that say, "This is the issue."
>
> So, um, then you go to the public defender's office, and then you got to go back to court. And then the public defender they gave me—he crazy, too! You know. He's yelling at you and stuff. I'm like, "Why is this man yelling at me?" You know, why is he yelling at me? The stuff is in there. If you look in there. He's like, "Oh, I'm so sorry."

Yvonne described the public defender as uninterested in the details of her case and eager for her to make a deal with the district attorney to pay back the money she had received from the welfare office.

> And he [the public defender] act like I'm still working. He said, "How much more can you give us?" I'm only getting what they're giving me—or what they're already not taking from me. You know. And he said, "Well, you gotta pay something else. So it'll just go away." How am I just not going to ever, ever go away because I had to go through a lot of mess? So how's it going to go away? It's gonna go away for him. It'll go away for them. But it's not going to go away for me. So, there's just so many mistakes.

Yvonne sounded confused about the whole process, even after the event:

> YVONNE: 'Cause they was talking about, oh, we just wanted—they just wanted money. Oh, you just want money back? You could have just told me over the phone you want money back! I shouldn't have to—they make you go to jail.
> INTERVIEWER: You went to jail?
> YVONNE: They make you stay in there for twelve hours. I got sick, you know, being up in there for twelve hours, just to go to court. Just to go to court. Now, you could have just told me to go to court. I already went to court. . . . You know. It don't make no sense.

These encounters, of course, were only the beginning of Yvonne's new relationship with not only the welfare system but also the criminal justice system. As a result of the overpayment and Yvonne's failure to report her earnings from ValueMart, Yvonne's aid was cut off for more than six months. When she could reapply for aid and her cash grant began again, the checks were reduced by a given amount every month to offset her earlier overpayment. She also had to go to the courthouse once a month and pay ten dollars toward the money she owed the county. If she failed to make her payments, the court would lodge a felony fraud conviction against her.

Even after her involvement in the legal process and nearly a year of repayment, she did not truly understand that the penalties were her fault for failing to report her earnings on her monthly report and to submit her check stubs. She expressed her belief that what she had experienced was retaliation by ValueMart for quitting her job. She said, "It didn't matter to them until ValueMart told them I was working—'cause I quit. And it was after ValueMart reported to them that I had been working for them that . . . that's when they made a big fuss." Her lack of education or computer literacy made it difficult for her to comprehend the government's ability to track her earnings. It was difficult for Yvonne to play by the rules because the whole system seemed unfathomable to her.

In Bayview County during the period of data collection, fraud investigators received between 250 and 600 fraud investigation referrals for active cases each month. Between March 2000 and 2002, about sixty-five persons were convicted of fraud each month. During those months, another thirty to forty persons entered a fraud diversion program. Bayview County was one of only a handful of California counties to offer fraud diversion. At its peak, the county processed as many as 150 fraud diversion cases per month. Through welfare fraud diversion, those facing welfare fraud charges admitted to wrongdoing and established a repayment plan for the amount of money they owed the county. Those who completed the diversion program had their fraud charges dismissed. The diversion program in Bayview County was available only to welfare recipients who owed less than five thousand in cash and food stamp repayments; whose fraudulent behavior was limited to unreported earnings; and who had no prior criminal histories or welfare fraud charges.

The Bayview County fraud diversion program was designed, through the encouragement of the local legal aid office, to be a less punitive option for those welfare recipients who engaged in welfare fraud. It is unclear, however, that the system was in fact less punitive. The fraud diversion program seemed to create a more efficient way for prosecutors to bring charges against first-time criminals charged with welfare fraud. In addition, the county kept little account of the number of those individuals who went through fraud diversion and had the charges dismissed versus the number who, unable to make their required payments, had the charges lodged against them. In Bayview County in 2003, individuals had to show up once a week to make a nominal payment at a window in the courthouse with a sign that read "Welfare Fraud Payments."

A discussion I had with the county public defender in charge of welfare fraud cases revealed that because the state fraud statute on the books at the time included no language about intent, the defenders had not yet determined whether welfare fraud was a general-intent crime or a specific-intent crime under the existing statute (which has since been modified). While this is a technical distinction for criminal lawyers, the distinction is important in these cases: a valid mistake—a good-faith misunderstanding of the law—can serve as a defense for a specific-intent crime, though not for a general-intent crime. These misunderstandings, however, are determined by juries. Welfare fraud defense attorneys in Bayview County considered welfare recipients charged with fraud so unsympathetic to juries that they refused to take those cases to trial—even when there might have been a valid defense. Instead, the practice was to reach plea agreements on all welfare fraud cases.

The costs of policing and prosecuting welfare fraud are high, though largely unmeasured. When a welfare recipient is charged with fraud, she or he adds costs to the criminal justice system, including the labor costs of investigators, prosecutors, public defenders, judges, and probation officers. If the recipient is assigned to a welfare fraud diversion program, then the county bears continuing administrative costs for collecting payments and monitoring her progress. If the recipient is sent to jail or prison, costs soar. The state cost of incarcerating an individual is dramatically higher than supporting a family on welfare. And if children are placed in foster care because the sole parent is serving time for welfare fraud, more costs are added. All of these costs are ignored in calculations of the costs of investigating and prosecuting welfare fraud.

One factor contributing to the high volume of welfare fraud prosecutions during the period of data collection appears to be the financial incentives the state provided California counties that prosecuted welfare recipients for fraud. The 2002-3 California budget, however, cut $5.1 million CalWORKs Fraud Incentive payments that had been provided to counties (G. Davis 2002,

48). Bayview County responded by scaling back its Welfare Fraud Investigation Unit, suggesting that the prosecutions were fueled as much, if not more, by money than by a sense that they were fighting crime and securing justice. District attorneys around the state continually request increased spending on welfare fraud prosecution, arguing that by ending payments to those convicted and by making claims for overpayments, the state makes money. However, the savings in payments are often speculative, relying on the questionable assumption that welfare recipients will remain on aid while receiving a maximum grant. In addition, most of the overpayments (80 percent statewide, according to the Bayview County district attorney) are reclaimed from the payments that continue to children, not through actual payment by the welfare recipient. In other words, dollars recouped generally come from reductions in government aid to still-needy families.

There are a number of additional unmeasured costs of criminally punishing those who are caught cheating the welfare system. One of those costs is the costs to families. Low-income families that include an adult charged with welfare fraud not only lose access to government benefits but also gain an adult with decreased earning capacity due to the criminal prosecution. In Bayview County, where welfare fraud prosecution rates were unusually high for the state, the rate of foster care usage was also unusually high. It is unclear whether the two rates are related or coincidental, but it raises questions that the county might want to pursue.

A poignant example of the unmeasured costs of welfare fraud occurred in the case of Jerome, an interviewee caring for a toddler. The toddler's mother ended up spending a year in jail after her sister called the welfare fraud hotline and reported that Jerome was living in the household. The sister had hoped that officials would kick Jerome out of the house. Instead, they arrested and prosecuted his girlfriend, a mother with a young child. Jerome, who had been unemployed while staying with his son and girlfriend, could not find employment after she went to jail. While Jerome received a sanctioned aid check for his son, the family was ineligible for child care assistance because of the earlier deception to the welfare office. Jerome and his son were renting a small room from Jerome's ex-wife. The boy would spend a year without his mother because she had agreed to house the boy's unemployed father.

One of the difficulties in evaluating the success of punitive and criminalizing approaches to welfare is that the goals of these strategies are often unstated, multiple, and even contradictory. And even if deterring fraud is treated as the main goal, success in achieving that goal cannot be easily measured. As Professor Dan Kahan writes, "Empirically, deterrence claims are speculative" (1999, 416). Deterrence theory assumes that individuals can foresee the penalties of rule breaking. But as the interviews in this book have revealed, the harsh penalties for welfare cheating are largely unknown by welfare recipients. This cost-benefit system of deterrence cannot function where neither the rules nor the consequences of rule breaking are known by individuals. The system also cannot function where immediate needs actually do outweigh the risks of long-term suffering.

Even the assistant district attorney (ADA) who headed the welfare fraud investigation unit in Bayview questioned the rationality of some of the practices. When interviewed in March of 1999, the ADA said that the welfare fraud unit was filing about 100 to 110 felony welfare fraud cases a month. The ADA criticized the state standard for fraud, saying that "it targets the wrong people" and that the system "traps and punishes the least culpable culprits," that it was hardworking and financially strapped mothers who were hardest hit by these policies and practices.

The ADA said that while the fraud investigation unit pursued cases identified through computerized income matching, the office also pursued a lot of cases reported anonymously through the welfare fraud hotline. The hotline paved an arbitrary track to welfare investigations for many people. The hotline was apparently used by individuals in personal disputes: "No one can snitch you off like your ex or your ex's girlfriend or your neighbor or your landlord." At the time of our interview, the ADA said the investigators had three hundred to five hundred hotline tips backlogged for investigation. Hundreds of poor parents were awaiting an unpleasant surprise.

Why People Disobey the Law

Why do people not comply with the welfare laws? The interviews reveal that welfare recipients for the most part find it either difficult or impossible to comply fully with the complex rules regulating their lives. The rules themselves are out of sync with their everyday economic needs and their unstable lives. Many of the interviewees also found it impossible to comply with the welfare rules because they had only vague notions what the rules were and what the repercussions were for breaking the rules.

The basic instrumentalist approach, asking whether the welfare rules regulate what they were intended to regulate, would find that the rules were not functioning as intended. Some of the rules—the time limits on cash assistance and the family cap rules, for example—were not widely known and therefore could not be expected to have effects on behavior. The reporting rules, widely known though often misunderstood, upset many a family's already fragile economic well-being.

Other rules were confusing, even for welfare caseworkers. Tanya described how the welfare office gave conflicting information to welfare recipients about whether money they earned in student work-study positions should be counted as earned income or not. She said that she knew several welfare recipients who were students but whose current benefits, future benefits, and student status were jeopardized by tussles with the welfare office over overpayments claims. About the confusion Tanya said, "It seems like you don't know whether you're going to be breaking the rules next month if you're within the guidelines this month. You know, what's okay today may not be tomorrow."

To Tanya, the actions of the welfare office appeared arbitrary. She explained:

> Last year every month my income changed—it went up, it fluctuated $150 month to month. One month I didn't get anything because they were, um, they did recertification and somebody started to enter the information in the computer and stopped halfway through my name. And so they said my case is inactive. So I stormed in there and the guy pulled it up on the computer, he goes, "I want to show you this." He said, "Look at this! Some idiot." And he goes, "I apologize for this—entered half of your name, part of your address, and just wandered off to have a coffee break or something, you know." So he goes, "You'll have your food stamps in X number of days and we'll get on the ball with this." And I said, "I want food vouchers! I don't have anything!"

The mistakes on the part of the welfare office exacerbated Tanya's existing financial problems. She viewed the system as in many ways counterproductive: "It is very frustrating. And what's supposed to be cost-effective and efficient ends up being . . . least efficient and least cost-effective." In other words, the system lacked the formal rationality of an effective bureaucracy.

The widespread lack of understanding of the grant calculations based on earnings deterred compliance. The system thereby lacked the means-end rationality of deterring cheating. This irrationality occurred because the specific sanctions for breaking the rules were generally misunderstood and underpredicted, preventing them from having any intended deterrent effects. While the possible penalties for failing to report income were listed on each recipient's monthly reporting form, the statement of penalties was just a blur in the chaotic, paper-filled lives of these families.

Not only was there a dissonance between the rules, intended behavior, and ability to comply with the welfare system, but there was also a context of interaction where those who were subject to the rules could not gain complete knowledge of the rules. Welfare recipients avoided seeking clarification of the rules for fear they would tip off officials to what they either already knew to be or suspected to be their noncompliant behavior. Many welfare recipients were trying to make their way through the complex rules in a fog, a fog that was thicker for some than for others.

In this context, law's power to guide the behavior of most of the welfare recipients was elusive. Kiki, for example, repeatedly described herself as someone who complied with the rules, who turned in all of her documents and check stubs in a timely matter and received only one welfare check. At the same time, despite apparently living with her boyfriend, she described herself as "homeless" to the welfare department, ostensibly to (1) receive a small supplement in her cash aid designed for homeless families; (2) avoid reporting her boyfriend's income to the welfare office; and (3) qualify for housing aid in an area where market-rate apartments were beyond her reach. In addition, she was working, but not under the welfare-to-work agreement she had signed with the employment specialist in the welfare office. While Kiki's financial need kept her from being entirely truthful with the welfare office, it was also true that the welfare grant provided a less-than-substantial benefit to her. The less money she received from the welfare office, it seemed, the less obligated she felt to abide by every single rule.

Criminologists use the term *neutralization* (Sykes and Matza 1957) to describe lawbreakers' attempts to rationalize their rule breaking. Welfare recipients who did not report outside sources of income to the welfare office displayed neutralization techniques in describing their knowing failures to report income to the welfare office. Many of the justifications revolved around need. Tanya neutralized her intentional rule breaking and the rule breaking of others on the basis of need, stating:

I believe that *anybody* and darn near everybody, darn near, I won't say a blanket term—most all the women I know and people I know who are on, you know, disability and all kinds—they have to do something to survive. Because you can't do it, you just can't do it. And whether it's working under the counter or, you know, getting a little money from your baby's father or a relative, or working the flea market on the weekend, you know, going to garage sales and, and doing that turnaround thing. People do what they got to to survive.

Tanya and the other interviewees were aware that reporting their income might diminish their government cash aid; they just could not determine when and how.

Pam, a thirty-three-year-old mother of an eight-year-old, mentioned that a man who worked in a business near the welfare office offered to buy families' food stamps for cash. When I asked Pam if it was a problem that adults sold their food stamps, she first hesitated and then replied, "Some really need it, some just need something else. But if they really need it . . . no, they don't give you enough money to do anything, you know. Especially if you gotta go to get the, uh, something to clean your body with. You know? That's bad." Food stamps can be used only for food; many welfare recipients had trouble buying necessities such as hygiene products. For many families, abject physical need trumped rule compliance.

Welfare fraud investigations appeared to change an individual's engagement with the rules. Welfare recipients who had been investigated for welfare fraud (and approximately 20 percent of the California caseload was investigated for fraud each year during the years of this study) tended to make a transition from Misinformed to Informed, or at least Semi-informed, recipients. Those who had been investigated were somewhat more cynical about the system and more aware of the web of surveillance cast over their day-to-day lives. These individuals were conscious of the predicament in which they are caught.

"The system makes you cheat" was the very first comment from the first interviewee in this study. It came from Annette, a woman who took care of five children—three her own, one a relative, and another a foster child. She realized that with only a high school diploma, years away from the workforce, and poor reading skills, she had little chance of finding a job that would pay enough to support her family. She sporadically worked cleaning houses or doing hair. She did not report to the welfare office that she did hair, however, because she lacked a hairdresser's license and therefore feared reprisal. She did not report the little money she made cleaning houses because it was not routine; the earnings would have been discounted from her check in future months, and she never knew whether she would have the ability to absorb the future reduction in her welfare grant.

Annette had been threatened a few years earlier with a charge for welfare fraud for failing to report earnings from a single day's work. On the day at issue she had helped her mother's employer when the business had more work than the employees could handle. Annette had also recently had an unannounced visit from someone from the welfare office. The woman who showed up was unfamiliar with the card key system used on the apartments in Annette's building. According to Annette, "She said that I put a lock over my door knob, so I didn't live there." The confusion delayed Annette's check. As a result of those experiences, Annette constantly feared the authority of the welfare office. However, she believed she could not follow the rules and survive.

To compromise, she followed the rules as closely as she believed possible and did not ask questions of welfare workers. As a result of her reticence in the welfare office, however, she missed out on the education, training, and child care benefits designed to help women like her transition into sustainable employment. Annette was fully informed of law's threat and aware of the impossibility of complying with the law. As a result of her fraud investigation, her prior belief in the legitimacy of the rules was fraying.

In the context of welfare, there is a complex interplay between lawmakers' multiple intentions and the construction of legality and identity among welfare recipients. The welfare reform measures were designed not only to regulate and discipline welfare recipients but also to stigmatize welfare recipients—and especially welfare cheaters—as lazy, no-good parents and citizens. The gap between needs and resources—or more generally between the welfare rules and the lives of welfare recipients—poses the possibility of neutralizing welfare recipients' beliefs in the legitimacy of law. But this was for most of the respondents not the case. How, one may wonder, can legal subjects believe in a set of rules with which they cannot comply?

The interviews revealed that while these welfare recipients found it impossible to comply with the rules and most considered it impossible for anyone to follow the rules, many of the interviewees nonetheless believed that the work requirements, the time limits, the family caps, the extensive reporting rules, and the stiff penalties for breaking the rules were good, necessary, and legitimate. Pam—a mother who complained that she could not find a stable job with adequate pay and benefits, who thought it was ludicrous for the welfare office to ask women in homeless shelters to dress like business professionals for their CalWORKs orientation meetings, and who was both working janitorial jobs for cash and working an afternoon job at her child's school without reporting her earning in the hope of saving enough for a security deposit for an apartment—demonized other welfare recipients. She complained that most welfare recipients were "just sitting there on they ass and using that money" and should be cut off aid. She added, "They laying up having babies and they ain't helping nobody. Basically it's [the grant is] for the kids anyway. They giving that money away to the dope man. Sometime that dope man is at the check-cashing places." The abstract and stigmatized image of a welfare recipient was clearer to her than her lived experience as a welfare recipient.

For the most part, the interviewees invested legitimacy in the complex rules by citing the necessity to regulate "those women": in other words, by invoking the stereotype of the welfare queen, a symbol given additional force by the welfare reform rules. Thus respondents' positive self-identities and their grants of legitimacy to rules that they individually found unworkable were constantly being constructed in opposition to the stigmatizing forces of the rules.

For the Misinformed, in particular, there appeared to be a strong inter-action between welfare rules and their own identities, an interplay that had several effects. First, it produced a dynamic that reinforced law's hegemony. Even in the face of impossible rules, welfare recipients granted their legiti-macy to the system of rules in order to ally themselves with dominant social values and mainstream political symbols. Second, the legitimacy that welfare recipients themselves granted to the system stifled formal resistance—both individual and collective. Third, welfare recipients' beliefs that those who were charged with welfare fraud were bad mothers reinforced widespread political sentiment against those who were—and who would be—caught breaking the welfare rules.

Thus the neutralization in which the interviewees engaged and their jus-tifications for rule breaking were individual. Interviewees neutralized their own actions and the effects of their own actions. Many, however, did not view their own rule breaking as something that neutralized the power or the legitimacy of the welfare rules and regulations.

Interrogating Existing Notions of Resistance

While resistance has been a prominent theme in the legal consciousness lit-erature, notions of it have yet to be developed thoroughly. Legal conscious-ness scholars often view resistance as action. The idea of resistance needs to be expanded to include not only actions but also beliefs and identity. A few legal scholars have in passing noted that this type of resistance to law could reinforce law's hegemony, contributing to law's power (Ewick and Silbey 1998; McCann and March 1996). Clear examples of the reinforcing power of resistance, however, have been sorely lacking.

The reinforcing power of what the scholar John Gilliom (2001) would label resistance—earning money and not reporting it to the welfare office—was evident in my study on various levels. Welfare recipients' failures to follow the rules reinforced law's punitive power when those failures were discovered. High rates of sanctions for failures to comply with work requirements and high rates of income underreporting merely contributed to lawmakers' declarations that noncompliance was a rampant problem. In addition, welfare recipients' impressions that many welfare recipients cheated reinforced their views that constant and detailed reporting and intrusive investigations were necessary. Interviewees' actions and omissions contradicted law's authority in the immediate term but contributed to negative symbolic constructions of welfare recipients in the long run.

This study suggests that discussions of resistance should be careful to differentiate between actions and beliefs. While sociolegal scholars have analyzed welfare recipients' behaviors and attitudes in studies of resistance, their practice of treating welfare recipients as an undifferentiated group has impeded efforts to analyze resistance. The categories described in chapter 6, however, may prove helpful in analyzing different kinds of resistance and in questioning whether certain actions or beliefs should be labeled resistance at all. Among welfare recipients, actions that some would describe as resistance to formal rules are in many ways completely compliant with and consistent with pervasive legal symbols, specifically the symbols of the good worker and good mother. There is nothing *defiant* in feeding one's children, even when it requires skirting bureaucratic rules. Moreover, some of the "resistant" action evident in the study was done without conscious violation of the formal rules and regulations.

An example of the problems inherent in an undifferentiated notion of resistance can be shown in the cases of Shanelle and Lisa, two close friends who were knowledgeable about the welfare work requirements and the sanctions that would result from failing to fulfill the requirements. Shanelle had met her work participation requirements under CalWORKs the month before our interview, which allowed her to receive her full cash grant. Her compliance with the rules, however, demonstrated her financial need and her ability to fulfill the requirements with ease rather than her belief that complying with the work requirements was a good per se. In fact, Shanelle advocated defiance of the work requirements, stating: "If you got a job and you don't like it, don't do it. Get out of it, you know what I'm saying, don't do it just because they telling you they going to cut your checks. Don't do it, 'cause it don't make no sense. You're just wasting time." Shanelle's compliance did not flow from a belief that the rules themselves had a moral sway over her. It was simply that compliance proved uncomplicated for her.

On the other hand, Lisa's failure to complete her work requirements the previous month was not the result of a decision to defy the rules but the result of a need to stay with her sick child at the hospital. And Lisa accepted her sanction not because she believed the sanction fair but because she had no idea that an exception to the general rule existed and that an administrative appeal was available to her. Just as Shanelle's compliance grew from her understanding and ability to comply with the rules, Lisa's noncompliance grew out of her misunderstanding and inability to comply.

This suggests that sociolegal scholars should redefine risk and resistance as enterprises situated in a context—particularly in a context of rule knowledge. In this study, I found that those individuals most strongly resisting law's hegemony by questioning the legitimacy of the welfare rules and the criminal rules used to punish welfare cheaters were those who were in many ways *most* compliant with the formal rules. Among the Informed, rule knowledge, rule compliance, rule breaking, and rule stretching were consciously defiant. At the same time, the Informed successfully evaded the rules and the penalties for breaking the rules. Their actions created the least systemic resistance because, for the most part, these actions went unperceived by welfare officials.

Those welfare recipients who were supposedly resisting law's force by breaking the rules often had the least consciousness of their rule breaking. They violated the rules and requirements of welfare reform not out of defiance but rather out of financial need and ignorance of the formal rules. Moreover, they were the welfare recipients most invested in the legitimacy of the system.

The sociolegal scholar Austin Sarat acknowledges that legal consciousness may not be universally shared among the welfare poor, "that legal consciousness among people on welfare may be as internally divided and plural as it is different from the legal consciousness of other social groups" (1990, 348). This plurality was borne out in my interviews, as was polyvocality among individual interviewees, who could describe the welfare system as both arbitrary and senseless in one breath and fair and sensible in the next. Sarat defines resistance simply as "behavior or actions seen to be at odds with the expectation of those exercising power in a particular situation" (1990, 347 n.15). This definition of resistance, however, overlooks will, intent, agency, or defiance as aspects of resistance. Under Sarat's definition, unintentional and systemically unperceived rule breaking is no different from intentional manipulation or violation of the rules.

Michael McCann and Tracey March (1996) have criticized sociolegal scholars' tendency to engage in uncritical discussions of resistance and note that resistance can take many forms. They explain that many factors differentiate types of resistance: the success in obtaining immediate relief; the success in transforming an individual's general material situation; the ability of an oppressed member of society to make a positive transformation in his or her group's relationship with the dominant society; and the ability to mobilize collective resistance (McCann and March 1996, 221). What they do not note, however, is that intent should be a factor, since some of the rule breaking among welfare recipients is uninformed and unintentional. Welfare cheating's only positive effects are on individuals and their children. It does nothing to improve the status of the poor collectively in relationship to the nonpoor.

McCann and March criticize those who write about resistance for overemphasizing the "undramatic" by "mak[ing] the everyday almost heroic" and "impu[ting] political significance to near futile incidents of coping and surviving" (1996, 223). While the noncompliance of most welfare recipients holds little political significance for them, it does have political significance in that it reinforces the law's drive to catch and punish welfare cheating. It also reinforces legally and politically relevant symbols such as that of the welfare queen.

Patricia Ewick and Susan Silbey (1998), in addition to analyzing and critiquing the literature on resistance, describe some responses to law as *deflection*. As an example of deflection they discuss the actions of one of their research participants, Millie Simpson, who was ordered by a court to perform community service but who simply assigned her routine and ongoing volunteer work at her church as her community service time. Ewick and Silbey write that Simpson deflected law's power. They note, however, that "dodges, ruses, and feints such as these rarely leave a structural imprint" (13). Simpson may have evaded law's commands, but her resistance neither challenged nor changed the larger legal system. This deflection is akin what happened all the time among welfare recipients, particularly those most familiar with the rules. They knew they were breaking the rules and getting away with it. For most of the interviewees, however, the rule breaking offered little personal empowerment.

An example: in baking and selling cupcakes to generate extra unreported income, Tammy successfully dodged the welfare system's reporting requirements, licensing requirements for food vendors, and the tax system's income-reporting requirements. She was pleased that her under-the-table employment allowed her to buy a car. Nevertheless, she feared the consequences of her actions should the welfare office ever find out. In other words, it was an incomplete ruse. Her actions, rather than rendering the welfare system impotent, left her feeling especially vulnerable to law's power. She perceived herself just as much a weak subject who stood *before the law* as she would have been without her cupcake sales.

In addition, many interviewees were violating the rules and mandates of welfare reform unknowingly. Previous studies of welfare recipients have generally excluded the group described above as the Preoccupied and Disengaged. What little discussion of these socially and economically marginal women exists has often speculated on the lives of these women rather than relying on the personal accounts of the women themselves or on direct observation. Kay Levine and Virginia Mellema (2001), for example, have critiqued Ewick and Silbey, arguing that not all types of social action occur with/before/ or against the law, as Ewick and Silbey have asserted. To support their position, Levine and Mellema point to the lives and actions of "street women," whose actions often run afoul of the law and who are in no position to call upon or mobilize the law for their own benefit. For the truly disenfranchised, Levine and Mellema argue, law is simply not "salient." Street women lack legal consciousness, they say, because they do not initiate engagement with the law.

This argument, however, misunderstands legal consciousness, or legality, in the way that Ewick and Silbey use the notions. Avoiding interactions with formal rules of legal institutions does not render law and legal understandings irrelevant to the everyday lives of marginalized people. Individuals who misunderstand the legal rules, who break the rules, or who fail to call upon legal resources are nonetheless living within a broader legal culture. They live with a given—and limited—set of legal resources, definitions, and concepts. In fact, even while dodging the rules or deviating from the rules, individuals may share the understandings that keep those rules in place.

Moreover, not all actions that are done in disregard of the law lie "outside" law and legal culture. In fact, they are often the very effects of law and legal culture. Women who have used government aid programs; who have been involved in domestic violence; who have given birth to and raised children without private medical insurance; who have been convicted of a crime or whose partners have been convicted of crimes; who have so much as faced an inquiry from Child Protective Services; who have been evicted and homeless—all have had their lives shaped by both law's action and law's inaction. Law is relevant even where it is not straightforwardly (or perceptively) directing individual behavior. For those who live at the margins of society, law's social control mechanisms have often played a crucial role in herding them to the margins.

Certainly the women described above as the Preoccupied and Disengaged bear a strong resemblance to the women Levine and Mellema describe as street women. These women were homeless or, in the best cases, temporarily sheltered; they had substance abuse problems; they "hustled" to survive; they were likely to have already lost children to the foster care system and faced a strong possibility of losing the children in their care. Law and legal institutions were ever salient for these women on a daily basis. Whether they were trying to find housing subsidies, trying to requalify for cash aid, or avoiding the police and Child Protective Services while hustling to pay for a hotel room to shelter their children, they were engaged in a constant tango with legal rules and legal sanctions.

The concept of resistance has been discussed and analyzed too generally, too uncritically. Without question, state power faces resistance in the practices of those who are subject to its power. Not all actors, however, resist that power with knowledge and intent. Not all actors resist in ways that have transformative effects on law. In parsing out different types of resistance and the multiple effects they may have on law's hegemony, scholars should start examining knowledge, will, intent, and effect as relevant—and separate— aspects of resistance. These are aspects most certainly relevant to the potential for political mobilization and for the empowerment of legal subjects.

The Limited Potential for Political Resistance by Welfare Recipients

John Gilliom, in his study of welfare recipients (2001), concluded that welfare recipients' reliance on language akin to that used in the legal realm of privacy rights holds the potential to become the catalyst of political mobilization. My analysis suggests this is not the case. Much of my disagreement goes back to the relative resources, political clout, and views of law's legitimacy held by each of the three categories of welfare recipients—the Informed, the Misinformed, and the Preoccupied/Disengaged. Even when these groups of individuals are examined separately, it is clear that not one holds the potential to bring about political transformation—at least not political transformation that will improve their daily lives or their power under the law.

The Informed interviewees hold the greatest potential for political mobilization. Their explanations for their poverty extended beyond their individual circumstances or actions. Jane, for example, offered a class-based political critique of welfare policies: "I'm a conspiracist. I think there's a conspiracy, because there's not enough room at the top, they gotta hold us down. And, um, the gap is getting bigger between rich and poor. No more middle class."

Lisa and Shanelle offered their theory that the welfare system was created as a system to keep African Americans quiet, specifically quiet about any demands to claim their "forty acres and a mule." While some of the individuals who were informed and critical of the rules overstepped them, they were also the group that would face the most political resistance if they did begin to mobilize. The public would likely view them as manipulating a system they did not necessarily need and as scoffing at legal mandates.

Tanya, for example, had been politically active in the Indian rights movement before she applied for welfare and appeared to carry that critical awareness and experience to her views of and experiences with the welfare system. Still, she attributed her expanding political critique of the welfare system to the system itself.

> I never viewed the aid that I got as a right. I always somehow felt that . . .
> I felt a degree of guilt because you know I had a lot of input from people,
> you know, the issue of nonproductivity and autonomy. But, um, it definitely has more of a Big Brother feel to it now. You know?

Tanya said that welfare reform had transformed her view of welfare: "the changes that have made me—*really* made me—look at the issues of how our government views or values motherhood. Or childhood even. And, you know, how little they value it." Unlike most of the interviewees, Tanya voted, explaining that she had voted for the Green Party candidate rather than Bill Clinton in the 1996 presidential election. The high levels of political awareness and participation of the Informed recipients, were, however, the exception rather than the rule. Most of the welfare recipients interviewed—the Misinformed and the Preoccupied/Disengaged—paid little or no attention to politics and rarely invoked the language of rights in their discussions.

In many ways, the Informed were those with the greatest potential for political mobilization. They tended to be better educated than other welfare recipients and to have stronger social networks, better communication skills, and better access to resources. At the same time, they were also the group that would face the most political resistance. Since they were the most privileged group of welfare recipients and the individuals savviest about skirting the rules and using the rules for their own benefit, the public would likely view them as manipulating and milking a system they might not desperately need. Their income-maximizing efforts evoked the hyper-rational aspect of the welfare queen, the image of someone trying to "get over" on the welfare system.

In addition, as the most privileged group of welfare recipients, the Informed tended not to know or associate with other welfare recipients. On the social level, they affiliated with people who were part of the economic mainstream. They were not leading their fellow poor. Their potential for engaging in collective political mobilization around welfare issues was therefore quite limited.

The Misinformed were situated as those with the most potential to mobilize public sentiment in their favor. They generally considered work requirements a good idea, and many were trying to comply with the requirements. When they were unable to comply, it was often out of the difficulty of doing so, not out of defiance. Their economic coping strategies, which may seem like resistance because they violated the rules, were sometimes done without knowledge and sometimes done purely out of need. Many, such as Veronica—a working mother caring for a large group of children but still unable to afford laundry detergent—offered sympathetic views of life on welfare. At the same time, the Misinformed were the group most invested in the system, in distancing themselves from the stigma associated with welfare receipt. Their noncompliance with the rules had no effect on the political commands of the state, did not spur them to view themselves as marginalized and stigmatized members of the populace, and did not prompt them toward political action.

In addition, the Misinformed recipients were easily transformed into criminal welfare queens. Their lack of detailed knowledge of welfare rules, surveillance techniques, and the consequences of rule breaking made them the group of welfare recipients most likely to be hit with welfare fraud charges. The Misinformed recipients did not resist the welfare system in any way that would question or disrupt the system's power over them; instead, they neutralized their own actions within the welfare system and continued to invest their beliefs in the legitimacy of both the punitive rules and the negative condensation symbols that justified the punitive system. The system itself went without transformation.

Most interviewees lacked the time and resources to engage in political mobilization. This was particularly true for the Preoccupied/Disengaged recipients. Even if they were to mobilize, they would likely face social and political stigma as a result of their economic coping strategies and life circumstances. Commonly homeless, persistently jobless, and frequently toothless, they were unlikely to draw the sympathy of those who had the power to enact systemic change but who would be easily put off by social and economic deviance. The Preoccupied recipients, who suffered the most severe deprivations of financial resources, were also the poorest prospects for mobilization.

Gilliom writes that as "the poor continue their poaching in the face of a massive governmental effort to detect and stop them, they are rejecting and challenging, often by evasion, the political commands of the state" (2001, 100). Not true. In their poaching, the poor are submitting to the commands of the state to fend for themselves. The great number of welfare recipients who are not working, the high sanction rates, and the number of welfare recipients charged with welfare fraud simply reinforce the cultural symbol—the welfare queen—and the discourses of crime and criminology that fostered difficult and punitive welfare rules in the first place.

Power and Resistance Reconsidered

Legal consciousness scholars sometimes refer to Michel Foucault's description of the "capillary functions of power" (1979, 198), which holds that power flows everywhere in the social organism, moving from and through both institutions on the macro level and bodies on the micro level. Power is fluid and ever-shifting. Moreover, it is not only repressive but also productive and constantly resisted (Foucault 1990, 95-98). In the context of welfare, instead of using water or blood as metaphors of law's power, it might be more apt to use electricity. A certain level of resistance is created whenever electricity flows through a medium, though different substances produce different levels of resistance. Some substances conduct electricity, while others are insulators, impermeable to electrical force. While electricity may be present, it may have more or less effect on its targets or media. Similarly, welfare laws that are punitive and that heavily regulate daily life are conducted toward and through the welfare population with different types and levels of resistance.

Some members of the welfare population, attuned to the impossibilities of full compliance with rules and mandates, insulate themselves from law's normative authority by adopting their own moral frameworks to distinguish acceptable rule violations from impermissible cheating. Still, those who insulate themselves from law's repressive power seldom offer resistance that will transform policies and procedures, much less challenge dominant ideologies. Other welfare recipients—even those who get caught in the welfare system's punitive policies—may conduct law's power and symbols, channeling the understandings that have produced the criminalization of poverty.

Various strains of power flow through the lives of welfare recipients: the policing power of welfare regulations; the repressive power of the criminal justice system; powerful ideologies such as neoliberalism; and the driving power of condensation symbols such as the welfare queen. To describe welfare recipients' relationships to these flows of power or their reactions to the criminalization of poverty as univocal or as simple would be deceptive. The welfare recipients in this study described various relationships with welfare law: as repressed and silenced objects of domination; as citizens politically empowered by the challenges they had withstood; as agents of micro-level resistance; and as individuals constructing complex ideas of themselves and others in relationship to the law.

Most notable was that many of the interviewees recognized the welfare queen as a condensation symbol that had some hold over their lives. They acknowledged the stereotype and recognized themselves as objects of its stigma. Sometimes they recognized that their conduct fit within the stereotype. Sometimes they challenged the stereotype. More frequently, they simply deflected its power in constructing their own identities. They often redeployed the stereotype in discussing the welfare system, the welfare rules, and other recipients. This study emphasizes that welfare law has been constructed, recreated, and transformed—at the level of politics and at the level of individual identity formation—not only through the beliefs and actions of elite policy makers but also through the actions and understandings of welfare recipients themselves.

Much of the work on welfare law simply examines policy changes and their effects. There is value, however, in examining individuals' relationships to law. Some of the recent critical work on welfare focuses on the state and state power, particularly on the growth of the repressive power of the state in policing the poor. Loïc Wacquant, for example, traces the rise of neoliberalism and the attendant withering of the welfare state and dramatic expansion of the penal state (2009b, 2001). He describes how the welfare policies in place in the United States discipline the poor, quell their political capacity, and express the demands of the neoliberal state (2009b). Others, rejecting state-centered analyses of the state, have examined the ways that power has influenced micro-level practices and beliefs and have traced the downward flow of power to the point where it permeates the knowledge and daily actions of individuals. Barbara Cruikshank, in her analysis of welfare and welfare cheating, employs Foucauldian notions of governance, examining "the ways we act upon ourselves" and the ways that power manifests itself without state exercise (1999, 4). Both of these approaches—the state centered and the individual focused—are useful; rather than treating them as unrelated, theory would grow stronger by treating them as complementary perspectives in shaping our understandings of welfare law. Indeed, understanding law means understanding the constant interplay among state practices, cultural understandings, and constructions of the self.

8

Cheating Ourselves

Cheating the Rule(s) of Law

Four decades ago, Lon Fuller wrote a book titled *The Morality of Law* that articulated a set of principles he considered essential to law's inner morality. Fuller wrote that for legality to exist—in other words, for both the legal system and legal rules to be considered legitimate—law must meet certain indispensable requirements. Fuller's work (1969, 39) describes eight failings that may undermine a legal system. These are as follows:

1. Failure to achieve rules at all
2. Failure to publicize rules, or at least to make available to the affected party the rules he is expected to observe
3. The abuse of retroactive legislation
4. Failure to make rules understandable
5. The enactment of contradictory rules
6. Rules that require conduct beyond the powers of the affected party
7. Introducing such frequent changes in the rules that the subject cannot orient his action by them
8. Failure of congruence between the rules as announced and their actual administration

While stated in the negative, Fuller's principles stress a number of basic assumptions about how law should work. In general, they require that rules make sense to the individuals who are subject to those rules. Specifically, they require that a system of rules is fully understood and consistently applied; that people subject to those rules know of them; that it is possible for individuals subject to the rule to comply with them; and that it is possible to follow a rule without breaking another rule.

While these essentials of legality may seem rather abstract, they are seldom put to the test in a grounded study. Analyzing each of these requirements reveals a welfare system that undermines rather than promotes legality. First, this study revealed that rules were not known. The Bayview County welfare office failed to achieve rules, publicize rules, or make them understandable to welfare recipients. All but a few of the interviewees lacked basic knowledge of or misunderstood many, if not all, of the key components of the 1996 welfare reforms. Obtaining information from welfare caseworkers was difficult during mass recipient intake meetings. Many recipients had no assigned caseworkers and had difficulty accessing anyone in the office who could or would answer questions. Interviewees also reported receiving wrong information about the rules and requirements from welfare officials. As a result of all this, recipients commonly conferred with misinformed friends or family members to obtain information about welfare rules, leaving some of the individuals with the strongest social networks the ones least informed about the rules. In addition, interviewees feared seeking clarification of the rules, concerned that asking questions about rules would draw official attention to their cases and reveal hidden flows of income or other problems.

There was a gap between the rules as they were announced and their actual administration. The "carrots" implemented under the welfare reforms—work supports, transportation assistance, child care assistance, and transitional support programs to help low-income parents transition from welfare to work—could not serve as incentives because they were largely unknown to welfare recipients or unavailable or too burdensome to obtain when they were available. The reformed welfare system also proved inconsistent. The system was supposed to create a system of mutual obligation between the welfare system and the welfare recipient. The obligations, however, were for the most part one-sided. Welfare recipients were required to work, to report their sources of income, and to meet a host of other stipulations. Frequently, though, interviewees reported submitting their paperwork only to have it lost. Many were not receiving the work supports, training opportunities, and ancillary benefits the county welfare office was supposed to make available to CalWORKs participants. In other words, the welfare recipients were often held to their obligations to the welfare system, while the welfare system failed to meet its obligations to the poor.

Some of the elements of federal welfare reform contradicted each other. While the system was designed to encourage economic self-sufficiency, the work-first policies pushed several interviewees out of the educational programs that would have given them the skills to become more financially secure. Without the degrees, they could not find work. Similarly, while the welfare legislation's stated goal was to create strong families, many families were strained by the rules. Mothers left their children home alone at night to fulfill their mandatory work hours. Welfare fraud convictions caused families to unravel.

It was difficult for many of the interviewees to comply with all of the rules and regulations because their day-to-day financial and family needs either prevented them or discouraged them from complying with the rules. In the end, the interviewees could not orient their actions to the welfare rules— or at least to the welfare rules alone. The Informed responded by flouting the rules; the Misinformed responded by following the rules, or what they believed were the rules, as best they could; the Preoccupied, distracted by the chaos of their lives, were oblivious to the rules. For the most part, the welfare recipients interviewed embraced and engaged with the dominant moral beliefs about the importance of law and the need to follow rules.

Furthermore, the get-tough penalties for welfare cheating, which have shifted penalties from the welfare system to the criminal justice system, could not deter rule breaking, since the penalties were not clear to those subject to them. The consequences of rule breaking were either unknown or underestimated, thereby masking the risks and costs of rule violation. For some rule violations, the actual costs were quite high. But these costs, and the many deterrent mechanisms designed to discourage both welfare use and welfare cheating, went largely unknown among welfare recipients. Welfare recipients had to make big decisions—about wage earning, about side jobs, about staying with their children, about staying with their lovers—amid a cloud of fuzzy rules, of foggy costs and benefits. Those who were the most confused ended up the worst off in the welfare system. As Shanelle said during her interview, "It's not that I'm welfare bashing or anything like that, but it's like the rules, the rules don't apply to everybody the same."

One might suppose that these frailties in the formal rules of the welfare system would jeopardize its legality in the consciousness of welfare recipients. For many, however, that was not the case. The Misinformed and the Preoccupied/Disengaged assumed that there must be more order to the welfare system than they could perceive. The interviews highlight that popular beliefs about the legitimacy of the welfare system, even where the system is based on a flawed set of rules, can militate against the collapse, or even questioning, of the system. The widespread beliefs among interviewees that welfare reform was working, and specifically that it was working to keep welfare queens in check, bolstered their faith in the reformed welfare system even when they could not meet its demands. The power of welfare law flowed from the power of condensation symbols to order beliefs about right and wrong, even in the face of lived experience to the contrary.

The welfare recipients interviewed hardly demonstrated the qualities for which welfare recipients are so often criticized: laziness and greed. Most of them worked hard, often at multiple jobs, put the essential needs of their children first, and generally lived lives without luxuries. Most of the interviewees aligned themselves with mainstream morality. What set them apart from the mainstream was that they were poor.

If we are going to create a system of welfare rules that adhere to basic principles of legality, we need to make sure that the rules are not contradictory or too complicated, that they are effectively communicated to the public, and that they can be followed. These are the basics of procedurally fair and just welfare laws.

Cheating Taxpayers

The welfare system and those who fall under its rules are increasingly governed by the logics of criminal law and increasingly entangled in the criminal justice system. Nonetheless, the costs of certain policies and procedures frequently go unmeasured by the government. For those people who measure the effectiveness of state policies by the measurable returns on their tax dollars, this should be of concern. Failure to note the increasingly blurry boundaries between the welfare system, the criminal justice system, and the foster care system—and failure to measure the costs that are increasingly transferred from one system to the other—means that the larger economic realities of welfare are being ignored. A lot of resources are now devoted to investigating welfare fraud. In 2008, the state of California spent $34 million investigating ongoing fraud in CalWORKs cases. For all that money spent on investigations, the state identified overpayments of only $19.6 million (California State Auditor 2009, 22). Perhaps it is time to take a closer look at how tax dollars devoted to "welfare" are being spent.

There are still other unmeasured costs to welfare fraud prosecution. When a welfare recipient is charged with fraud, she adds costs to the criminal justice system. In addition to the costs of investigation, the county has to pay for the time of both a prosecutor and a public defender. If the recipient goes through a welfare fraud diversion program, the county bears continuing administrative costs for collecting payments and monitoring her progress in the diversion program. If the welfare recipient is convicted and sent to jail or prison, then government costs soar. It is much more expensive to house a single inmate for a year than it is to provide for a typical family on welfare. If the head of a household does end up serving time in jail or prison, her children may be placed in the foster care system, where more money will be spent on the children than under the welfare system. All of these costs are ignored in calculations of the costs of investigating and prosecuting welfare fraud. In sum, the government cost savings that policy makers associate with punitive and criminalizing welfare policies may actually only be cost shifting—either between federal, state, and local coffers or from the welfare system to the criminal justice and foster care systems.

The broader social costs of the criminalization of poverty—for example, the effects on family life and communities—have similarly been underexamined. Fiscal studies fail to measure costs associated with increasing the number of parents in the criminal justice system, costs to state and local governments of policing the poor, and the long-term costs of stigmatizing public assistance and allowing poverty to go unalleviated. While this study cannot quantify most of these unmeasured costs of welfare rules and regulations, it may suggest some of the areas where some of the extra costs may be going unnoticed. Evaluators should develop a holistic accounting method that examines both cost shifting and the human costs of criminalization.

Cheating Social Science

The ethics of policy implementation and social scientific research is rarely discussed, but that discussion is desperately needed. This study suggests that those who design and implement policy and those who measure the effects of policies should take great care when it comes to rules. For rules to have an effect on action, they must be known by the actors. For the interviewees, rule knowledge was a huge barrier to informed decision making and to compliance with the mandates of the welfare system. Complicated rules, frequent changes in the rules, and failures to communicate rules and penalties to welfare recipients have produced an ineffective system of incentives and disincentives. Researchers must assess rule knowledge when evaluating policies.

There are other warnings good researchers might heed. First, social scientists and policy makers should be reluctant to initiate or endorse policy changes that negatively affect welfare recipients simply for the sake of behavioral or economic experimentation. The conflation of policy goals informed by ideology with policy goals informed by heedless social scientific zeal has become problematic in welfare reform programs. Cutting benefits or stiffening rules to see what happens ignores the material and psychological effects on families. Second, much of the recent welfare research draws upon the databases of state agencies and can at best reveal correlations between variables. As other scholars have noted, many of these studies cannot resolve the more important issue, causality (Brady, Nicosia, and Seto 2002). It is not enough for researchers to document that poor people are doing something or experiencing something and to offer speculations about the reasons; they must do more to explain *why*.

Third, researchers should be careful to engage in ethical research. The limited qualitative research that specifically focuses on welfare recipients' compliance with welfare rules raises serious ethical concerns. The only published qualitative research with its central question revolving around the issue of welfare rule compliance has been sponsored by government agencies that police such behavior. A study of welfare fraud rates conducted in Orange County, California, measured fraud by staking out the houses of a random sample of 450 welfare recipients (California Department of Social Services 1997). Research investigators examined whether there were regular members of the household whom recipients had not reported to the welfare office, whether there were signs of additional sources of income, and whether welfare recipients left their houses at regular times, suggesting unreported employment.

Such research methods raise a number of ethical concerns. First, the research subjects were not aware of the investigations and certainly did not provide their informed consent to participate in the research. Second, the research not only posed the risk of harm but actually harmed the research subjects. Welfare recipients who were found to be breaking the rules were cut off welfare or pursued by the district attorney with criminal fraud charges (California Department of Social Services 1997, 2-3). Third, the research methods were ostensibly quite intrusive, infringing on the private realms of home and family. In addition to these ethically questionable tactics, the value of the research findings appears limited. While the Orange County study found fraud in 45 percent of the cases (1997, 2), the study did nothing to explain the reasons why some welfare recipients break rules and why others do not. And by no means did the study explore whether welfare recipients knew and understood the rules that applied to them or whether they understood the consequences of breaking the rules, two critical requirements of a moral law. Such studies, offering heavy risks to research subjects and limited knowledge value, should not be conducted.

Welfare is an interesting topic for social scientists. But curiosity and available research funding should not drive social scientists to breach ethical protocols, to let funders determine the research questions and research findings, or to engage in insubstantial research. This is not to say that research about welfare should cease. Indeed, more research is needed on poverty and on the convergence of the criminal justice system and the welfare system. The sociologist Loïc Wacquant warns researchers to use caution in our rhetoric and in our policy recommendations so that we are not uncritically contributing to the expansion of the penalization of poverty (2001, 410). Researchers should approach their work with care, attentive to the interests served by their findings and aware of the discursive and political implications of their research.

Cheating Welfare

The American public has invested heavily in the creation of a new welfare system, as well as in the perpetuation of the symbol of the welfare queen. We have developed a culture that stigmatizes, even criminalizes, the poor. We have instituted public benefits programs that do not lift people out of poverty or even ease the experience of poverty. We have created complex and contradictory rules that criminalize the poor. We have not, however, considered how those who are the objects of this state power experience criminalization. Nor have we asked how they describe their own experiences, their views on law, their perceptions of agency, and their own identities.

This study has revealed that welfare recipients possess little knowledge of the welfare system and that their ignorance often comes at a high cost. Both the general public and policy makers have ignored the realities of the daily lives of welfare recipients and their difficulties negotiating their way through, and out of, the welfare system. My hope is that this book might move readers who have so far been misinformed, preoccupied, or disengaged to become informed and engaged about welfare policy and the experiences of low-income families.

This book has attempted to highlight some of the problems associated with the criminalization of poverty. At the same time, I do not want to leave the reader with the impression that simple reforms of policy or procedure would offer grand solutions. The criminalization of poverty—the notion that the poor are latent criminals and that anyone seeking government assistance should be treated as a criminal—serves as a distraction from the underlying issue: poverty. The criminalization of poverty simply describes the institutionalization of ideologies of neoliberalism, racism, sexism, and the dehumanization of the poor. In many ways, the policy goals of punishing non-working welfare recipients, welfare cheats, and aid recipients who engage in unrelated crimes has diverted public attention away from poverty and from the nearly forgotten policy goals of protecting low-income adults and children from the effects of economic instability.

At the time of this writing, the economy is in crisis and the welfare caseloads are growing. We have created a society where families, particularly lower-income families, bear a disproportionate share of economic risk and where limited government resources are devoted to their material welfare. Many people who thought they were financially secure have sadly discovered that they were not clear on all of the rules, that they may have misjudged economic risks. My hope is that we will return to a discussion of welfare—not just welfare policies (though that might be a good idea)—but a deeper discussion of how we protect the general welfare.

Appendix A: Critical Methodology

My Approach

The core of my research involved interviews with welfare recipients, individuals who must negotiate compliance with increasingly complex welfare regulations. My data collection was limited to one county in Northern California, a county I call Bayview. Bayview County was an attractive research site because of its size, racial and ethnic diversity, and its coverage of both urban and rural areas, and because other researchers have conducted welfare research in the county, allowing me to draw upon existing studies. Studying the policies in only one county allows me to control for policy variations that may occur from county to county.

While limiting the scope of research to one county may limit some of the findings, the general nature of the questions I asked and the similarities of welfare policies and practices across both the state and the country allow reasonable generalizations about many of my findings. Rules, regulations, and their enforcement all vary from county to county. Limiting the interviews to welfare recipients in only one county is most likely to hinder the generalizability of the interviewees' responses about rule knowledge. It is likely that welfare recipients' access to institutional sources of information varies from locale to locale, as office practices and caseloads vary from county to county. Still, the degree to which welfare recipients obtain information from unofficial sources may or may not vary across counties or sites. More importantly, examining the degree to which welfare recipients skirt the rules and their perceptions of the welfare system's legality offers revelations of until-now-hidden behaviors and beliefs.

I began recruiting and interviewing welfare recipients in November 1998 and conducted the final interview in April of 2002. This meant that all the interviews occurred between the time the CalWORKs program was instituted in the county and December 31, 2002, the day that the sixty-month lifetime welfare limit was reached for California families who had been receiving welfare since the beginning of my study. The welfare recipients I interviewed were recipients of TANF and were the heads of household in an aid unit. Not all of the interviewees, however, received cash assistance themselves. Some either were having their cash grant sanctioned at the time of the interview or were excluded from the aid unit. Welfare time limits and work requirements were inapplicable to the excluded cases where only the child or children received aid. Still, all of the interviewees were responsible for compliance with the other welfare rules, including the reporting rules. Moreover, while some of the adults were excluded from the aid calculations done by the welfare office, they all shared the collective income resources with the other members of their households.

With the consent of the research participants, I audiotaped the interviews. (Only one interviewee, Carmen, wished not to be recorded. I took notes by hand during her interview.) After each interview, I either wrote or recorded additional notes or observations about the interview and the interviewee. I also discarded any contact information I had for the interviewee and changed his or her name in my notes. I transcribed the recorded interviews, a time-consuming (and for the half I had professionally transcribed, expensive) endeavor that allowed me to more thoroughly and accurately review and analyze the interviews.

I followed each interview with a debriefing, explaining to the participants that I was most interested in their knowledge and assessment of the welfare rules. I carried with me a list of legal and community service referrals and, after the interview, provided research participants with appropriate contact information based on information they shared with me during the interview.

The interviews with the welfare recipients generally lasted one to two hours. Most of the interviews occurred in the back corners of restaurants or cafes, though I interviewed four of the participants in their homes. (I interviewed Lisa and Shanelle, who were best friends, in Lisa's house.) I interviewed one participant, Viola, in a conference room at her drug treatment program.

The interviews were semistructured and covered welfare recipients' knowledge of the rules and of the sanctions for violating the rules and requirements; their means of support and household composition (both reported and unreported); their socioeconomic, educational, and work histories; their experiences with the welfare office and with its fraud and error control measures; and their attitudes about the welfare rules, the welfare system, and other welfare recipients (see the Interview Schedule, Appendix B). I asked probing questions about sources of income and ways of making ends meet when the money got tight. I asked follow-up questions to find out if they knew that some of the things they were doing were against the rules and how they regarded their actions that fell outside the rules. I also asked what they thought about people who broke the rules; whether they thought the work requirements, time limits, and reporting requirements were fair; and what changes, if any, they would make to the welfare system if they could.

Much of the information the participants shared with me would be impossible to obtain through administrative data and difficult to obtain in a survey. I asked participants what they might have considered sensitive, personal questions. In addition, I often asked them about hidden practices that they may not have wanted others, especially welfare officials, to know. Certainly, the strength of my data and conclusions relied upon my ability to obtain revealing information from the participants in my research. I describe some of my experiences with the interviewing process below.

While some of the interview questions involve theory testing—for example, testing the assumption that welfare recipients possess accurate knowledge of the rules and the consequences for breaking them—many of the questions and the study as a whole are designed to peek into dark, unexplored crevices, to generate rather than test theories.

Gaining Access

This description of my methodology differs in one significant way from many of the social scientific and legal texts written about welfare in that much of this section is written in the first person. My choosing to write in this voice is no error or oversight but rather a deliberate decision to reveal the research process. That process involves a continual back-and-forth between honing the research questions, developing the appropriate methods, and, in response to everyday practicalities and new revelations, readjusting both. The criticism and danger I face in rendering the research process transparent is exposure of the problems I encountered and therefore the weaknesses in the research. However, every researcher faces similar problems, whether she or he chooses to reveal them or not. I hope that by revealing the problems I can make the efforts of other researchers easier.

I had originally hoped to solicit a random sample of welfare recipients in my research county by letter. I thought this would allow me to reach more reliable general conclusions about welfare recipients in my research county. I drafted a proposal to the county welfare department in 1997, requesting minimal contact information for three large samples (one thousand households) of welfare recipients, with the samples drawn in different quarters of the year. I requested that administrators destroy the samples after providing them to me. From these samples, I hoped to subsample one hundred cases, making it virtually impossible for the administrators to trace who my sampled research participants would be.

Shortly after I submitted the proposal, the county and the state both drafted new policies about providing identifying information about welfare recipients to researchers. These county and state policies were ambiguous and, in some ways, contradictory. As a result, officials were hesitant to release the samples, though they admitted that doing so would have been simple. After more than seven months of discussions with county officials, I realized that this sampling technique was not going to occur. (Admittedly, I had anticipated a very low response rate by writing solicitation letters to welfare recipients.) I ultimately tried another strategy.

The strategy had two parts. First, I contacted and left recruiting leaflets at legal aid and welfare rights organizations in the county in an effort to contact welfare recipients who might be more "rights conscious" than the average welfare recipient. Through this method I located only two participants—Jane and Tanya. Second, I recruited participants by approaching individuals who were exiting the primary county welfare office. I parked myself on the sidewalk outside the offices and did my best to approach every adult who left the office. To protect participants from possible embarrassment, I did not approach individuals if others were within earshot. After catching individuals' attention, I stated that I was a researcher from the nearby university and was conducting a study of people's experiences with the welfare system. I explained that participation involved an interview of approximately an hour and a half and that the interview would be scheduled at a convenient time and place.

When recruits expressed interest in participating, I assured them that I was not employed by or otherwise affiliated with the welfare office. I explained that there were two requirements to participation—current receipt of welfare benefits and an age of eighteen or older. Because my interview questions concerned familiarity with welfare rules, and because I did not want to contaminate the responses I received, I did not tell participants before the interviews began that my research particularly focused on welfare rule knowledge and compliance.

Participants usually set up a meeting time on the spot, though a couple asked me to call them at home so that they could coordinate their schedules or check their calendars. I told participants that my questions addressed sensitive personal information, specifically questions about money and questions about problems they might have experienced with the welfare system. I also told them that I was interested in facts that the welfare office might not know and that I was taking measures to minimize the risk of the welfare office finding out any of this information. I informed participants that their participation was completely voluntary and that their consent could be withdrawn at any time.

The Interviews, Trust, and the Presentation of Self

At the 1998 American Sociological Association Meeting, I discussed my early thoughts on this research project with a social scientist who had related research interests. She warned me that I would have a lot of trouble gaining trust and getting people to reveal honest information. My experience working with welfare recipients was quite the contrary. Not only did people tell me things about themselves that were not particularly admirable, they also commonly shared much more information than I wanted to know.

I have come to realize that I was not only studying rule breaking but also engaging in a sort of rule breaking in the course of research. In doing the type of qualitative research that I did, I violated social scientific norms about who does research, guidelines about researcher neutrality, social expectations of fixed social status, and everyday norms that caution people against asking personal questions. Failing to acknowledge these violations would, I believe, give an air of dishonesty to my data presentation and analysis.

The very fact that I was a graduate student surprised many of my research participants. For the record, I am an African American woman who uses a wheelchair. At the time I began recruiting research participants, I was visibly pregnant. For the first six months after my daughter's birth, I toted her along with me both when recruiting research participants and when conducting interviews. As a researcher, I was engaged in an unusual and ambiguous status relationship with my research subjects.

The renowned sociologist Erving Goffman described status as "a pattern of appropriate conduct, coherent, embellished, and well articulated" (1959, 75). The status I held as a researcher was sometimes at odds with the intersecting axes of privilege and subordination that construct my identity, as well as with the image I projected to strangers. No matter how coherent my *conduct* as a researcher, my appearance to some degree undermined my researcher *status*. The result of my various positions: status ambiguity.

Textbook training for aspiring social scientists is geared toward those individuals who have traditionally been aspiring social scientists: white, socially and economically privileged students and researchers who lack visible disabilities. Advice on interviewer comportment and interaction is based on the assumption that researchers already project a certain image. Practical training for qualitative research is often hard to come by. Instructors offer the advice that new studies should look like existing studies and that methods and approaches to research should not stray toward innovation for risk of compromising study comparability and data integrity. For those of us who do not look like most other American social scientists, however, our bodies may become influential media in the inquiry process.

When I began this research project, I was not prepared for the ways that the image, or images, I project would affect my interactions with the research participants. The fact that identity plays a role in research would come as no shock to most social scientists. Identity affects both research interests and comfort in pursuing certain research agendas. Social researchers who conduct interviews or engage in direct observation tacitly take into account their social identities when gauging their ability to gain access and trust. The interplay between researcher identity and research subjects' identity is rarely discussed in methodological literature, except as something to be overcome. (For a notable exception to this general rule, see a collection of research stories by Francis Winndance Twine [2002].) A researcher's identity, though, is a variable in the research. While this variable is sometimes brought to light by the researcher (Brunskell 1998), this occurs far too infrequently.

My unusual social location affected basic issues of methodology, including recruitment; interviewer neutrality; openness and trust; critical distance; and interviewer self-disclosure. In fact, my initial contact with research participants was unusual. Many of the individuals I recruited approached me before I approached them. Apparently concerned to see a disabled woman sitting outside the welfare office, a number of people walked right up and asked whether I needed help. Sometimes when my infant daughter was with me in the early days of recruiting interviewees, people came up to make baby talk to my daughter. A couple times, as I was making my way from the car to the sidewalk, women approached me and asked, "Are you going to the welfare meeting?" In these situations, my response that I was a university researcher and my solicitation of their participation came as unexpected. Though I did my best to look the role of the researcher—dressed-up but not dressy; glasses rather than contacts; folio or clipboard in hand as a prop—my race, disability, motherhood status, and perhaps even gender seemed to undermine my "performance" of the researcher (Goffman 1959). Thus my interactions with research participants began with the experience of status ambiguity.

Many of the qualitative studies of the poor and their experiences with the welfare system that have been published in the last two decades (e.g., Berrick 1995; Edin and Lein 1997; Sarat 1990; Seccombe 1999) have been conducted— like most academic studies in the United States—by white, financially stable, able-bodied researchers. For these researchers, their social status both put them at a distance from their research participants and served as a known barrier going into the research. For example, John Gilliom, in his study of welfare mothers in Appalachia (2001), quickly realized that his age, gender, economic status, and regional accent were all barriers to data collection and hired recent welfare recipients from the area to conduct the research interviews. Gilliom and the other researchers knew they would have difficulty gaining the trust of individuals who might consider themselves (or be considered by the researchers) as social subordinates. My ambiguous social status, however, meant that there were no established interaction rituals, no clear indications of which of us should be playing the subordinate and therefore deferential role.

My status ambiguity also fogged the issue of researcher neutrality in my study. The traditional literature on qualitative research methods stresses the need for the appearance of neutrality on the part of the researcher. Interviewers, in particular, are instructed not to give off any signs of political stances, provide clues about their socioeconomic background, or provide hints about their feelings about interviewees' responses (Singleton and Straits 1999, 262, 269-70). But this traditional advice seems specifically aimed at traditional-looking interviewers. There is nothing neutral about the image I gave off; it called out to have stereotypes projected upon it. Moreover, there was only so much of my image that I could control. The people I interviewed commonly assumed from my race, gender, disability, and motherhood status that I had direct experience with government aid programs. This affected our interactions, leading interviewees to assume that we shared experiences and perspectives that we might not have actually shared. Anne-Marie Fortier writes that the images we researchers project are unstable and are commonly negotiated and renegotiated in the course of our interactions with research subjects (1998, 49). There may be, however, a point where unstable images become so unstable that they destabilize traditional modes of social inquiry.

Qualitative researchers do not universally agree upon appropriate research methods or even on the epistemological assumptions underlying the research. Departing from classical social science methods, some feminist methodologists not only take a less rigid stance on neutrality but even encourage researchers to reveal more about their agendas and themselves in efforts to gain trust and obtain personal information from interviewees (Acker, Berry, and Esseveld 1991; Oakley 1981). These researchers, aware of gender biases in the substance and methods of traditional research, are constantly engaged in continual "epistemological debate about the nature of legitimate inquiry" (Brunskell 1998, 43). Feminist methodologists argue that only by identifying with the research subject can the researcher find "truth." If truth includes interviewees' admissions of deception, then my nonclassical approach to methodology was effective in eliciting the truth about rule breaking. For the most part, however, the "truth" I was searching for in the interviews had less to do with interviewees' descriptions of their behaviors than with their beliefs about the welfare rules and the welfare system—the view from the inside.

My breaches of convention extended further. In the course of my research, I violated social norms by asking strangers personal questions about finances and family, as well as invasive questions about lying and cheating. Before conducting my research, I believed that eliciting this information from research participants would take some time and effort. I found, to my great surprise, that welfare recipients were quite forthright in disclosing rule-breaking behavior. Often the women volunteered such information before I even asked. My guess is that my apparent subordinate social location as defined by my gender, race, and disability made me nonthreatening.

"Nonthreatening," though, may not completely describe the interaction. I sense that, despite my role as researcher, the participants I interviewed considered me neither a social superior nor an equal. My identity was, and is, so marginal that the possibility that I might develop negative judgments of them did not seem to concern them. I did not fall within their social peerage. As a result, they offered deeply personal information about their finances, families, and social failings.

I also found that the interviewees had no hesitation in turning the tables, making me the object of their questions. The magnifying glass became a two-way lens. While self-disclosure by interviewers is typically discouraged (Weiss 1994, 79), I found it unavoidable. Being asked personal questions seemed to be the price I paid for doing the same. While I bristled at these questions and tried to give short, dampening responses, the counterquestions were a persistent aspect of my interviews. Again, my status ambiguity seemed to inspire curiosity. In some interviews, I felt as if I were asked to ante up with some degree of self-disclosure for each sensitive question I put forth. These were experiences for which my graduate school research methods courses had not prepared me.

I noticed two effects of my violating the conventions of social interaction and social scientific research. First and foremost, I was able to obtain rich data. The people I interviewed described their frustrations with not understanding complex welfare rules; their pain at having little education and poor reading skills; their mundane and extraordinary strategies for coping economically; their fears of being caught by "the system," a term that seemed to envelop welfare fraud investigations, child protective services, and the criminal justice system; and their admissions of mental illness, drug use, prostitution, and victimization by abuse. There is, I believe, no way that I could have captured this information through less interactive methods.

Moreover, the interviews tended to go long, and the interviewees seemed quite comfortable participating in the research. Classical methodologists view an interviewer's response effects as a systematic error in research, a source of bias (Singleton and Straits 1999, 267). My experience suggests, however, that response effects may be neutral or even positive aspects of an interview if the effect is merely the interviewee's divulging of honest information.

The second effect of my approach, however, was my frequent discomfort, even prompting my hesitation to pursue similar research in the future. Both delving into the lives of others and revealing so much of myself to my research participants were emotionally draining. Sometimes I found myself dreading to ask interviewees follow-up questions about personal matters, anticipating that they would feel free to ask equally touchy questions of me. I believe that my marginalized social location also raised the psychic costs of interview research.

Qualitative research is particularly well suited to revealing actors' understandings and misunderstandings, motivations, and hidden behaviors. The types of data gathered in the course of social research are affected not only by the types of questions that are asked but also by how the questions are asked and by whom they are asked. While reflexive social inquiry has been gaining ground, few social scientists acknowledge that the researcher herself (or himself) is a variable in the research process, both as a data gatherer and as a data analyst. For much of U.S. academic history, there has been little variation in the social status of those researchers pursuing sociolegal or public policy questions. Social scientists are wedded to the idea that for data to reflect truth it most be possible for all inquirers to be able to gather and observe the same data.

Patricia Hill Collins writes that African American women have often held an "outsider within" status because they have been nonparticipant observers in mainstream, white society (1990, 11-13; 1991). For African American women intellectuals, she argues, marginality provides a distinctive perspective on social life and theory. Collins suggests that this status affects analysis and interpretation of data, as well as engagement with and evaluation of social theory. In developing my research agendas, my research questions, and my methods of research, I commonly find myself an outsider within. As a social scientist studying traditional theory and methodology, I find that my minority identities are not represented in those theories, those methods, or the society composed of my disciplinary colleagues.

I am additionally an "outsider within" as a researcher doing fieldwork. My multiply subordinate social location offered me some entrée into the circle of welfare recipients I was interviewing. At the same time, my ambiguous social status and my status as a social scientist maintained my place as an outsider. This status created unusual researcher-subject interactions, allowing me to explore data that have been until now gone unexplored. (My sense is that Sudhir Alladi Venkatesh, a sociologist studying life in low-income, African American neighborhoods in Chicago, has been able to gain unusual access because of his "outsider" status as a man of South Asian descent [Venkatesh 2000, 2006].)

My experiences as an interviewer suggest that qualitative researchers— of all races, ethnicities, ages, genders, abilities, and sexual orientations, not just minorities—should reveal their social locations in presenting their findings. These statuses are significant variables in the ability to observe, to ask. Until researchers reveal these variables, they will not be given the attention in methodology that it deserves. Second, more diversity in the pool of qualitative researchers might reveal layers of social phenomena that are yet unexplored. Bringing more outsiders into the discipline of sociolegal studies might just open up new areas of understanding.

The Research Sample

The response rate for the research was admittedly low. I approached more than two hundred potential interviewees to obtain the thirty-four interviews. Fewer than half of the individuals who initially agreed to be interviewed actually followed through. In addition, in many of the cases of successful interviews, it took multiple attempts at meeting to finally complete the interview.

Most of the interviews lasted approximately an hour and a half. During the interviews, I asked questions about what had led the interviewees to apply for welfare, about their familiarity with the rules and requirement of the welfare system, and about their knowledge of the consequences of violating welfare's rules or failing to meet the requirements. I asked the interviewees to explain how they made ends meet financially. I also asked whether they thought specific rules were fair and necessary, whether they had particular rules, regulations, or aspects of the welfare system they wanted to change.

This study departs from most qualitative studies of welfare recipients in that I tried to interview a cross section of welfare recipients. I did this by recruiting near the county welfare office, approaching every person who left the building. My lack of fluency in any language other than English certainly prevented me from sampling from a broad ethnic and linguistic spectrum that Bayview enjoys. Still, I found great variation in levels of rule knowledge, in things respondents did to make ends meet, and in perceptions of the law to convince me that I was gathering rich and valuable information.

In addition, some of the sociolegal studies with the poor tend to sample individuals who may be distinct—those who have mobilized the law through legal services. For example, Austin Sarat (1990) interviewed welfare recipients in a legal services office in his article on the welfare poor. Welfare recipients seeking legal services, however, are likely to have a certain degree of knowledge of the rules, or at least of the procedural rules, and are arguably in the office with the belief that they have some access to law that they can use in their favor. In short, they are using rules strategically. They also have a certain orientation toward the legal system in general. They must invest some legitimacy in the rules and the procedures for calling upon or challenging those rules, even if they view the system as biased.

While Sarat attends to rights and due process as legal symbols at play in the legal consciousness of welfare recipients, he does not attend to other social and cultural symbols that may also be relevant to welfare recipients. In the context of the American welfare system, gender, race, and motherhood are not merely axes of individual identity but also axes of cultural experience and markers of social status. To discuss rights as salient symbols without discussing "welfare queens," "deadbeat dads," or "vagrants" as salient cultural symbols limits the analysis of the complex cultural milieu, where various symbols and stereotypes inform individual action, individual identity, and individuals' relationships to the law.

Qualitative studies of welfare recipients that use snowball sampling techniques (e.g., Edin and Lein 1997; Gilliom 2001; Seccombe 1999) also select a particular group of welfare recipients: those who have social networks that include other welfare recipients. While some of the individuals

I interviewed did know other welfare recipients, others did not. In some cases, in fact, the respondents were quite socially isolated, with limited or nonexistent social networks. One of the biases that may exist where interviewees are part of a network of welfare recipients is that they are likely to share knowledge, or at least understandings, of the welfare system. Since part of my goal was to assess welfare recipients' knowledge of welfare rules, I wanted to avoid conducting interviews that followed established circuits of shared knowledge.

In some ways my recipients reflect the local population of welfare recipients; in some ways they do not. Admittedly, my sample does not reflect the racial and ethnic diversity of the county, in large part because of my limited language ability. In 1999, 31 percent of the welfare recipients in the county used a language other than English as their primary language. My research therefore excluded a sizable population of Vietnamese, Chinese, Laotian, Cambodian, and Spanish-speaking welfare recipients. It also excluded small but significant populations of Afghan and Ethiopian welfare recipients.

While a disproportionate percentage of my interviewees were African American, I do not consider this weighty oversampling a liability in the research design. The political scientist Martin Gilens (2003) has conducted research finding that many Americans hold a racialized view of welfare, associating welfare with African Americans, especially urban African Americans. And at the time of the data collection, slightly more welfare recipients—58 percent (Coulton 2003, 95)—lived in urban areas rather than rural areas. But race and racism are particularly salient to studies of welfare recipients. In fact, focusing on how African Americans respond to the legal and moral regulation that occurs through welfare policy is compelling because they have become the focus of welfare policies. Kenneth Neubeck and Noel Cazenave write that the stigmatization of African American women in discourses about welfare has been fostered by the media, academics, and the general public (2001, 31). Studies by Ange-Marie Hancock (2004) and Martin Gilens (1999, 2003) reveal that negative public attitudes about welfare correlate with, and perhaps rise from, negative stereotypes about African Americans. While focusing on this population poses the risk of perpetuating the myth that poverty and welfare use are limited to city-dwelling African Americans, research about the very group most associated with welfare in the public consciousness will provide a clearer picture of the lives these families lead. In short, holding interviews with individuals who fit not just the stereotype but the very archetype of welfare recipients is of some value in bringing a lens of reality to the myth.

The Data Analysis

This study was guided by Barney Glaser and Anselm Strauss's notion of *grounded theory* (Glaser and Strauss 1967). In a grounded-theory approach, a researcher generates theory from data rather than testing a priori theories against found data. To do this, according to Glaser and Strauss, "one generates conceptual categories or their properties from evidence; then the evidence from which the category emerged is used to illustrate the concept" (23).

My interview schedule and my interviews thus included numerous questions about how and where welfare recipients received information about welfare rules, what they knew about the rules, how they navigated the rules, what their financial needs were each month, and how they made ends meet. I reviewed the interview schedule after each interview to assess which questions and topics were effectively generating information and which ones were not. I then adjusted the interview schedule to better obtain useful information. For example, after a handful of early interviews where I asked very detailed questions about monthly income and expenses, I discovered that often the interviewees simply could not recall even approximate dollar amounts well enough for specific time-consuming questions to be particularly useful assessments of need. More general questions such as "How do you make ends meet?" or "How do you feed your family?" were somehow better able to capture the economic dynamics in the family—especially if those questions were repeated at different points in the interview.

I developed conceptual categories during the course of data collection and well afterwards. I periodically reviewed the interview tapes and transcripts to refresh my familiarity with the material and wrote analytical notes based on the recurrent issues I found. Common issues and themes emerged from the interviews. For the most part, these themes became and headings and subheadings of data chapters.

I began analyzing the data by turning the conceptual categories into a detailed coding scheme. I coded a number of the transcripts and tried a qualitative software program to analyze the coded data. Once I had developed the categories, however, I found that most of the analytic work had been done and that taking the time to code the remaining transcripts offered little value to the project. With a sample of only thirty-four recipient interviewees, much of the data could be organized in Excel spreadsheets without the use of software specifically designed for qualitative analyses. Some of the basic characteristics of the interviewees—age, education, marital status, number of minor children—I compiled in distribution tables.

One of the frustrations of collecting rich data in the course of lengthy qualitative interviews is that so many of the details of individual experience are necessarily lost in the effort to confine the discussion to the topics of the research. That loss seems particularly poignant in this study because the men and women who were the subjects of this research lead lives that are often invisible to middle-class Americans. My hope is that in the future other types of projects will allow those who are economically privileged to gain more complete and complex impressions of the lives of those who are economically disadvantaged. More importantly, I hope that others—scholars, members of the press and popular media, and policy makers—will better allow poor families the opportunities to express and share their experiences with everyone else.

As the author, I have no way that I can write without my voice being the dominant one in this manuscript. My framing of the issues and my choices in selecting quotes particularly filter the view of the recipient interviewees. Still, the discussion borrows from the lives and views of many other individuals. In an attempt to make their voices come through, I include a lot of unpolished quotes that are in many cases longer than the scholarly norm. I encourage the reader to engage with these quotes rather than treat them as textual distractions.

Appendix B: Interview Schedule

I'm going to ask you some questions about your experiences with the welfare office. You are, of course, free not to answer any questions or to end the interview at any time.

Household/Family Composition

Do you live with other people? (How many? How are they related to you? How old are they? What kinds of income do they receive?)

Are the members of your household receiving welfare this month? (What kind[s]? Can I ask how much you receive?)

How many people do you have to support in your household?

Do you have kids in school or child care? (How many? What kind of school or child care program?)

Are you yourself included or excluded from the people receiving aid in your house?

Welfare History

When did you first go on welfare? (Why was that? What types of aid have you received?)

How did you know to go on aid?

Were you on welfare anytime before? (Why did you go off? What type of aid? How long were you off? When did you next go on welfare again? Why?)

Have you ever received other types of benefits such as Workers' Comp., Unemployment, or Social Security? (When? For how long? What were the circumstances?)

Did your family receive welfare when you were growing up?

Predictions of Continued or Future Welfare Use

How much longer do you think you'll need to be on welfare?
How much longer do you think you will actually receive welfare?
What would have to happen for you not to have to use welfare?
What would happen if something happened to your welfare?

Neighborhood and Social Support Information

How would you describe the neighborhood where you live?
How long have you lived there?
Are most people in your neighborhood working? Receiving aid?
Do you have relatives or friends nearby? Do they help you out in any way?
Do you receive any help from your kids' father(s)?

Meeting Essential Needs

I would imagine it's tough to get by on welfare.
    How do you make ends meet?
        Child support?
        Help from relatives?
        Help from friends?
        Share household expenses?
        Work? (What type? How much does it pay? On or off the books?)
        Other ways?
It's hard to feed a family. How do you manage?
        School breakfast/lunch programs?
        Food stamps?
        Food pantries or giveaways?
        Share food?
        Shopping strategies?
Have you and your family had medical care? How do you cover the costs?
        Medi-Cal?
        Private insurance?
        Other?
What do you do for transportation?
    How much does it cost you?
    Is transportation a problem for you now or has it been in the past?

Housing/Homelessness

Do you have stable housing?
>Do you feel safe where you live?
>How much do you pay for rent each month?
>How much do you have to pay for utilities?
>Have you had problems with housing?

Amount of Welfare Benefits

You mentioned before that you receive ($_____) a month in welfare
(or How much welfare do you get?)
>Is this enough?

Ancillaries

Do you receive any other help from the welfare office?
>Help with transportation?
>Help with child care?
>Help with educational expenses?
>Substance abuse or domestic violence counseling?

Perception of Need

How much money would you need to get by in a month?

Unofficial Sources of Information

Do you know other people who are on welfare? What sorts of things do they
do to make ends meet?
Do you talk with other people on welfare and share information on rules,
caseworkers, or different programs?
Did you ever get or give any advice on how to apply for programs or how to
report information?

Familiarity with Welfare Rules

When you went on welfare, did someone in the office explain the rules to you?
Did you understand them all?
Are some confusing?
> If so, which?
If you had questions about the rules, who would you ask?

Knowledge of the Rules

I imagine you have to report information about your income to the welfare office from time to time.
> How often do you have to do this?
> What do you have to report and do you have to submit proof?
> Is there some money you do not have to report?
> Do you have to report who is living in your house?
> Do you have to report about what other people in your house are earning?
> Does the welfare office have rules about receiving money from friends?
> Do you know of any rules about how long you can be on aid (time limits)?
> Do any time limits apply to you? Why or why not?
> What are the time limits?
> When does your time run out?
> Do you know if the welfare office adjusts your aid if you have a baby?
> Do you know if anything happens to your aid if you are charged with having or using drugs?

I imagine there are a lot of rules and requirements about training and work.
> What does the welfare office require you to do each month for work? (How many hours? What type of activities?)
> Are you in school?
> Do you receive any kind of educational assistance from the welfare office?
> Did you drop out of school while on welfare?
> Do you think you need more schooling or training?
> Are you working now? (What do you do? How many hours? What's your pay? Do you report this to the welfare office?)
> Have you had (other) jobs in the past? (Types? Pay? Length of employment?)

Questions of Noncompliance and Resistance

What do you think happens if someone fails to meet their work requirements?

What do you think happens if someone breaks the rules?

Have you ever knowingly had to break the rules? (Did anything happen? What?)

Do you know of other people who have broken the rules? (Do you know any of them personally? Do you know if something happened as a result? What?)

Have you ever kept things from your eligibility worker or bent the truth about money you received during the month in order to improve your benefits?

Have you had any unreported cash income? (Why or why not? If so: When? For how long?)

Did you get caught? (If so, how do you think you got caught? What happened?)

What should be against the welfare rules?

What should happen to the people who break those rules?

Have you ever kept things from your eligibility worker or bent the truth about who was living in your house?

Have you ever kept things from your eligibility worker or bent the truth about working or going to school?

Rule Legitimacy

Do you think the reporting rules are fair?

Do you think the work and requirements are fair?

Do you think sanctions are fair?

Do you think the time limits are fair?

Do you think the family cap is fair?

Risk Assessment

How do you think people get caught for bending or breaking the rules?

How often do you think this happens?

Do you think if someone broke the rules, she or he would be likely to get caught?

Experiences with Welfare Authorities

Did the welfare office ever contact you about problems with your case?
  (Why? How did the office contact you? Phone, letter?)
What happened?
How do you feel about it?
Was this fair?
Have you ever gotten any letters or had to see the district attorney about your
  welfare? (Why? What happened? How do you feel about it?)
How do you feel about people who don't fully report their income or resources?

Rights Consciousness and Mobilization

Have you ever filed an appeal in the welfare office?
Have you ever gotten advice from a law office? (What was the reason? What
  happened? Why did you use that office?)
Have you ever been involved in a lawsuit? What were the circumstances?
Have you dealt with the district attorney with any paternity child support
  matters?
Have you ever been involved in a welfare rights organization?
Are you involved in any community groups? Church groups?
Do you vote? (Which political party do you belong to?)

Personal Information and Background

How far have you gone in school? Are you in school now? (Kind, level)
How old are you?
How would you describe your racial/ethnic background?
Are you currently single, married, divorced, or separated?
Have you ever been married or been married before?
Are you currently in a relationship? How long has the relationship been
  going on?
Is the other person living with you?

Debriefing

If you could make changes to the welfare system, what would they be?
Has this interview raised any questions you want me to answer or made you
think of other things you'd like to mention?

Works Cited

BOOKS, ARTICLES, AND REPORTS

Abramovitz, Mimi. 1988. *Regulating the Lives of Women: Social Welfare Policy from Colonial Times to the Present*. Boston: South End Press.

Acker, Joan, Kate Berry, and Johanna Esseveld. 1991. "Objectivity and Truth: Problems in Doing Feminist Research." In *Beyond Methodology*, edited by Mary Margaret Fonow and Judith A. Cook, 133–53. Bloomington: Indiana University Press.

Advisory Council on Public Welfare. 1966. *"Having the Power, We Have the Duty": Report to the Secretary of Health, Education and Welfare*. Washington, DC: Government Printing Office.

Allard, Patricia. 2002. *Life Sentences: Denying Welfare Benefits to Women Convicted of Drug Offenses*. Washington, DC: Sentencing Project.

Anderson, Steven G., Anthony P. Halter, and Brian M. Gryzlak. 2004. "Difficulties after Leaving TANF: Inner-City Women Talk about Reasons for Returning to Welfare." *Social Work* 49:195–194.

Asian Pacific American Legal Center. 2000. *Barriers to Food Stamps*. Los Angeles: Asian Pacific American Legal Center.

Auerbach, Jerold S. 1976. *Unequal Justice: Lawyers and Social Change in Modern America*. New York: Oxford University Press.

Bailis, Lawrence Neil. 1974. *Bread or Justice*. Lexington, MA: Lexington Books.

Bane, Mary Jo, and David T. Ellwood. 1994. *Welfare Realities: From Rhetoric to Reform*. Cambridge, MA: Harvard University Press.

Beccaria, Cesare. 1963. *On Crimes and Punishments*. Translated by Henry Paolucci. Library of Liberal Arts 1764. Indianapolis: Bobbs-Merrill.

Bell, Winnifred. 1965. *Aid to Dependent Children*. New York: Columbia University Press.

Berrick, Jill Duerr. 1995. *Faces of Poverty*. New York: Oxford University Press.

Bloom, Dan, Laura Melton, Charles Michalopoulos, Susan Scrivener, and Johanna Walter. 2000. *Jobs First: Implementation and Early Impacts of Connecticut's Welfare Reform Initiative*. Washington, DC: Manpower Demonstration Research Corporation.

Boris, Eileen. 1993. "The Power of Motherhood: Black and White Activist Women Redefine the Political." In *Mothers of a New World*, edited by Seth Koven and Sonya Michel, 213–45. New York: Routledge.

Brady, Henry E., Nancy Nicosia, and Eva Y. Seto. 2002. "Establishing Causality in Welfare Research: Theory and Application." Interim Report, prepared for the California Department of Social Services and the Administration for Children and Families, U.S. Department of Health and Human Services. December. http://ucdata.berkeley.edu/pubs/CWRIS1.pdf.

Britton, Dana M. 2000. "Feminism in Criminology: Engendering the Outlaw." *Annals of the American Academy of Political and Social Science* 571:57–76.

Broder, David S. 1981. "Still Learning to Be the Opposition." *Washington Post*, February 15.

Brodkin, Evelyn Z. 1986. *The False Promise of Administrative Reform*. Philadelphia: Temple University Press.

Brunskell, Heather. 1998. "Feminist Methodology." In *Researching Society and Culture*, edited by Clive Seale, 37–47. Thousand Oaks, CA: Sage Publications.

Bumiller, Kristin. 1988. *The Civil Rights Society*. Baltimore: Johns Hopkins University Press.

Burnham, Linda. 2002. "Welfare Reform, Family Hardship, and Women of Color." In *Lost Ground: Welfare Reform, Poverty and Beyond*, edited by Randy Albelda and Ann Withorn, 43–56. Cambridge, MA: South End Press.

California Department of Social Services and Orange County Social Services Agency. 1997. *County of Orange Fraud Incidence Study*. Santa Ana: California Department of Social Services and Orange County Social Services.

California Department of Social Services, Program Planning and Performance Division. 2000. *CalWORKs Leavers Survey: A Statewide Telephone Survey of Former CalWORKs Recipients*. Sacramento: California Department of Social Services. www.dss.cahwnet. gov/research/res/pdf/calreports/Leavers.pdf.

California State Auditor. 2003. *Statewide Fingerprint Imaging System: The State Must Weigh Factors Other Than Need and Cost-Effectiveness When Determining Future Funding for the System*. California State Auditor Report 2001-015. Sacramento, CA. www.bsa.ca.gov/ pdfs/reports/2001-015.pdf.

————. 2009. "Department of Social Services: For the CalWORKs and Food Stamp Programs, It Lacks Assessments of Cost-Effectiveness and Misses Opportunities to Improve Counties' Antifraud Efforts." California State Auditor Report 2009-101. November. Sacramento, CA. www.bsa.ca.gov/pdfs/reports/2009-101.pdf.

Camasso, Michael J. 2007. *Family Caps, Abortion, and Women of Color: Research Connection and Political Rejection*. New York: Oxford University Press.

Cancian, Maria, Robert H. Haveman, Daniel R. Meyer, and Barbara Wolfe. 2002. "Before and after TANF: The Economic Well-Being of Women Leaving Welfare." *Social Service Review* 76 (December): 603–41.

Casey, Timothy J., and Mary R. Mannix. 1989. "Quality Control in Public Assistance: Victimizing the Poor through One-Sided Accountability." *Clearinghouse Review* 22:1381–89.

Chau, Michelle, and Ayana Douglas-Hall. 2008. *Low-Income Children in the United States: National and State Trend Data, 1997–2007*. New York: National Center for Children in Poverty, Columbia University.

Cherlin, Andrew J., Karen Bogen, James M. Quane, and Linda Burton. 2002. "Operating within the Rules: Welfare Recipients' Experiences with Sanctions and Case Closings." *Social Service Review* 76 (September): 387–405.

Chi, Keon S. 1984. *Fraud Control in State Human Services Programs: Innovations and New Strategies*. Lexington, KY: Council of State Governments.

Cloward, Richard A., and Frances Fox Piven. 1966. "A Strategy to End Poverty." *Nation*, May 2.

Cohen, Thomas H., and Tracey Kyckelhahn. 2010. *Felony Defendants in Large Urban Counties, 2006*. Washington, DC: U.S. Department of Justice, Office of Justice Programs.

Collins, Patricia Hill. 1990. *Black Feminist Thought.* New York: Routledge.

———. 1991. "Learning from the Outsider Within." In *Beyond Methodology,* edited by Mary Margaret Fonow and Judith A. Cook, 35–59. Bloomington: Indiana University Press.

Coulton, Claudia. 2003. "Metropolitan Inequities and the Ecology of Work: Implications for Welfare Reform." *Social Service Review* 77 (June): 159–90.

Cruikshank, Barbara. 1999. *The Will to Empower: Democratic Citizens and Other Subjects.* Ithaca: Cornell University Press.

Daly, Kathleen, and Michael Tonry. 1997. "Gender, Race, and Sentencing." *Crime and Justice* 22:201–53.

Davis, Gray. 2002. *California Governor's Budget Highlights.* Sacramento: State of California Governor's Office.

Davis, Martha. 1993. *Brutal Need: Lawyers and the Welfare Rights Movement, 1960–1973.* New Haven: Yale University Press.

Donzelot, Jacques. 1997. *The Policing of Families.* Baltimore: Johns Hopkins University Press.

Durose, Matthew R., and Patrick A. Langan. 2004. *Felony Sentences in State Courts, 2002.* Washington, DC: U.S. Department of Justice, Office of Justice Programs.

Dyer, Wendy Tanisha, and Robert W. Fairlie. 2004. "Do Family Caps Reduce Out-of-Wedlock Births? Evidence from Arkansas, Georgia, Indiana, New Jersey, and Virginia." *Population Research and Policy Review* 23:441–73.

Edelman, Murray. 1964. *The Symbolic Uses of Politics.* Urbana: University of Illinois Press.

Edin, Kathryn, and Christopher Jencks. 1993. "Welfare." In *Rethinking Social Policy,* by Christopher Jencks, 204–35. New York: HarperCollins.

Edin, Kathryn, and Laura Lein. 1997. *Making Ends Meet: How Single Mothers Survive Welfare and Low-Wage Work.* New York: Russell Sage.

Ellwood, David T. 1988. *Poor Support: Poverty in the American Family.* New York: Basic Books.

Engel, David M., and Frank W. Munger. 1996. "Rights, Remembrance, and the Reconciliation of Difference." *Law and Society Review* 30:7–54.

Ewick, Patricia, and Susan S. Silbey. 1992. "Conformity, Contestation, and Resistance: An Account of Legal Consciousness." *New England Law Review* 26:731–49.

———. 1998. *The Common Place of Law.* Chicago: University of Chicago Press.

Fineman, Martha Albertson. 1991. "Images of Mothers in Poverty Discourses." *Duke Law Journal* 1991:274–95.

———. 1995. *The Neutered Mother, the Sexual Family and Other Twentieth Century Tragedies.* New York: Routledge.

Fortier, Anne-Marie. 1998. "Gender, Ethnicity and Fieldwork: A Case Study." In *Researching Society and Culture,* edited by Clive Seale, 48–57. Thousand Oaks, CA: Sage Publications.

Foucault, Michel. 1979. *Discipline and Punish: The Birth of the Prison.* New York: Vintage Books.

———. 1990. *The History of Sexuality.* Vol. 1. *An Introduction.* New York: Vintage Books.

Fragile Families Research Brief. 2002. *Mothers' Beliefs about Welfare Rules.* Princeton, NJ: Bendheim-Thomas Center for Research on Child Wellbeing.

Fuller, Bruce, Sharon Lynn Kagan, and Susanna Loeb. 2002. *New Lives for Poor Families? Mothers and Young Children Move through Welfare Reform.* Berkeley: Growing Up in Poverty Project, University of California, Berkeley.

Fuller, Lon L. 1969. *The Morality of Law*. Rev. ed. New Haven: Yale University Press.

Gallman, Vanessa. 1995. "'Sit Down and Shut Up': Welfare Debate Turns Testy." *Miami Herald*, March 25.

Gardiner, John. 1984. *The Fraud Control Game: State Responses to Fraud and Abuse in AFDC and Medicaid Programs*. Bloomington: Indiana University Press.

Gardiner, John, and Theodore Lyman. 1984. *Responses to Fraud and Abuse in AFDC and Medicaid Programs*. Washington, DC: National Institute of Justice.

Garland, David. 2001. *The Culture of Control*. Chicago: University of Chicago Press.

Gilder, George. 1981. *Wealth and Poverty*. New York: Basic Books.

Gilens, Martin. 1999. *Why Americans Hate Welfare: Race, Media, and the Politics of Antipoverty Policy*. Chicago: University of Chicago Press.

———. 2003. "How the Poor Became Black: The Racialization of American Poverty in the Mass Media." In *Race and the Politics of Welfare Reform*, edited by Sanford F. Schram, Joe Soss, and Richard C. Fording, 101–30. Ann Arbor: University of Michigan Press.

Gilliom, John. 1996. *Surveillance, Privacy and the Law*. Ann Arbor: University of Michigan Press.

———. 1997. "Everyday Surveillance, Everyday Resistance: Computer Monitoring in the Lives of the Appalachian Poor." *Studies in Law, Politics, and Society* 16:275–97.

———. 2001. *Overseers of the Poor: Surveillance, Resistance, and the Limits of Privacy*. Chicago: University of Chicago Press.

Glaser, Barney G., and Anselm L. Strauss. 1967. *The Discovery of Grounded Theory: Strategies for Qualitative Research*. New York: Aldine de Gruyter.

Goffman, Erving. 1959. *The Presentation of Self in Everyday Life*. New York: Anchor Books.

Goldberg, Heidi, and Liz Schott. 2000. *A Compliance-Oriented Approach to Sanctions in State and County TANF Programs*. Washington, DC: Center on Budget and Policy Priorities.

Gordon, Linda. 1994. *Pitied but Not Entitled: Single Mothers and the History of Welfare*. New York: Free Press.

Greenberg, David F. 1993. "The Causes of Crime." In *Crime and Capitalism*, edited by David F. Greenberg, 57–99. Philadelphia: Temple University Press.

Greenberg, David, and Douglas Wolf. 1986. *Using Computers to Combat Welfare Fraud: The Operation and Effectiveness of Wage Matching*. New York: Greenwood Press.

Gurmu, Shiferaw, and William J. Smith. 2006. "Recidivism among Welfare Recipients: The Role of Neighborhood and Access to Employment." *Atlantic Economic Journal* 34:405–19.

Gusfield, Joseph R. 1986. *Symbolic Crusade: Status Politics and the American Temperance Movement*. 2nd ed. Champaign: University of Illinois Press.

Gustafson, Kaaryn. 2009. "The Criminalization of Poverty." *Journal of Criminal Law and Criminology* 99:643–716.

Hagert, Celia. 2001. Testimony before House Committee on Human Services, 77th Texas Legislature. February 12.

Hancock, Ange-Marie. 2004. *The Politics of Disgust: The Public Identity of the Welfare Queen*. New York: NYU Press.

Handler, Joel F. 1987–88. "The Transformation of Aid to Families with Dependent Children: The Family Support Act in Historical Context." *New York University Journal of Law and Social Change* 16:457–533.

———. 1998. "Poverty, Dependency, and Social Welfare." In *Justice and Power in Sociolegal Studies,* edited by Bryant G. Garth and Austin Sarat, 136–65. Evanston, IL: Northwestern University Press.

———. 2002. "Commentary: Quiescence: The Scylla and Charybdis of Empowerment." In *Laboring below the Line,* edited by Frank Munger, 271–80. New York: Russell Sage.

Handler, Joel F., and Yeheskel Hasenfeld. 1991. *The Moral Construction of Poverty.* Newbury Park, CA: Sage Publications.

———. 2007. *Blame Welfare, Ignore Poverty and Inequality.* New York: Cambridge University Press.

Hasenfeld, Yeheskel, T. J. Ghose, and Kandyce Hillesland-Larson. 2004. "The Logic of Sanctioning Welfare Recipients: An Empirical Assessment." *Social Service Review* 78:304–19.

Haskins, Ron, Isabel Sawhill, and Kent Weaver. 2001. *Welfare Reform: An Overview of Effects to Date.* Washington, DC: Brookings Institution.

Hirsch, Amy. 2003. *Every Door Closed: Facts about Parents with Criminal Records.* Washington, DC: Center for Law and Social Policy.

Horsburgh, Beverly. 1996. "Schrödinger's Cat, Eugenics, and the Compulsory Sterilization of Welfare Mothers: Deconstructing an Old/New Rhetoric and Constructing the Reproductive Right to Natality for Low-Income Women of Color." *Cardozo Law Review* 17:531–82.

Hutton, Gary W. 1985. *Welfare Fraud Investigation.* Springfield, IL: C. C. Thomas.

Jackson, Larry R., and William A. Johnson. 1973. *Protest by the Poor.* Report R-791-NYC. Santa Monica, CA: Rand Institute.

Jagannathan, Radha, and Michael J. Camasso. 2003. "Family Cap and Nonmarital Fertility: The Racial Conditioning of Policy Effects." *Journal of Marriage and the Family* 65:52–71.

Jayakody, Rukmalie, Sheldon Danziger, Kristin Seefeldt, and Harold Pollack. 2004. *Substance Abuse and Welfare Reform.* Policy Brief #2. Ann Arbor: National Poverty Center, University of Michigan.

Jensen, Jane. 1990. "Representations of Gender: Policies to 'Protect' Women Workers and Infants in France and the United States before 1914." In *Women, the State, and Welfare,* edited by Linda Gordon, 152–77. Madison: University of Wisconsin Press.

Joyce, Ted, Robert Kaestner, Sanders Korenman, and Stanley Henshaw. 2004. "Family Cap Provisions and Changes in Births and Abortions." *Population Research and Policy Review* 23:475–511.

Kahan, Dan M. 1999. "The Secret Ambition of Deterrence." *Harvard Law Review* 113:413–500.

Kalil, Ariel, Kristin S. Seefeldt, and Hui-Chen Wang. 2002. "Sanctions and Material Hardship under TANF." *Social Service Review* 76 (December 2002): 642–62.

Katz, Michael B. 1989. *The Undeserving Poor.* New York: Pantheon Books.

———. 1998. *The Price of Citizenship: Redefining the American Welfare State.* New York: Metropolitan Books.

Kidwell, Kaye D., and Paul A. Gottlober. 1999. *Temporary Assistance for Needy Families: Educating Clients about Sanctions.* San Francisco: Office of Inspector General, Department of Health and Human Services.

Kingfisher, Catherine Pelissier. 1996. *Women in the American Welfare Trap.* Philadelphia: University of Pennsylvania Press.

Kornbluh, Felicia. 2007. *The Battle for Welfare Rights: Politics and Poverty in Modern America*. Philadelphia: University of Pennsylvania Press.

Kyckelhahn, Tracey, and Thomas H. Cohen. 2008. *Felony Defendants in Large Urban Counties, 2004*. Washington, DC: U.S. Department of Justice. Office of Justice Programs.

Ladd-Taylor, Molly. 1994. *Mother-Work: Women, Child Welfare and the State, 1890–1930*. Urbana: University of Illinois Press.

Lange, Andrea G. 1979. *Fraud and Abuse in Government Benefit Programs*. Washington, DC: U.S. Department of Justice, Law Enforcement Assistance Administration.

Leff, Mark H. 1973. "Consensus for Reform: The Mothers'-Pension Movement in the Progressive Era." *Social Service Review* 47:397–417.

Leiby, James. 1978. *A History of Social Welfare and Social Work in the United States*. New York: Columbia University Press.

Lelyveld, Joseph. 1985. "Hunger in America; The Safety Net Has Shrunk But It's Still in Place." *New York Times*, June 16.

Levine, Kay, and Virginia Mellema. 2001. "Strategizing the Street: How Law Matters in the Lives of Women in the Street-Level Drug Economy." *Law and Social Inquiry* 26:169–207.

Lewis, Oscar. 1959. *Five Families: Mexican Case Studies in the Culture of Poverty*. New York: Basic Books.

———. 1968. "The Culture of Poverty." In *On Understanding Poverty: Perspectives from the Social Sciences*, edited by Daniel Patrick Moynihan, 187–200. New York: Basic Books.

Little, James S. 1983. "An Examination of Data on Welfare Fraud." *Clearinghouse Review* 16:1005–8.

Lipsky, Michael. 1984. "Bureaucratic Disentitlement in Social Welfare Programs." *Social Science Review* 58:3–27.

Long, Russell B. 1972. "Welfare Cheating: Address of Hon. Russell B. Long, Chairman, Committee on Finance and Supporting Materials." *Congressional Record*, 92nd Cong., 2nd sess. (September 30): 33010.

Los Angeles Grand Jury. 1999. *Welfare Fraud Prevention and Investigative Functions of the Department of Public Social Services*. Report. Los Angeles: Los Angeles Grand Jury. http://grandjury.co.la.ca.us/gjury99/REPORtgj-15.htm.

Lower-Basch, Elizabeth. 2000. *"Leavers" and Diversion Studies: Preliminary Analysis of Racial Differences in Caseload Trends and Leaver Outcomes*. Washington, DC: Office of the Assistant Secretary for Planning and Evaluation, U.S. Department of Health and Human Services.

Lower-Basch, Elizabeth, and Mark H. Greenberg. 2009. "Single Mothers in the Era of Welfare Reform." In *The Gloves-Off Economy: Workplace Standards at the Bottom of America's Labor Market*, edited by Annette Bernhardt et al., 163–90. Champaign, IL: Labor and Employment Relations Association.

Lubiano, Wahneema. 1992. "Black Ladies, Welfare Queens, and State Minstrels: Ideological War by Narrative Means." In *Race-ing Justice, En-gendering Power*, edited by Toni Morrison, 323–63. New York: Pantheon Books.

Luna, Erik G. 1997. "Welfare Fraud and the Fourth Amendment." *Pepperdine Law Review* 24:1235–90.

Manza, Jeff, and David Uggen. 2006. *Locked Out: Felon Disfranchisement and American Democracy*. New York: Oxford University Press.

McCann, Michael, and Tracey March. 1996. "Law and Everyday Forms of Resistance: A Socio-Political Assessment." In *Studies in Law, Politics, and Society*, edited by Austin Sarat and Susan Silbey, 210–36. Greenwich, CT: JAI Press.

McConahay, John B. 1988. "Pornography: The Symbolic Politics of Fantasy." *Law and Contemporary Problems* 51:31–70.

Mead, Lawrence M. 1986. *Beyond Entitlement*. New York: Free Press.

———. 1992. *The New Politics of Poverty*. New York: Basic Books.

Melnick, R. Shep. 1990. "The Politics of the New Property: Welfare Rights in Congress and the Courts." In *Liberty, Property, and the Future of Constitutional Development*, edited by Ellen Frankel Paul and Howard Dickman, 199–240. Albany: SUNY Press.

Merry, Sally Engle. 1995. "Resistance and the Cultural Power of Law." *Law and Society Review* 29:11–26.

Meyers, Marcia K., Bonnie Glaser, and Karin MacDonald. 1998. "On the Front Lines of Welfare Delivery: Are Workers Implementing Policy Reforms?" *Journal of Policy Analysis and Management* 17:1–22.

Miller, Eric J. 2004. "Embracing Addiction: Drug Court and the False Promise of Judicial Interventionism." *Ohio State Law Journal* 65:1479–1576.

Mink, Gwendolyn. 1990. "The Lady and the Tramp: Gender, Race, and the Origins of the American Welfare State." In *Women, the State, and Welfare*, edited by Linda Gordon, 92–122. Madison: University of Wisconsin Press.

Moynihan, Daniel Patrick. 1965. *The Negro Family: The Case for National Action*. Washington, DC: Office of Policy Planning and Research.

———. 1973. *The Politics of a Guaranteed Income*. New York: Random House.

Murray, Charles. 1984. *Losing Ground: American Social Policy, 1950–1980*. New York: Basic Books.

Nelson, Barbara J. 1990. "The Origins of the Two-Channel Welfare State: Workmen's Compensation and Mothers' Aid." In *Women, the State, and Welfare*, edited by Linda Gordon, 123–51. Madison: University of Wisconsin Press.

Neubeck, Kenneth J., and Noel A. Cazenave. 2001. *Welfare Racism*. New York: Routledge.

New York Times. 1974. "Welfare and Pension Swindle Laid to Woman of Many Aliases." December 15.

———. 1977. "Chicago Relief 'Queen' Guilty." March 19.

———. 1978. "'Queen of Welfare' Ordered Jailed in $239,500 Fraud." December 29.

———. 1980. "Woman's Aid Claims for 38 Children Are Examined." December 21.

———. 1983a. "Coast Woman Admits $377,458 Welfare Fraud." March 17.

———. 1983b. "Reagan Signs Bill Providing '84 Funds for Legal Services." November 29.

Nielsen, Laura Beth. 2004. *License to Harass: Law, Hierarchy, and Offensive Public Speech*. Princeton: Princeton University Press.

Oakley, Ann. 1981. "Interviewing Women: A Contradiction in Terms." In *Doing Feminist Research*, edited by Helen Roberts, 30–61. London: Routledge and Kegan Paul.

Office of Inspector General, U.S. Department of Agriculture. 2000. *Operation Talon, October 2000 Update*. Washington, DC.

———. 2006. *Semiannual Report to Congress: FY 2006—2nd Half* 22. Report No. 56.

Office of Inspector General, U.S. Department of Health, Education and Welfare. 1979. *Annual Report: January 1, 1978–December 31, 1978*.

Office of State Systems. 1997. *Report to Congress on Data Processing and Case Tracking in the Temporary Assistance to Needy Families (TANF) Program*. Washington, DC: Department of Health and Human Services.

Okin, Susan Moller. 1989. *Justice, Gender, and the Family*. New York: Basic Books.

Ong, Paul. 1996. "Work and Automobile Ownership among Welfare Recipients." *Social Work Research* 20:255–62.

Orleck, Annelise. 2005. *Storming Caesars Palace: How Black Mothers Fought Their Own War on Poverty.* Boston: Beacon Press.

Paddock, Richard C. 1986. "Gov. Reagan's Workfare: No 'Gang Busters' in a Short Life." *Los Angeles Times,* February 10.

Pager, Devah. 2003. "The Mark of a Criminal Record." *American Journal of Sociology* 108:937–75.

Patterson, James T. 1994. *America's Struggle against Poverty, 1900–1994.* Cambridge, MA: Harvard University Press.

Pavetti, LaDonna, Michelle K. Derr, Gretchen Kirby, Robert G. Wood, and Melissa A. Clark. 2004. *The Use of TANF Work-Oriented Sanctions in Illinois, New Jersey, and South Carolina.* Washington, DC: Mathematica Policy Research.

Pear, Robert. 1982. "Reagan's Social Impact." *New York Times,* August 25.

Peterson, Janice. 2002. *Feminist Perspectives on TANF Reauthorization: An Introduction to Key Issues for the Future of Welfare Reform.* Washington, DC: Institute for Women's Policy Research.

Piven, Frances Fox, and Richard A. Cloward. [1971] 1993. *Regulating the Poor.* New York: Vintage Books.

———. [1977] 1979. *Poor People's Movements.* New York: Vintage Books.

Pollack, Harold A., Sheldon Danziger, Kristin S. Seefeldt, and Rukmalie Jayakody. 2002. "Substance Use among Welfare Recipients: Trends and Policy Responses." *Social Service Review* 76 (June): 256–74.

Pope, Jacqueline. 1989. *Biting the Hand That Feeds Them: Organizing Women on Welfare at the Grass Roots Level.* New York: Praeger.

Quadagno, Jill S. 1984. "Welfare Capitalism and the Social Security Act of 1935." *American Sociological Review* 49:632–47.

———. 1994. *The Color of Welfare.* New York: Oxford University Press.

Rank, Mark Robert. 1994. *Living on the Edge: The Realities of Welfare in America.* New York: Columbia University Press.

Reaves, Brian A. 2001. *Felony Defendants in Large Urban Counties, 1998.* Washington, DC: U.S. Department of Justice, Office of Justice Programs.

Reich, Charles A. 1963. "Midnight Welfare Searches and the Social Security Act." *Yale Law Journal* 72:1347–61.

———. 1964. "The New Property." *Yale Law Journal* 73:733–87.

———. 1965. "Individual Rights and Social Welfare: The Emerging Legal Issues." *Yale Law Journal* 74:1245–58.

Rivera, Carla. 1994. "Fingerprint Program to Target Aid Fraud." *Los Angeles Times,* April 7.

Roberts, Steven V. 1981. "Food Stamp Trims Sought by Reagan." *New York Times,* September 23.

Romero, Diana, and Madina Agénor, 2009. "US Fertility Prevention as Poverty Prevention: An Empirical Question and Social Justice Issue." *Women's Health Issues* 19:355–64.

Romero, Diana, Hannah Fortune-Greeley, Jorge Luis Verea, and Debbie Salas-Lopez. 2007. "Meaning of the Family-Cap Policy for Poor Women: Contraceptive and Fertility Decision-Making." *Social Work in Public Health* 23:165–82.

Ryan, Suzanne, Jennifer Manlove, and Sandra L. Hofferth. 2006. "State-Level Welfare Policies and Subsequent Nonmarital Subsequent Childbearing." *Population Research and Policy Review* 25:103–26.

Sapiro, Virginia. 1990. "The Gender Basis of American Social Policy." In *Women, the State, and Welfare,* edited by Linda Gordon, 36–54. Madison: University of Wisconsin Press.

Sarat, Austin. 1990. "'. . . The Law Is All Over': Power, Resistance and the Legal Consciousness of the Welfare Poor." *Yale Journal of Law and the Humanities* 2:343–75.

Scheer, Robert. 1992. "Question and Answer: Clinton Sketches Scenarios for Easing Urban Problems." *Los Angeles Times,* May 31.

Schein, Virginia E. 1995. *Working from the Margins: Voices of Mothers in Poverty.* Ithaca, NY: ILR Press.

Scheingold, Stuart A. 1974. *The Politics of Rights.* New Haven: Yale University Press.

Schexnayder, Deanna T., et al. 1997. "Lone Star Image System Evaluation Final Report: Executive Summary." Center for the Study of Human Resources, University of Texas at Austin. www.utexas.edu/research/cshr/pubs/html/lsisfinalexsum.htm.

Schram, Sanford F. 2000. *After Welfare: The Culture of Postindustrial Social Policy.* New York: NYU Press.

———. 2002. "Race and State Welfare Reform Choices: A Cause for Concern." In *From Poverty to Punishment: How Welfare Reform Punishes the Poor,* edited by Gary Delgado, 89–107. Oakland, CA: Applied Research Center.

Schram, Sanford F., and Joe Soss. 2001. "Success Stories: Welfare Reform, Policy Discourse, and the Politics of Research." *Annals of the American Academy of Political and Social Science* 577:49–65.

Seccombe, Karen. 1999. *"So You Think I Drive a Cadillac?": Welfare Recipients' Perspectives on the System and Its Reform.* Needham Heights, MA: Allyn and Bacon.

Services, Immigrant Rights and Education Network (SIREN). 2000. *Immigrant Family Access to Food Stamps in Santa Clara County.* San Jose, CA: SIREN.

Silbey, Susan. 2001. "Legal Culture and Legal Consciousness." In *International Encyclopedia of the Social and Behavioral Sciences,* edited by Neil J. Smelser and Paul B. Baltes, 8623–29. New York: Elsevier.

Simon, Herbert A. 1997. *Administrative Behavior.* New York: Free Press.

Simon, Jonathan. 2002. "A Colloquium on Community Policing: Introduction: Crime, Community, and Criminal Justice." *California Law Review* 90:1415–22.

Simon, William H. 1983. "Legality, Bureaucracy, and Class in the Welfare System." *Yale Law Journal* 92:1198–1269.

Singleton, Royce A., Jr., and Bruce C. Straits. 1999. *Approaches to Social Research.* New York: Oxford University Press.

Skocpol, Theda, Marjorie Abend-Wein, Christopher Howard, and Susan Goodrich Lehmann. 1993. "Women's Associations and the Enactment of Mothers' Pensions in the United States." *American Political Science Review* 87: 686–701.

Soss, Joe. 2000. *Unwanted Claims: The Politics of Participation in the U.S. Welfare System.* Ann Arbor: University of Michigan Press.

Sparer, Edward. 1965. "The Role of the Welfare Client's Lawyer." *UCLA Law Review* 12:361–80.

Stack, Carol B. 1975. *All Our Kin.* New York: Harper Paperback.

Sykes, Gresham M., and David Matza. 1957. "Techniques of Neutralization: A Theory of Delinquency." *American Sociological Review* 22:664–70.

Trattner, Walter I. 1994. *From Poor Law to Welfare State: A History of Social Welfare in America.* New York: Free Press.

Twine, Francis Winddance. 2002. *Race-ing Research, Researching Race.* New York: Routledge.

Tyler, Tom R. 1990. *Why People Obey the Law.* New Haven: Yale University Press.

———. 1994. "The Psychology of Legitimacy." Working Paper No. 9425. American Bar Foundation, Chicago.

Tyler, Tom R., and John M. Darley. 2000. "Building a Law-Abiding Society: Taking Public Views about Morality and the Legitimacy of Legal Authorities into Account when Formulating Substantive Law." *Hofstra Law Review* 28:707–39.

U.S. Department of Health and Human Services, Administration for Children and Families. 2010. *TANF Caseload Data.* www.acf.hhs.gov/programs/ofa/data-reports/caseload/caseload_archive.html.

U.S. General Accounting Office. 1997. *Food Stamps: Substantial Overpayments Result from Prisoners Counted as Household Members.* Washington, DC.

———. 1998. *Food Stamp Overpayments: Households in Different States Collect Benefits for the Same Individuals.* Washington, DC.

———. 1999. *Food Stamp Program: Various Factors Have Led to Declining Participation.* GAO Report 02-716. Washington, DC.

———. 2002. *Welfare Reform: Implementation of Fugitive Felon Provisions Should Be Strengthened.* Washington, DC.

U.S. Government Accountability Office. 2005. *Drug Offenders: Various Factors May Limit the Impacts of Federal Laws That Provide for Denial of Selected Benefits.* Report GAO-05-238. Washington, DC.

Venkatesh, Sudhir Alladi. 2000. *American Project: The Rise and Fall of a Modern Ghetto.* Cambridge, MA: Harvard University Press.

———. 2006. *Off the Books: The Underground Economy of the Urban Poor.* Cambridge, MA: Harvard University Press.

Verma, Nandita, and Richard Hendra. 2003. *Monitoring Outcomes for Los Angeles County's Pre- and Post-CalWORKs Leavers: How Are They Faring?* New York: Manpower Demonstration Research Corp.

Viadero, Roger C. 2001. *Statement in Formulation of the 2002 Farm Bill: Hearings before the H. Comm. of Agriculture and Its Subcomm.* 107th Cong., 1st sess., pp. 643–57. March 14.

Wacquant, Loïc. 2001. "The Penalisation of Poverty and the Rise of Neo-Liberalism." *European Journal on Criminal Policy and Research* 9:401–12.

———. 2008. "Ordering Insecurity: Social Polarization and the Punitive Upsurge." *Radical Philosophy Review* 11:9–27.

———. 2009a. "The Body, the Ghetto and the Penal State." *Qualitative Sociology* 32:101–29.

———. 2009b. *Punishing the Poor: The Neoliberal Government of Social Insecurity.* Durham: Duke University Press.

Washington Post. 1978. "Woman Guilty of $240,000 Welfare Fraud." December 2.

Weiss, Robert S. 1994. *Learning from Strangers: The Art and Method of Qualitative Interview Studies.* New York: Free Press.

West, Guida. 1981. *The National Welfare Rights Movement.* New York: Praeger.

White, Julie A., and John Gilliom. 1998. "Up from the Streets: Handler and the Ambiguities of Empowerment and Dependency." *Law and Social Inquiry* 23:203–22.

Williams, Lucy A. 1994. "The Abuse of Section 1115 Waivers: Welfare Reforms in Search of a Standard." *Yale Law and Policy Review* 12:8–37.

Wilson, William Julius. 1987. *The Truly Disadvantaged.* Chicago: University of Chicago Press.

Wolf, Douglas, and David Greenberg. 1986. "The Dynamics of Welfare Fraud: An Econometric Duration Model in Discrete Time." *Journal of Human Resources* 21:437–55.

Zedlewski, Sheila R., and Sarah Brauner. 1999a. *Are the Steep Declines in Food Stamp Participation Linked to Falling Welfare Caseloads?* Washington, DC: Urban Institute.

———. 1999b. *Declines in Food Stamp and Welfare Participation: Is There a Connection?* Washington, DC: Urban Institute.

CASES CITED

Beno v. Shalala, 30 F.3d 1057 (9th Cir. 1994).

Brown v. Board of Education of Topeka, 347 U.S. 483 (1954).

Dandridge v. Williams, 397 U.S. 471 (1970).

Goldberg v. Kelly, 397 U.S. 254 (1970).

Jefferson v. Hackney, 406 U.S. 535 (1972).

King v. Smith, 392 U.S. 309 (1968).

Marchwinski v. Howard, 113 F. Supp. 2d 1134 (E.D. Mich. 2000), *rev'd*, 309 F.3d 330 (6th Cir. 2002), *vacated by rehearing en banc,* 319 F.3d 258 (6th Cir. 2003), *aff'd*, 60 Fed. Appx. 601 (6th Cir. 2003).

Rosado v. Wyman, 397 U.S. 397 (1970).

Sanchez v. County of San Diego, 464 F.3d 916 (9th Cir. 2006), *rehearing denied and rehearing en banc denied,* 483 F.3d 965 (9th Cir. 2007), *cert. denied*, 522 U.S. 1038 (2007).

Shapiro v. Thompson, 394 U.S. 618 (1969).

LEGISLATION

Family Support Act of 1988, Public Law 100-485, 102 Stat. 2343 (codified as amended at 42 U.S.C. § 668 et seq.).

Food Stamp Act of 1977. Public Law 106-171, 114 Stat. 3 (codified as amended at 7 U.S.C. §§ 2011-2036).

Housing Act of 1937. Public Law 93-383, 88 Stat. 653 (codified as amended at 42 U.S.C. §§ 1437 et. seq.).

Improper Payments Information Act of 2002. Public Law 107-300, 116 Stat. 2350 (codified as amended at 31 U.S.C. § 3321).

Inspector General Act of 1978. Public Law 95-452, 92 Stat. 1101 (codified as amended in 5 U.S.C. App. 3 §§ 1-13).

Omnibus Budget Reconciliation Act of 1981. Public Law 97-35, 95 Stat. 357 (codified as amended in scattered sections).

Personal Responsibility and Work Opportunity Reconciliation Act of 1996. Public Law 104-193, 110 Stat. 2105 (amending 26 U.S.C. § 32).

Social Security Act of 1935. Public Law 74-271, 49 Stat. 620 (codified as amended in 42 U.S.C. § 301 et seq.).

Index

dependency: welfare dependency, 38, 39, 43, 44, 48, 49-50; interdependence of caretakers and dependents, 8

deserving poor, 17, 18-19, 20, 24

deterrence, 57-58, 160-61, 165, 167, 183

devolution, 41, 44-45

disabilities: as a barrier to employment, 87-89; among dependents, 89-90; among recipients, 79-80

disability benefits. *See* Social Security Disability Insurance

discretion in determining eligibility for benefits, 20, 22-23, 24, 31, 32. *See also* special needs grants

discrimination, racial, 25; in welfare provision, 20, 23, 24

disqualification consent agreements, 66

diversion programs, 68, 163-64

domestic abuse/violence, 76-77, 84, 85, 86, 126, 175

Donzelot, Jacques, 52

drugs: drug felony exclusion, 53-56; drug testing, 59-60; substance abuse treatment, 55-56, 78; use among interviewees, 78, 139; use among welfare recipients generally, 60, 176; use by family members, 76

due process, 135

Earned Income Tax Credit (EITC), 43, 61

Edin, Kathryn, 10-11

education: access to educational opportunities, 46, 84, 87, 126; educational backgrounds of interviewees, 83-84; enrollment in education programs, 113, 122, 123, 132

Ellwood, Paul, 43

empowerment, 14, 174, 180

employment: barriers to, 87-92; exploitative, 103; histories, 85-87; legitimate, 98-101, 137-38; side jobs, 93, 95-96, 101-3, 117, 127, 138, 155, 169, 174-75; types of, 80, 85-87, 98-101, 101. *See also* work requirements

Engel, David, 13

ethical issues in social research, 42-43, 185-87

Ewick, Patricia, 13-14, 173-75

extended family members: as an encumbrance, 107; support from, 106-7

fairness: of welfare rules, 127, 128, 142, 147-50; of penalties for cheating, 150; of sanctions, 146; of time limits, 148-49; of work requirements, 128, 149-50

family cap policies, 42, 46, 62-63; effects of, 43; fairness of, 150; knowledge of, 135-37, 141, 145

Family Assistance Plan (FAP), 31

Family Support Act, 40-41

fathers: deceased, 75; domestic violence, 76, 78; incarcerated, 75-76, 77, 78; interviews with, 78-79; invisible men, 74-79. *See also* child support

fear: of getting caught cheating, 174-75; of time limits, 149; of welfare officials, 159

federalism, 37

Fineman, Martha, 8

fingerprinting/fingerimaging, 56-59

food: food assistance, 20, 37; food insecurity, 48, 94-95; use of food pantries, 80

food stamps: policies, 31, 33, 37, 44; selling, 140, 169; use of, 48, 80, 107

foster care, 143, 169, 176

Foucault, Michel, 155, 179

Fourth Amendment, 59-60, 65, 157, 160

free-market economy, 17

fraud, 7-8, 33; charges, 131; costs of policing, 57-59, 69, 164-66, 184-85; hotlines, 40, 166; investigations, 38, 40, 63-65, 123, 156-60, 163, 169, 169-70, 184; investigators, 69; prevention, 56-58, 64-65, 96-97, 157; prosecutions and convictions, 3, 4, 21, 34-36, 67-68, 68-69, 105, 160-65, 183, 184. *See also* home visits by welfare officials; midnight raids

fugitive felon prohibitions, 52-53

Fuller, Lon, 181

Garland, David, 6, 51
gender, 36
Gilder, George, 39
Gilens, Martin, 61, 200
Gilliom, John, 14-15, 51, 171, 176, 179
Goffman, Erving, 193
Great Depression, 19
guaranteed income, 30, 31

Hancock, Ange-Marie, 200
Handler, Joel, 14
Hasenfeld, Yeheskel, 62
health: mental, problems of, 89; physical, problems of, 87-89, 124-26, 141
home visits by welfare officials, 18, 29, 32, 40, 65, 158-59, 169
homelessness: experiences of, 78-79, 88, 91-92, 93-94, 98, 138, 139, 144, 145; homeless shelters, 94
housing: difficulties finding, 94, 144-45; housing insecurity, 92, 140
housing, subsidized. *See* Section 8

identity: self-, welfare receipt and, 81, 171, 180; theft, 121-22, 152
illegal activities, 94, 109-10, 139, 142, 143-44, 153, 176
immigrants, 18, 74
incentives, 124, 134, 151, 182; to cheat, 121-22, 127; to leave welfare, 61-62, 123, 127, 155; to work, 121, 132, 133-34
informed welfare recipients, 119-29, 176-79, 183
incarceration, interviewees' experiences of, 78, 143, 162. *See also* fathers, incarcerated
invisible men. *See under* fathers

Jencks, Christopher, 10-11
job training, 40, 46
Johnson, Lyndon B., 25

Kahan, Dan, 165-66
Katz, Michael
Kennedy, John F., 23

knowledge: of administrative penalties for cheating, 130-31, 146, 150; of criminal penalties, 68, 122, 127, 129, 130-31, 133, 183; of fraud control efforts, 129-30; of rules and requirements, 11, 110-12, 124-29, 130, 132, 133-39, 143, 145-47, 166-71; of sanctions, 114, 141, 146; of work supports, 139, 182

lawyers, 24-29, 30, 37
leaver studies. *See under* welfare research
legal consciousness, 3, 10, 11-13, 171-76, 199; defined, 11
legal services, 25, 31, 37
legality, 10, 181-84
legitimacy: of the welfare rules, 151-54, 170; of the welfare system, 11, 43, 183. *See also* legality
Levine, Kay, 175-76
Long, Huey, 61
Long, Russell, 34

"man-in-the-house" rules, 21, 29, 40
March, Tracey, 14, 173-74
marital history of interviewees, 73-74
Maximum Family Grant (MFG). *See* family cap policies
McCann, Michael, 14, 173-74
Medicaid, 24, 44, 107
MediCal. *See* Medicaid
medical insurance, 44, 80, 100-101
Mellema, Virginia, 175-76
mental illness, 89
methodology: description of, 189-202; grounded theory, 201
Mead, Lawrence, 39
Mica, John, 61
midnight raids, 21, 40
misinformed welfare recipients, 129-39, 176-79, 183
Mobilization for Youth (MFY), 26-27, 28
morality: of law, 181-84, 186; morality requirements for aid recipients, 18, 21; regulating, 48-49, 52; among welfare cheaters, 179, 183, 184

motherhood, 30

Mothers' Pensions, 18, 20

Moynihan, Daniel Patrick, 29-30, 38, 40

Munger, Frank, 13

Murray, Charles, 38-39, 43, 44

National Welfare Rights Organization (NWRO), 31

networks: of rule knowledge, 182, 199-200; social, 177

neutralization, 168-70, 171

Nielsen, Laura Beth, 13

Nixon, Richard, 31, 32, 34, 37

Ohlin, Lloyd, 26

"Operation Talon," 52, 54

overpayments of benefits, 33, 34, 56, 64, 145, 163

parenthood, 71-73. *See also* fathers; substitute parenting

paternity determinations, 47, 76, 96

personal responsibility, 44, 73

Personal Responsibility and Work Opportunity Reconciliation Act (PRWORA), 44, 45, 46, 63

Piven, Frances Fox, 28

policing the poor, 1, 40, 42, 52, 60, 180

poverty, 25, 185; causes of, 38, 39; culture of, 38, 82; feminization of, 36; poverty rate, 37, 48. *See also* War on Poverty

power, 179-80

preoccupied/disengaged welfare recipients, 139-47, 176-79, 183

privacy: discussions of, 137, 150, 158; welfare recipients' rights to, 59-60. *See also* Fourth Amendment

property: crimes, 7; "The New Property" (Reich article), 27-28

Puerto Ricans, as recipients of aid, 21

punitive policies, 3, 46, 47, 60-69, 70, 151, 183

quality control, 32, 38

race and ethnicity: of interviewees, 81-82; racial/ethnic composition of research county, 71

racism, 200

rationality: bounded, 5-6, 117, 131, 168, 170; economic, 114, 117, 126-27, 145, 166, 184; legal, 49; mean-ends, 167; rational actor model, 3, 39, 117, 160-61, 183

Reagan, Ronald, 35, 37, 40; on welfare policies, 37; on welfare queens, 35-36

recidivism, 52

Reform Era, 18-19

Reich, Charles, 27

resistance, 3, 14, 171-76, 178, 179-80; individual, 120-21, 123; political, 174, 176-79

rights: due process, 199; privacy, 176; right to live, 27, 29, 30; right to welfare, 27-28, 123, 177. *See also* civil rights; welfare rights movement; welfare rights organizations

risk: economic risk, 17, 26, 155, 156, 188; perceived risks of noncompliance with welfare rules, 116-17, 119, 122, 131, 173, 183; to research subjects, 186-87

rules: rule breaking, 4, 5, 6-7, 64, 118, 121-22; rule engagement, 119, 147; rule knowledge, 5-6, 118, 123, 119-29, 129-39, 173, 183, 185

Sarat, Austin, 9, 173, 199

sanctions, 9; defined, 47; experiences with, 76, 103, 120, 122-23, 124-26, 141, 146; research on, 4, 61-62; sanction rates, 62, 172

Schram, Sanford, 48, 61, 81

Seccombe, Karen, 11

Section 8, 44, 94, 107-8, 144, 145

segregation, 22

sexual behavior, policed by welfare rules, 21, 42

sexual harassment, 85-86

Scheingold, Stuart, 15

Silbey, Susan, 13-14, 173, 74

Simon, Herbert, 5

Simon, Jonathan, 51

Social Security Act of 1935 (SSA), 19, 26, 29; amendments to, 23, 24, 25, 33

Social Security Disability Insurance (SSDI): applications for, 123; eligibility, 88; policies, 44; receipt of, 87, 90, 108

Soss, Joe, 48
Sparer, Edward, 27
special needs grants, 22, 29, 31
stereotypes of welfare recipients, 36, 40, 82, 152-53, 170, 180, 200
stigma of welfare receipt, 25, 83, 91, 153, 164, 170, 171, 178, 185, 187
substitute parenting, 72-73
substitute father rules, 21, 29
suitable home requirements, 18, 20, 21, 22
Supplemental Security Income Program (SSI), 31, 88, 107-8
surveillance, 18, 40, 97, 169, 177
symbols, 3, 171, 172, 174, 179, 187, 199; symbolic power of law, 171, 172, 174, 183. *See also* condensation symbols; "welfare queen"

Temporary Assistance to Needy Families (TANF), 44, 45
"three strikes and you're out," 65
time limits, 45; knowledge of, 113, 123, 124, 129, 134, 142, 145, 146
transportation: assistance, 41, 46; barriers, 91
Tyler, Tom, 10

underclass, 38, 39, 51
unemployment, 23, 44
Unemployment Insurance, receipt of, 79, 87

Venkatesh, Sudhir Alladi, 198

Wacquant, Loïc, 6, 180, 187
waivers, state, of federal requirements under § 1115, 41-42
War on Poverty, 23-24
"welfare queen," 1, 15, 34-35, 35-36, 152, 170-71, 174, 177, 179-80, 183, 187, 199; individuals described as in popular media, 34-36
welfare reform. *See* Personal Responsibility and Work Opportunity Reconciliation Act
welfare research, 9; gaps in, 4-9; leaver studies, 4; qualitative research, 6-7, 10-11, 195-97, 199; quantitative research, 4-5
welfare rights movement, 24-32
welfare rights organizations, 123
welfare use: cycling on and off welfare, 79, 83; entry triggers, 79-80; by interviewees during childhood, 82-83
Wilson, William Julius, 39
workers' compensation program, 44
work requirements: generally, 47, 48, 124-26; compliance with, 98-101, 106, 122, 172-73; exemptions from, 46, 88, 124-26; knowledge of , 113-14, 120, 123, 132; proposals to institute, 33, 43, 44, 45-46; "work-first" policies, 120, 126, 182
Women and Infant Children food supplement program (WIC), 80

About the Author

KAARYN S. GUSTAFSON is a professor at the University of Connecticut School of Law.

CPSIA information can be obtained at www.ICGtesting.com
Printed in the USA
LVOW091243310512

284007LV00001B/10/P